THIS IS
FENCING!

ADVANCED TRAINING AND PERFORMANCE PRINCIPLES FOR FOIL

THIS IS
FENCING!

ADVANCED TRAINING AND PERFORMANCE PRINCIPLES FOR FOIL

Ziemowit Wojciechowski

THE CROWOOD PRESS

First published in 2019 by
The Crowood Press Ltd
Ramsbury, Marlborough
Wiltshire SN8 2HR

enquiries@crowood.com

www.crowood.com

This impression 2020

British Library Cataloguing-in-Publication Data
A catalogue record for this book is available from the British Library.

ISBN 978 1 78500 595 4

Dedication
To my father who introduced me to this beautiful sport.

Acknowledgements
I would like to thank all my fencers for giving me such good feedback and all the coaches from whom I have had the pleasure of taking lessons and discussing aspects of coaching. In particular, I would like to mention Stanislaw Krucinski, Andrzej Przezdziecki, Zbigniew Czajkowski, Zbigniew Skrudlik, Wladyslaw Kurpiewski, Stanislaw Szymanski, Longin Szmidt, Alex Zuyev, Alexander Press, Livio Di Rosa, Alexander Pierekalski and Oleg Matseychuk.

Without the help and support of many, many individuals this book would not have been possible. I would like to thank all those who have contributed their time and effort. Thanks to Jamie Kenbar for his considerable contribution to performance analysis; to the photographic contributors – Augusto Bizzi, Jornnawat (P'Mod) Limprasert, Karen Saunders, and especially Niki Bruckner, Kevin Nixon, Chris Turner, Dawn Uhalley – and to those who have consented to have their images used and indeed to Richard Kruse and James Davis for demonstrating numerous fencing positions; to Malcolm Fare for help with content and English; and to Paula Huckle for her incredible help with all things editorial – it's been a long road! I would also like to express my deep gratitude to Australian international fencer and expert linguist Christopher Flood Nagle for the massive task of proof reading – his input has been invaluable.

Frontispiece: Ziemowit Wojciechowski. (Photo: Chris Turner)

Typeset by Kelly-Anne Levey
Printed and bound in India by Replika Press Pvt Ltd

CONTENTS

PREFACE

There is nothing so practical as a good theory.

Kurt Lewin (1890–1947)

As we all love foil so much, the purpose of this book is to add some theory to the practical aspects of coaching. Over twenty years have passed since I wrote my first book – Theory, Methods and Exercises in Fencing – and the experiences and knowledge I have gathered since then are reflected in this new book.

The incredible results achieved by some of my many talented fencers are proof positive of the benefits of my coaching philosophy. The list is far from exhaustive, with many of my other fencers receiving medals at European, World Cup and Grand Prix events.

Although the book is primarily targeted at coaches, I hope everyone who likes fencing will find something useful in it. Certain things are repeated in various chapters, in part as a result of overlapping theory and to enhance the usage and practicality of this book. In addition, it is good practice to read the same thing again, as repetition is one of the basic methods of learning.

Year	Fencer/Team	Event/Position
1981	Linda Mcmahon (née Martin)	World Championships – top 8
1992	Fiona Mcintosh	Olympic Games – top 8
1997	Ben Montague	Cadet World Championships – Bronze
2001	Lawrence Halstead	Junior European Champion
2002	Richard Kruse	Junior European Champion
2003	Richard Kruse	Senior World Championships – top 8
2004	Richard Kruse	Olympic Games – top 8
2006	Richard Kruse	Senior European Championships – Silver
2008	Lawrence Halstead	Senior European Championships – Silver
2009	Richard Kruse	Copenhagen World Cup Champion
2009	Richard Kruse	Venice Grand Prix Champion
2009	Edward Jefferies	Junior European Champion – Silver
2010	Richard Kruse	Copenhagen World Cup Double Champion
2010	GB Team (Kruse, Halstead, Jefferies, Mepstead)	Senior European Championships – Bronze
2013	James Davis	St Petersburg Grand Prix Champion
2014	James Davis	Senior European Champion
2014	James Davis	Senior World Championships top 8
2015	Alex Lloyd	Commonwealth Junior Champion
2015	Alexander Tofalides & Richard Kruse	European Games Team Champions
2016	Alex Lloyd	World U20 Team Championships – Bronze
2016	Richard Kruse	Olympic Games – 4th
2017	Alexander Choupenitch	European U–23 Champion
2017	Richard Kruse	Cairo World Cup – Champion
2017	Richard Kruse	Shanghai Grand Prix – Champion
2017	Richard Kruse	Senior World Championships – top 8
2018	Richard Kruse	Shanghai Grand Prix – Double Champion
2018	Richard Kruse	World Championships – Silver
2018	Alexander Choupenitch	Senior European Championships – Bronze
2018	Richard Kruse	Lion of Bonn – Gold
2019	Richard Kruse	Tokyo World Cup Champion

Achievements table.

ABOUT THE AUTHOR

Ziemowit (known as Ziemek) Wojciechowski, born in Gdansk, Poland in 1948, is both a fencer and a coach. Encouraged by his father and inspired by the sword fighting in a TV series about King Arthur and the Knights of the Round Table, Ziemek took up fencing when he was twelve years old. He went on to study in Warsaw where he was preparing to follow a career in plant biology. It was in Warsaw that Ziemek met the greatest influence on his fencing career: Zbigniew Skrudlik, Poland's national fencing coach, a truly dedicated man with a genuine interest in his fencers.

By his early twenties Ziemek had to make a decision: to follow a career in research or dedicate himself to his passion – fencing. There was no choice! By the age of thirty, Ziemek had been the Polish Foil Champion eleven times, had won numerous tournaments and had competed in the individual and team foil events at the 1976 Summer Olympics.

In 1978 Ziemek was smuggled out of Poland and came to Britain, where his coaching career began. Just like Zbigniew, Ziemek's quiet dedication to his sport and interest in his fencers saw him become the national coach for GB men's and ladies' foil squad for 1979–93 and 2006–13. He has also coached the GB team in most junior and senior World Championships since 1979. However, his career highlight, without doubt, was being chosen to coach the GB Olympic team (Kruse, Davis, Halstead and Mepstead) for the 2012 games. In fact, Ziemek has individually coached members of the GB Olympic team for the 2012/2016 games for a cumulative seventy years! Testament to Ziemek's coaching skill and style, these long and successful relationships deliver results – Kruse taking fourth place in the 2016 Olympics and most recently taking gold at the 2019 Tokyo World Cup, achieving World No. 1 status – a first for a UK fencer.

Today, Ziemek is one of the world's most renowned and sought-after foil coaches with a long and illustrious record of success, currently and perhaps most notably as coach to some of the world's top fencers – Richard Kruse (world number 2), James Davis and Alexander Choupenitch. Ziemek continues to develop up-and-coming talent with his club, ZFW Fencing Club, and regularly travels the world giving coaching masterclasses.

FOREWORD

I hope to die on the piste!

Ziemek Wojciechowski

Ziemek Wojciechowski's life has always been driven by his passion for fencing. Those who have witnessed him on the domestic or international circuits will all attest to his vociferous enthusiasm for the sport. It could be Richard Kruse in the final of the Shanghai Grand Prix, or Dominic 'Dragon' De Almeida in the final of the Czech Republic's U20 circuit tournament; Ziemek's animated cries of 'This is fencing!' resound through the hall. Such a man could only spend his hours away from fencing writing about it. The result is in your hands: an exhaustive encyclopedia of a lifetime's wisdom.

Ziemek delights in sharing his insights with not just his students, but also the wider fencing community. Counter-intuitively, he is often seen exchanging ideas with his rivals, whom he considers friends. Here, the reader will find countless insights: why should we line up our whole body with our opponent and not just our point? Why should you count the number of off-target lights you score? These insights are shared in the generous spirit of wanting to contribute to the wider progress of our sport.

This is Fencing! takes the form of a manual. You can use it to look up specific information, exercises, or ideas without having to read all of them. This isn't an accident: it is how Ziemek arranges all these ideas for himself. Ziemek's original intuitions have been distilled by decades of experience, and organised by an instinctive drive to categorize everything. The consequence is a meticulously curated mental catalogue of principles. Ziemek solves problems by combing this catalogue of principles and finding the best one to apply. This approach is distinct from a purely creative ad hoc system, where a new solution is invented for every new problem. Ziemek's creativity is focused on framing new problems as archetypes so that he can solve them with his tried-and-tested principles. Such a system is more easily shared with others, and importantly, it naturally suits this book/manual format. It has given us a remarkably faithful representation of his thinking in structure as well as content.

Ziemek's passion for taxonomy has also produced a rich lexicon of fencing terms and epithets. Everyone who has been involved with him remembers his humorous but earnest names for different moves and tactics. Some favourites include Romanian, Two Waves, Spike of the Cactus, and Spaghetti Arm. While all this might seem innocent and comical, it is in fact based on the powerful idea that a common vocabulary creates a common identity.

All the amusing and idiosyncratic terms used throughout This is Fencing! are explained in the Glossary. You should enjoy them and know they come from a living, very popular, and now rather mature fencing language spoken in North London.

The author's long record of success at the top gives him and his book a justified confidence in their ideas. And it is this confidence that allows him to stake out clear and bold positions for those ideas. The concrete nature of the views in this book serves not only to facilitate understanding, but also to further debate. Even if you disagree that fencers can be divided into technicians and fighters, the natural question of 'why not?', will challenge and develop your opinions in a constructive way.

This is Fencing! is the fruit of a life-long empirical study. Ziemek's approach has been honest, conscientious, and rigorously inquisitive. The results are plain to see, and here to read!

Christopher Flood Nagle,
Australian International Fencer

1 | PRINCIPLES OF COACHING

Throughout my career, I have found it helpful to support my coaching with certain core principles. This chapter details these principles, which I use as a starting point when developing my students' fundamental fencing skills.

FEELING AND CONTROLLING DISTANCE

Footwork controls everything: distance, timing and scoring. There can never be enough footwork. When I came to Britain to coach in 1978 my first major focus was to improve footwork; when that happened, results improved significantly. The good thing about working on footwork is the fencer can do it by themselves and, as legs respond to training, the fencer is rewarded by seeing and feeling the results. Improving footwork includes the ability to move at various speeds while maintaining the correct position, so the fencer is ready to attack at any moment with a strong lunge or flèche, can change direction with minimum loss of time or keep a particular distance (see Chapter 7).

Photo opposite by Niki Bruckner.

The James Bond connection!

Richard Kruse was an under-twenty fencer and had nobody to train with; he would come to the club in Highgate School and just practise footwork on the metallic piste. Incidentally, this was the piste used in the James Bond movie *Die Another Day*, very kindly given to us by Leon Paul.

In fencing, distance is the most fundamental factor affecting winning hits. In training (especially in lessons) and competitions, coaches should help fencers develop a feeling for distance.

Dancing with wolves!

The famous sabreur Vladimir Nazlymov told me that when he was in the Soviet team, he used to practise footwork by himself for three hours a week. Indeed, Russian coaches and fencers compare the mobility of fencers to wolves; both wolves and fencers rely on the speed, strength and stamina of their legs for reward – food for wolves and medals for fencers.

Perfecting a feeling for distance is a continuous process and requires superb footwork and eye–leg coordination supported by accurate anticipation. The timing of actions is inseparable from feeling and judging the correct distance.

Responsive legs are crucial in controlling the distance, reacting in time, and moving at various speeds – whether or not the fencer is consciously aware of this. If a fencer delays responding to the beginning of an opponent's attack, the opponent's chances of scoring will increase. Equally, when a fencer starts an answering attack too late, their chances of reaching the target diminishes. On the other hand, if the answering attack starts too fast, there is more chance of the counter-attack succeeding. Therefore, the first step forward of the fencer who starts an answering attack cannot be faster or longer than the first step back of their adversary. It is important to control the distance from the fencer whose attack finishes short – if it is too close, the original attacker has a good chance of succeeding with a counter-attack against an answering attack.

Having responsive legs is critical as they help improve control over the timing of actions, thus decreasing the number of out-of-time responses.

The importance of distance is huge and sometimes allows fencers to score hits just with good footwork. Using distance against an opponent's offensive action can be called defence with distance or **shah-put**. It is particularly apparent in sabre and is increasingly used in foil.

In a fight, the distance changes constantly. Fencers are advised to fight for 'their' distance which varies according to their own physique. The task of a tall fencer is to keep the distance long, while a shorter fencer will try to close the distance.

There are five types of distance: close-quarters, riposting, lunging, step-lunging, and long. The 'distance' in fencing can refer to the distance between targets and also from the point of the weapon to the target. **Tochka** is a Russian term referring to the change of distance that happens when, or just before, a fencer tries to hit. The opponent will often change this distance very late, therefore the fencer must be ready to cope with this change and adjust their hitting action.

When a fencer is about to hit, their opponent can stand still, move back or move forward. In these cases, the fencer can hit by medium *tochka* (lunge), long *tochka* (step-lunge), or short *tochka* (hitting with just the arm). The specific hitting action is particular to each fencer; *tochka* refers specifically to the challenge of anticipating and adjusting to late changes in distance just before hitting the opponent.

Riposting distance is hitting with only a fully extended arm, in a perfectly balanced position. This enables the fencer to transition to the next movement with minimal delay. (Photo: Kevin Nixon)

Lunging distance is hitting with a fully extended arm on a full lunge. (Photo: Kevin Nixon)

It is important to anticipate not only what action an opponent will choose when threatened, but also how they will try to change the distance in critical moments.

Just as coaches should mix their defensive strokes as a fencer tries to hit, they should also change the distance, encouraging the fencer to anticipate and adapt to both.

Fencers should search for a natural on-guard position to facilitate maximum mobility and balance. It should give a fencer the quickest change of direction, with the ability to control rhythm and speed. It should also be a position which facilitates the execution of a lunge or flèche with minimum delay. It is often the case that a fencer could have scored if their position had been correct. In the heat of the bout, many fencers lose the position from which to launch an effective offensive action. Those fencers who are able to maintain their position are better placed to succeed.

As every fencer has a unique physique, different positions will suit different people; generally fencers should sit lower and wider with the bulk of their weight on the balls of the feet.

Longer distance in offence and shorter in defence

Fencers have a tendency to come too close when preparing their attacks and to move too far away when defending their opponent's attacks; consequently they receive too many hits by counter-attacks or attacks. When defending, a shorter distance gives more opportunities to capitalize on any mistakes made by the fencer who is pressing forward. Some fencers tend to keep a longer distance while retreating because they feel safer. Such feelings are false as the opponent has more freedom to prepare their attack while gaining more speed. Thus, the distance in defence should be such that the fencer who is advancing feels under pressure.

On the other hand, the reason for getting too close while pressing is a strong desire to hit, using a faster and longer step to get momentum for the attack while the opponent strives to stay close while retreating. Coaches should pay close attention and regularly remind fencers about their distance.

Closer distance – shorter steps

Fencers have a tendency to make their steps too long, and therefore become exposed to counter-attacks. They should develop the habit of taking small steps, particularly while closing the gap to the target. While making shorter steps the fencer remains further away from the opponent and is able to change direction earlier as their steps are more frequent. As previously mentioned, a wide on-guard position helps develop this habit. If the size of steps differs, it will affect distance.

Feeling for distance

It is quite common for less experienced fencers to make too big a step forward on the coach's step back and get too close. Correcting this is one way of developing a feeling for distance. For that reason, it is useful if coach's steps back are small.

Closer distance – wider weapon movements

At a longer distance, a fencer can make very small movements of the point in order to avoid an opponent's blade. But, at close distance, the guard and arm are in the way so the point movement has to be wider. Similarly, avoiding octave at close distance can be executed with a smaller movement than when avoiding seconde (2). Also parries taken at a longer distance can be smaller than parries taken at close-quarters.

To hit at close-quarters the hand often has to travel some distance in order for the point to land, similar to a **bear hug**, or a **scoop**. Bear hug and scoop refers to the position where the sword arm is the farthest away from the target in order for the point to make contact (reminiscent of the beginning of a friendly bear hug). The blade movement is rounded to increase the chances of contact.

Leaning forwards while moving backwards – staying upright while advancing

While moving backwards a fencer has to be ready to change direction at any moment and be close enough to find the blade or hit with a stop hit. The best position is leaning forwards while moving backwards. When moving forwards, a fencer is better off keeping an upright position; this offers more control of the weapon, more power to lunge and it makes it easier to change direction.

Move as if on a railway line, not a bumpy road

It is better for a fencer to move smoothly forwards and backwards, as this limits an opponent's opportunity to attack. Fencers who move too much vertically are giving their opponents more time to hit. This is because while a fencer is airborne they are unable to move until they are back in contact with the piste. Of course, the element of surprise can make ripostes while high in the air very effective; **airborne ripostes** are rare but should be encouraged as they can be spectacular.

Some fencers like bouncy footwork, but their bounces should have small amplitude and high frequency. An advantage of bouncing is that it is harder for an opponent to notice the beginning of any real actions, thus deceiving the opponent and creating the element of surprise and impact; the disadvantage is vulnerability while in the air.

There is much merit in a seated lesson when the legs are completely relaxed, as the fencer's entire attention is on their hand whilst their legs are disengaged. Thus, the strength, speed and accuracy of the hand can be improved quickly. Additionally, the muscles of the back are more relaxed, enabling the arm movements to be freer. Such lessons are also useful when there is a leg injury. Even in a seated lesson, the coach can vary the distance.

REACTING IN TIME

Actions 'in time' can be defined as movements synchronized with those of the opponent. The above description refers mainly to the physical side of timing. However, there is also a psychological side of timing – choosing the action and the moment the opponent least expects for an attack. Accurately reading the intentions of the opponent is important to achieve surprise.

An airborne riposte positions the fencer higher than the opponent, opening up the upper target area – ideal for flicking and hitting the shoulder or back. This also elevates the fencer's target, making it harder to be hit by the opponent. (Photo: Kevin Nixon)

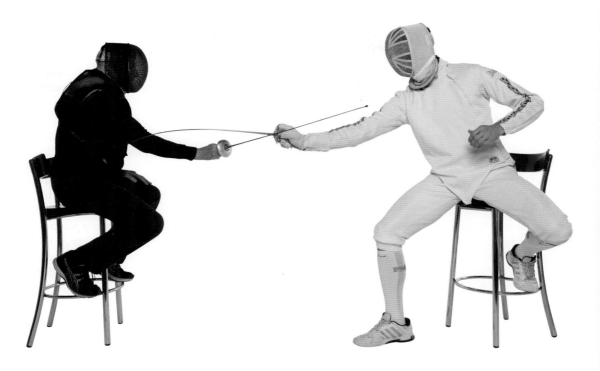

A sitting down lesson completely disengages legs from the action, enabling total focus on the sword arm. It is an excellent method to improve technique, speed and accuracy. (Photo: Kevin Nixon)

Coaches and fencers should pay attention to initiating and finishing foot and weapon movements in time, as only then do they have a chance to win or avoid the hit.

A feeling for time can be improved with practice; musical fencers have an easier task here. A feeling for time, like distance, is most important in fencing and it is crucial to have good footwork to be able to develop it. From the beginning, coaches should encourage fencers to perform actions in time – during lessons, exercises in pairs, training bouts and competitions.

There are four key areas where timing is vital:

1. Starting and finishing attacks
2. When to parry
3. Direct or indirect hits
4. Making compound actions.

Starting and finishing attacks

The most effective time for an attack is on preparation, when the opponent's foot just begins to move forward, so the attack arrives no later than the moment when the opponent's foot lands; this requires acute judgement to anticipate the difference between the beginning of a preparation and the beginning of an attack. Sharp perception is required, as is the ability to read pre-signals, or 'tells', which are often subtle. Experience is the best way to develop this sense of judgement – very experienced fencers can even fake tells. Such skill and experience is particularly valuable in situations where priority is in question.

The second most effective time for an attack is immediately after the opponent pauses or

17

finishes their development of an offensive action; this can be called an 'answering attack' or 'taking back the initiative'. There could be various reasons for an opponent to stop, such as their blade being found, not being sure how to finish their attack, or they may even pause in order to provoke an answering attack from the fencer. Here reading the opponent's intention is crucial.

The third attacking situation is when the fencer is advancing and looking for the moment to finish after getting within lunging distance to the opponent; this involves more risk as opponents often seek to draw such an attack in order to respond to it, particularly while having space behind them to retreat into.

The timing of attacks can also be determined by the movement of the opponent's weapon. While defending, an opponent will open and close various targets by moving their weapon; a fencer must finish in a particular sector *in time* – not after, but as an opponent is in the process of opening it. In a lesson the coach, while making various openings, can usually tell if a fencer finishes an attack too early, or too late, because the fencer's blade will be parried by the coach.

The coach can feel how much time there is to defend and what chance the fencer's attack has of succeeding. Ultimately, for more advanced fencers the coach should not simply wait for an offensive action to reach the open target, but ensure the fencer is hitting *in time*.

When to parry

The best time to parry is either at the first moment (usually by beating or parrying with a step forward) or at the last moment when an opponent finishes an offensive action (usually with holding parries and riposting along a closed line to avoid being hit by renewals). At such moments it is particularly hard for an attacker to deceive the parries.

Parries in the first moment are usually less expected and their beating nature towards the opponent's blade make them harder to deceive. Parries at the last moment are hard to deceive as they are taken right at the end of the attack when it is usually too late for an opponent to change line.

Direct and indirect hits

The timing of hitting with a direct riposte or direct attack (particularly an answering one) should be such that the fencer starts an offensive action before their opponent starts a defensive one because the fencer's point will arrive at the target before the opponent can parry. On the other hand, when making a simple disengage riposte or attack, it is best to start as the opponent begins a simple parry. The coach should always try to parry or avoid being hit and, if the timing is correct the hit should land, giving the fencer accurate feedback.

Compound actions

When a fencer wants to hit with a compound riposte or attack, in the case of a second-intention action they need to induce the opponent to react to the parry and wait until their reaction begins. Compound actions can be premeditated first-intention, in which case the fencer does a deep feint assuming the opponent will react in a habitual way, favouring a certain parry or counter-attack. Such a feint can also be synchronized with a back foot movement (completing a step forward) and the subsequent disengage will hit if the timing is right, but if the reaction of the opponent is unexpected, the fencer will have to switch to a continuation (either counter-parry or renewal).

Expected and unexpected

Against an unexpected or sudden action, an opponent usually reacts in a particular, habitual way. Against an expected action, an opponent may react differently. Knowing how an opponent reacts to an unexpected action is useful for winning hits. Among premeditated, compound first-intention actions, a feint cutover is very effective as it avoids most typical parries.

The timing for a stop hit is the moment when an opponent takes their point away from the target area. The stop hit should arrive before the opponent's point starts moving towards the target.

Reacting in time also applies to foot actions

Simply by following a coach's steps, a fencer should react as quickly after the time of the coach's movement as possible. According to Turecki, the time taken from the moment of initiating an attack to the moment of initiating a retreat is around 400 microseconds. This is enough time to avoid being hit if the attack is from a slightly longer than lunging distance. However, the execution time of the retreat will depend on whether the fencer must change direction, and at what speed they are already moving. Obviously, fencers who are defending have to constantly make decisions between moving back, parrying or counter-attacking and any hesitation can give an opponent time to hit. Any exercises which involve changes of direction or keeping the distance are useful.

The principle of reacting in time also applies to blade and point movements. For instance, a fencer should avoid an opponent's blade at the moment it travels across the target in such a way that the fencer's blade stays in line with the target. Fencers often move their point from the target area while deceiving, they can also mis-time the moment the point makes contact with the target; both should be corrected. For instance, the ideal flèche attack would have the point reaching the target at the end of the propulsion force from the front leg at a 45-degree angle and just before the end of the arm extension. Ultimately, the coach should not wait for the fencer's point to arrive but parry or take the target away if it is late.

FEELING FOR THE POINT; HITTING WITH ACCELERATION

The best tactics and the best frame of mind are useless if a fencer cannot hit. Therefore, the simple ability to control the point and hit with optimal strength is fundamentally important. The fencer who wants to be successful has to have a feeling for where the point is and what it is doing.

In fencing, the most important thing is to hit the target accurately. To achieve this a fencer has to know and feel where the point is as well as the target.

Ideally, a fencer should have a good awareness of the position of their point in relation to the opponent's target. Usually, a fencer's feeling for the blade does not extend all the way to the point. Over time, a fencer's feeling for the blade will extend up along the blade, eventually including the point. When a fencer has a good feeling for where their point is, they are usually fencing at their best.

Generally, there is a tendency to grip the weapon too tightly and hit too hard while

The point!

The Italians have a saying, **pensa alla punta**, which means 'think about the point'. In Poland coaches often call the point the 'rifle sight' through which the opponent's target is observed.

Holding foil with two fingers, back view. There is a general tendency with all fencers to hold the weapon too firmly, which then limits the ability to manipulate the foil. This exercise of holding the foil with two fingers is an excellent way to restore a lighter grip. (Photo: Dawn Uhalley)

Holding foil with two fingers, front view. Place the last three fingers on the guard and hold the grip with the thumb and index finger. This leads to greater point control and accuracy with small finger movements. (Photo: Dawn Uhalley)

guard moving more easily than the point, therefore it will be harder for the opponent to deceive a parry when there is no movement of the guard in relation to the point. Therefore, all beating parries with the point and guard moving along the same line are effective, as well as circular and semi-circular parries where it is mainly the point moving. When hitting the outside sectors in the case of same-handed fencers from a low **Muhammad Ali** position, when the point moves upwards, an opponent will see the movement later than if the whole arm is moving. Likewise, beats and engagements are harder to avoid if they are executed mainly by moving the point of the weapon. However, feints are more visible and effective if a target is threatened from different line positions with a clear sideways movement of the guard and additional body movements.

The most effective way of moving the point is when the pivoting point is just in front of the fingers. Finger play combined with extensions of the elbow give the best combination for maximum acceleration and speed of point movement in any direction. Whenever the shoulder 'interferes', the point travels more slowly and less accurately.

Independent and spaghetti arm

Ideally, the sword arm should be relaxed and independent from the legs, able to hit any target from any position at variable distance and speed. A loose arm is faster than a tense arm and coordination is better. It has more power and the point can be accelerated more easily. This can be achieved by working on lunging pads, practising during lessons, participating in pairs exercises, training bouts and competitions with a focus on keeping a loose arm. Fencers and coaches should actively seek the best position of the sword arm to facilitate maximum power and speed of the point. Many exercises from the Muhammad Ali position come in handy here, as it necessitates a

throwing the point rather than leading it. In order to get a better feel for directing the point and hitting correctly, the coach may ask a fencer during hitting practice to hold the weapon only with the index finger and thumb, while keeping the other three fingers on the outside part of the guard. The index finger is naturally used for pointing at things and therefore plays an important role in directing the point.

Almost every movement of the weapon should be initiated by the point, particularly when taking parries. An opponent sees the loose arm. Even when taking parries, fencers should try to keep their arm relaxed, giving them the feeling of a more powerful riposte than a tense one. A loose arm will be more accurate, particularly when using the fingers and optimal strength of grip. Developing the habit of accelerating the point increases the chances of winning hits.

Mace and chain

I like to compare a fencer's arm to a mace and chain. The mace is the hand and the arm is the chain. In general, we want to develop a sword arm that is independent of the legs according to the classical formula that in offence the arm moves before the legs, and in defence, the legs move before the arm. However, there are some useful coordination points of fencing actions between arm and leg movements, such as:

- Feint or beat synchronized with the back foot landing.
- Extension of the arm synchronized with the back foot landing.
- Parry with step forward synchronized with the front foot landing.
- **Engagement of the blade** synchronized with the front foot landing (ideally the point should start moving slightly before the foot).

Relax!

Just like working on perfecting the lunge or any other movement, relaxation of the arm is a continuous process goal. Muscles often involuntarily contract and this occurs throughout a fencer's career. Keeping the feet moving up and down (**mashing grapes** exercise) helps relax the upper body.

Coaches and fencers must always pay attention to the quality of hitting (optimal strength and perpendicular to the target) and to leading of the point rather than throwing (or waving). In lessons, coaches and fencers should not be satisfied with just making contact with the target, but should strive to hit correctly every time. This will result in greater accuracy, and a higher number of scoring hits in matches.

The ability to hit the target accurately is a huge part of technique. Using the fingers and having a relaxed and independent arm is a process goal which contributes significantly towards accuracy. Off-target lights are not just unlucky, they are directly related to a fencer's ability to hit the target accurately. This can be easily measured by comparing the number of hits on target with right of way, to the total number of off-target and on-target hits in time. To simplify measurements, do not include out of time actions. This index of accuracy usually varies between 40 per cent and 70 per cent, although better fencers can achieve a higher score; James Davis (GBR) often reaches over 80 per cent.

Correct hitting occurs when the point comes into contact, perpendicular to the target area, with optimal strength causing the blade to bend several centimetres. (Photo: Kevin Nixon)

Generally, accuracy depends on balance and correct position. Small rotating movements of the hips, vertically or laterally, can significantly affect the direction of the point. The back hip should stay level with the front hip, especially during a lunge. Small involuntary movements of the wrist, or tension in the shoulder can also induce wayward movement of the point.

Ideally, a fencer should retain accuracy, even if they are off-balance, which can occur during a fight. Fencers should be aware of the need to keep a loose arm (particularly the shoulder).

On target

In the 2004 World Cup, Cassara (ITA) fencing Ferrari (FRA) placed every hit on target, a rare event.

Accuracy

One way of concentrating on accuracy with younger fencers, is for fencers to perform one press-up for every off-target hit. This is regularly used by the US National Coach Greg Massialas during practice.

There are numerous accuracy tests, among them: one fencer moves 2 metres forwards and backwards often changing the hand position, while their partner randomly opens a gloved hand at various distances. The task of the fencer is to hit the palm of the hand as quickly as possible using optimum strength, adequate footwork and a fully extended but relaxed arm. Minimum number of attempts 3 × 10, calculating results as follows: very good 25–30, good 20–25, average 15–20, poor 10–15. There are two basic ways of hitting: placing the point and flicking.

In lessons all exercises from a low hand position help, because the arm has to be loose. Initiating actions from a low position automatically relaxes the sword arm and disconcerts opponents who like to take the blade. Practising lunging pad exercises from a low line position helps with relaxation and adds to the variety of positions from which it is desirable to develop accuracy.

A speeding bullet

In Olympic sports, the point of a foil has been named the second fastest object after a bullet, because of flicking.

A fencer's performance should be built on the fundamental ability to lead and place the point. Flicking is more of a lottery and is easier for taller fencers – Chamley-Watson (USA) is a good example. If a particular fencer scores frequently with flicks, it is worth practising them in lessons, but only after classical hitting is ingrained. Also, it is useful to automatically add another movement immediately after a flick hit, in case the flick does not work.

FEELING FOR THE BLADE

In foil, a feeling for the opponent's blade plays a more important role than in other weapons. Since a tactile reaction is faster than a visual one, a feeling for the opponent's blade is particularly relevant when there is little time to make a decision, and a fencer must react to the contact – or lack of contact – with an opponent's blade.

Coaches should introduce exercises to develop this skill; for example, a fencer engages the coach's blade and if the coach reacts early the fencer deceives two parries and if late, only one, but if there are no parries or reaction the fencer has a longer contact with the blade and finishes direct. Similarly, when a fencer takes a holding parry, the riposte will depend on a feeling for the blade. Exercises with closed eyes are very effective in developing that feel. Other exercises can develop explosiveness; when a fencer reacts to a lack of touch with a direct thrust from engagement. Also, reflex responses to a beat with a change beat or engagement are based on a sense of touch and are often executed automatically as a result of control from the lower parts of the nervous system.

DIRECTING THE POINT AWAY FROM THE TARGET AT A LONG DISTANCE AND TOWARDS THE TARGET WHEN THE DISTANCE IS CLOSING

This is an important principle to help fencers become more effective. It is common for fencers to take their point away from the target as the distance is closing, increasing the chances of a successful counter-attack against them.

A fear of being parried is the reason for this; however, the answer is for the fencer to keep a longer distance while preparing an attack,

Baldini (ITA) – Auclin (FRA). In the 2015 San Jose Grand Prix, Auclin in this particular moment has not applied the classic principle of keeping the point on target and receives a hit from Baldini. (Photo: Dawn Uhalley)

whilst constantly improving the ability to go round an opponent's parries and to retake the right of way while being parried. Fencers should consider being parried as an opportunity to score with a counter-riposte, renewal, counter-attack or defence with distance.

This principle is logical – at a longer distance an opponent needs more time to hit, so there is time to bring the point on target; time diminishes as the distance decreases. It is important to have the hand independent of the legs while anticipating the correct distance, to enable the hand to deliver the hit irrespective of what the legs are doing. Fencers with better anticipation and coordination can bring the point on target later and still be successful; this often results in hitting the target with an arm still bent. Obviously, the speed of moving forwards is relevant as at higher speeds, while keeping the point away, the chances of a successful counter-attack are higher than at lower speeds. It is therefore important to develop the ability to press slowly. Pressing slowly with an absence of blade is difficult to deal with but also difficult to do while maintaining the ability to finish in time against a counter-attack or parry.

Coping with pressing

To cope with such pressing a fencer has the following options:

- Going for near-simultaneous actions and trying to be in a position to press.
- After a feint attack closing the distance with a **sweeping parry** *or* **Romanian**.
- Using the line as a deterrent or for any actions (derobement, parry, attack, counter-attack).
- Making numerous feint attacks or counter-attacks and taking the risk of trying to hit after one of them with Romanian forwards or backwards (alternatively, waiting for an opponent to react to the feint and depending on the nature of the reaction performing an adequate counter-action – either attack, parry-riposte or counter-attack; there might be a case for simple beat attack if the opponent does not respond to the feint).
- Offering the blade and trying to hit afterwards with a counter-parry-riposte or Romanian, depending on the character of the opponent's movement (Romanian forwards is usually against a faster movement and backwards against a slower one).
- Keeping the distance without reacting until the opponent decides to hit and then trying to parry at the last moment – this requires a high level of control and confidence in taking parries.
- Suddenly increasing and decreasing the distance to open one sector of the target and thus force the opponent to finish into the opening, then parry and hit at close quarters.
- Constantly breaking the distance, encouraging the opponent to finish when the distance is closing and parry, or move faster when the distance is increasing and Romanian.

Sometimes at close-quarters a fencer, after taking a parry, withdraws the hand and moves the point away as the opponent tries to protect their target with the weapon and by wriggling the target area. This exceptional situation can only work if the opponent is very defensive and taking the sword arm away is the only way at close-quarters to land the point.

However, *keeping the point on target* is the fundamental principle of thrusting weapons and particularly important when the distance is closing. Fencing actions are often executed extremely fast; if the point moves out of line with the quickly moving target as well as the opponent's weapon, there might not be time to hit again. A fencer should always feel where the point is in relation to the target. Keeping

First phase of Romanian – hit. The key to a successful Romanian is to hit and parry in one swift movement. The ideal condition for a Romanian is when the opponent (in this case the coach) is moving quickly forward while taking the point away from the target, at medium or short distance. When presented with these conditions a fencer has a good chance of success. Here the fencer is responding with a swift hit which is the first phase of the Romanian. (Photo: Kevin Nixon)

Second phase of Romanian – parry. In the second phase the fencer follows the swift hit with a parry. (Photo: Kevin Nixon)

the point on target has become a little under-appreciated in recent times, but in my opinion, it is a fundamental principle of fencing.

STRONG BASIC FOUNDATION

The importance of a strong basic foundation is particularly relevant when a fencer is under significant pressure, short of time and distance. Fencers with a stronger basic foundation will have more chance of maintaining the correct positions and movements and will therefore have more chance of winning.

It is important to drill into fencers the habit of adopting:

- a solid on-guard position;
- a strong lunge or flèche;
- balanced movements;
- correct weapon and body positions.

On-guard position

In the on-guard position, the fencer should be sitting low, so the plumb line from the knee ends at least where the toes begin, with the bulk of the weight on the balls of the feet. The feet should be shoulder-width distance apart, the elbow of the sword arm should be one hand's width in front of the front hip bone, and the sword forearm in line with front leg knee and toes.

Strong lunge or flèche

Every successful fencer has to have a good attack, which means building up a strong lunge.

However, a good flèche can be a useful addition to the lunge. For instance, the Austrian fencer Joachim Wendt naturally had tense muscles and a rather short, ineffective lunge; he therefore developed a very effective strong flèche. The Soviet Elena Belova, from the former republic of Belarus, before one important tournament, injured her hip and was unable to lunge; she won by using an effective flèche.

A good lunge is characterized by a fully extended arm, hips, shoulders, sword arm and front thigh parallel to the ground, while the back leg is extended and the back arm is parallel to the back leg.
(Photo: Kevin Nixon)

In the first phase of a flèche, start by extending the sword arm, followed by pushing from the back leg in order to transfer weight to the front leg from where the energy for the flèche comes from. (Photo: Niki Bruckner)

For the second phase, the hit is delivered in the final push from the front leg. The vector of force from the front leg is approximately 45 degrees to the ground. (Photo: Niki Bruckner)

Balanced movements

Sometimes a fencer's unbalanced position gives an opponent the opportunity to score while preventing a fencer from hitting with a lunge or flèche; by the time balance is regained it is usually too late. The same thing applies to riposting. Therefore a fencer should always be ready to immediately lunge, even while engaged in changes of direction at high speed.

Correct weapon and body positions

Coaches teaching a solid basic foundation need to remember the importance of *fixing the correct position* at the beginning as well as at the end of a movement. Since every movement starts from a particular position, it is imperative for the movement and position to be correct at the end; if they are not, then the movement itself cannot be correct.

Another area to give a fencer a solid foundation is developing the ability to make a *smooth transition from one movement to another* should a situation rapidly change. For example, a fencer executes a direct thrust with a step forward; from time to time the coach increases the distance and takes a parry; the fencer finishes the step forward and deceives the parry with a smooth transition to another foot action (step or lunge depending on distance). A fencer practises a prime parry and riposte by flicking to shoulder. From time to time the coach defends the shoulder and the fencer makes a smooth transition by riposting to flank or chest.

Remember!

Almost every movement should start with the point.

Developing *maximum efficiency of movements* is key to a solid foundation, as this is the most accurate and easiest way of controlling speed and rhythm. Moreover, efficient movements need less energy and are better disguised; in other words, opponents see them later than the ones requiring greater effort.

As our nervous system registers movements of different speeds coaches should teach the execution of movements with the right rhythm and *maximum acceleration*, while maintaining high intensity. Developing a habit of accelerating the final movement of the point is also important as this gives a fencer more chance of scoring the hit. Acceleration comes mainly from the movement of the sword arm (shooting with the arm), and this should be independent of the legs. Acquiring a habit of slower and shorter steps forward is another part of building a solid foundation.

Safin (RUS) losing balance against Davis (GBR). Safin on the left is losing his balance. Most likely, Safin was surprised by Davis and responded by pushing from the front leg. (Photo: Dawn Uhalley)

Responsive legs

An active back leg controlling distance while moving backwards is very important. It is common to see fencers who are taken by surprise and have to rapidly move back, leaning backwards while pushing back with the front leg. This happens when there is too much weight on the front leg; the front leg responds first with a strong push and the legs cross – this is often the only way to avoid being hit, but it is very hard to make any actions forward.

Fundamental aspects for a solid foundation

- Make small preparation steps and weapon movements while keeping the point on target when closing distance.
- Maintain optimal strength of hitting and directing the point with the fingers rather than throwing it with the arm.

The situation can arise, often at crucial moments, when a poorly directed point bounces off the target without triggering the light, therefore practice of the above is critical.

SLOW BEGINNING

The principle of beginning slowly has emerged because many attacks on preparation and counter-attacks are successful. A lack of control over speed is often caused by a strong desire to hit the target and since young fencers tend to rush more than the older ones there is a high percentage of successful counter-attacks among the younger age groups.

Moving the point away from the target while getting closer is because of a fear of being parried and is another important reason why an opponent's counter-attacks succeed. Steps are often too long, which is what suits

> **Did you know?**
>
> In the early stages of a competition, there are more counter-attacks than in the later stages as fencers are more anxious and consequently more reactive.

the counter-attacker. There are other reasons why fencers start too quickly when preparing attacks. Other than a pure desire to hit, a lack of explosiveness in the legs results in the fencer needing fast steps to get enough momentum to achieve a desirable speed for the final lunge or flèche. Beginning more slowly helps a fencer switch to a parry and contributes towards a greater change of speed and hence a greater chance to hit.

Therefore developing a habit of beginning slowly is very important, but at the same time difficult as it is not instinctive.

> **Vary the speed**
>
> It is useful in some footwork sessions to completely eliminate fast steps forward and only move at a variable speed, including maximum speed backwards and only slow steps forward.

There is also merit in introducing **Avola steps** forward, meaning starting a step forward with the back leg and sometimes developing an attack from it. Such a sequence is quite natural with complete beginners. Also, advocating a wider on-guard position compels a fencer to do smaller steps and hence develop this important habit. This principle is more relevant for fencers with a long reach than shorter fencers, who have to be more dynamic and often do a **patinando**.

CHANGING RHYTHM AND SPEED – TWO WAVES

The ability to change rhythm and speed can significantly improve the effectiveness of a fencer's actions. It applies to both hand (point and blade) and leg movements.

Developing this ability is difficult as it requires moving at various speeds for a variable duration of time. Coaches and fencers need to work on this continuously as it is a skill that can take opponents by surprise. Everyone has a certain rhythm of moving and an opponent can get used to it; the ability to change is important. It is also important not to allow an opponent to impose their rhythm – from which they can perform better.

Sometimes, if an opponent's rhythm is predictable, a fencer can capitalize on it in order to find the perfect moment to initiate an action – an example of fencing from the opponent's initiative. There is a timing when executing actions can be described as 'breaking the opponent's rhythm' – for example, a beat attack executed just before the end of a preparatory attack while the opponent is still moving forward. Also, a one-tempo attack after defending with distance has to be faster than the opponent's recovery and can be called the answering attack.

The point should always accelerate as it closes in onto the target. In the case of a one-two-three movement, the action will be more effective if there is either a quick one-two followed by a short delay before the final three or a longer one followed by a quick two-three, rather than the same duration one-two and three.

When there is a direct exchange of blade actions, the second movement has to be clearly faster than the first. If indirect, there should be a small pause before the second action.

Changing rhythm: two waves

Two waves is a particular way of changing the rhythm; it applies to situations when a fencer is in the process of developing an attack, but the opponent manages to break the distance by accelerating backwards and the attacker realizes they are not going to reach the target. At this stage slowing down while still moving forwards can be effective, as often the opponent will slow their retreat accordingly and then there is a good chance of getting within striking distance (preferably one-tempo) and making an explosive finish (second wave). This is a classic situation and a few other options are possible; note that charging fast is unlikely to be successful, however, due to the high risk of receiving a counter-attack. Charging fast is an instinctive behaviour that has to be unlearned.

Two or more waves can be a premeditated way of preparing an attack. As it uses more energy, it can be an effective way of getting fit. On the other hand, if a fencer wants an opponent to react quickly, they must start a movement quickly, for example, when making a second-intention parry-riposte.

Remember!

A slow signal induces a slow reaction and a fast signal a fast reaction. If a fencer wants an opponent to react slowly, they should start slowly and accelerate smoothly. This is why an accelerating lunge is so effective, as well as any slow starting attack. (If we want to catch a fly sitting on a table, we can only achieve it by starting slowly and accelerating

DECEPTIVENESS

The later an opponent sees an action, the less time they have to respond. This applies mainly to stop hits and attacks without the blade, in addition to some footwork movements. A fencer can use body movement to create a false image of their intentions, camouflaging the real movement so the opponent sees it too late to respond.

Tactical steps

Show the opponent a backwards movement with the back leg, but immediately move forward with the front leg. Likewise, make a feint forward movement with the front leg, but actually move backwards with the back leg to complete a step back. Avola steps also have an element of deceptiveness.

Many fencers have developed a deceptive stop hit. Often after an initial preparatory movement partly extending the sword arm on an opponent's advance, they move their target backwards while leaving the sword arm where it is, so the opponent confuses the movement of the sword arm (straight) with the main target (backwards) and consequently the stop hit is seen quite late or only after being hit.

Deception

Chereminisov (RUS) has developed a deceptive attack with a lunge whereby he starts to retreat by moving the back leg backwards, but then makes a lunge which is seen too late, so has a good chance of succeeding.

The Ukrainian fencer Golubitski had a wide range of deceptive counter-attacks, particularly a flèche from retreating when he showed opponents he was moving backwards, but was able to change direction smoothly by putting the front leg behind the centre of gravity to trigger a flèche seen rather late.

To some extent, a **half-step flèche** is deceptive, as the opponent just sees the beginning of a step, which rapidly changes into a flèche. Also, the so-called **hop-lunge** (from sabre) is deceptive as the opponent sees the beginning of a lunge which is extended by hopping on the front leg further forward than expected; the rhythm of such an extension can be varied but is different from a step and lunge. Initiating an attack by moving the back leg forward before starting with the front leg is also deceptive as the back leg gains distance and the opponent sees it late.

THE RIGHT ACTION AT THE RIGHT MOMENT

Based on what is known about a particular opponent, a fencer has to find answers to two fundamental tactical questions: what to do and when? Here we can identify three types of fencing: intuitive; tactical (thinking); and visual (touch).

Intuitive fencing

Sometimes a fencer chooses the right strokes and sets up the right situation based on a *feeling* for the fight rather than on conscious thought. This artistic feel should be fostered, but generally, coaches should encourage thinking from the earliest stages of development.

Tactical fencing

This means getting fencers to use **premeditated actions** of first- or second-intention. This type of fencing is most effective against those who keep a short distance while being fast and are themselves players of premeditated actions. Some coaches develop a logical progression of premeditated actions based on the most probable response of an opponent to the next action depending on the previous action. For example, follow a successful compound attack with a simple attack or a second-intention parry-riposte.

Visual fencing

There is a third way of fencing, which is based on the so-called **open-eyes** approach. This way of fencing relies not only on vision but also on touch. Usually, a fencer starts a particular movement and, depending on an opponent's reaction, counteracts in order to hit while having right of way. Starting with the blade engages the sense of touch. The reaction to touch is faster than the reaction to sight. Visual fencers will sense or feel when the blade engages and respond on time based on their accurate selective perception. This method of fencing should be encouraged. Fencers who have fast, simple reactions should base their game on premeditated actions.

The three types of fencing

Overall, all three ways of fencing should be developed:

- **Feeling:** creative fencing based on feeling the fight and opponent.
- **Tactical (thinking):** premeditated first and second-intention (progression of actions with decisions made on an analytical (prognostic) level).
- **Open-eyes:** fencing based on vision and touch (decisions made on senso-motoric level) usually after creating a situation where the opponent has to respond.

ALTERNATING ACTIONS

A fencer is in a stronger position when their opponent is uncertain what is going to happen next.

Coaches should encourage fencers to have more than one response in any given situation, as by varying their actions an opponent will be in a weaker position, unable to accurately anticipate the next move. Varying actions is possible when a fencer has control and expects or creates a particular situation. However, it is always possible to surprise an adversary and in these cases, it is useful to identify the way an opponent reacts when surprised, which is usually habitual. For example, many fencers habitually search for the blade after it has been presented and quickly taken away. A fencer can alternate between actions in various ways.

Alternating between attacks on preparation and answering attacks

Both of these attacks are timed from the adversary's initiative. The fencer is following the opponent's steps forward and backwards and either attacks with one lunge at the beginning of the opponent's step forward or in the same situation they step back while taking the blade (if available) and followed by an answering attack with step lunge, usually of premeditated nature.

Alternating between simple and circular parries

This is useful against an attack in the high line. A fencer can sometimes take a parry of quarte (4) and sometimes counter-sixte (c6). Some coaches advise taking a circular parry if the attacker's blade is close to the defender's blade and a simple parry if further away. I prefer not to make such a distinction, as this might give an opponent a clue as to which parry to expect.

Alternating between first- and second-intention attacks

A fencer can alternate between an attack with an intention to hit or to draw a riposte and then have a variety of responses to it.

Parry-riposte and defence with distance or finishing an attack in time

These actions can be initiated after drawing a counter-attack or an attack on preparation and varying a parry-riposte with defence, distance and finishing an attack in time.

ACTIONS AND COUNTER-ACTIONS

This is a helpful principle in developing tactical thinking and should be applied from an early stage.

Against every action, there is at least one type of effective counter-action. A fencer who thinks in terms of action and counter-action

For every action there is a counter-action

For example:

- Against a direct attack there can be a simple parry.
- Against a compound attack, a counter-attack.
- Against a counter-attack, a parry-riposte.
- Against a riposte, a counter-riposte.
- Against a compound riposte, a counter-attack.
- Against an absence of blade slow pressing, point-in-line.

has a better chance of choosing the right stroke to counteract their opponent.

ANALYSE AND MEMORIZE AFTER EACH HIT

Coaches should teach fencers to analyse each hit, remember how fights progress and what actions scored the hits. This will enable a fencer to make the right decisions regarding what to do next and when.

Pay attention!

If a fencer does not pay attention to what has happened during a bout, they are likely to see the fight as a chain of accidental hits not connected with each other.

It is important to remember and analyse hits during training fights. Fencers need to remember during practice how they scored or received a hit and what they should do for the next touch. Similar questions can be asked during competition. While teaching an action the coach should explain when such an action is best applied, why and what counter-actions to expect. Developing thinking in terms of action and counter-action should help decision-making during a match, and also when analysing performance afterwards.

ANTICIPATE IN ORDER TO STAY AHEAD

In every conflict situation, it is crucial to be ahead of an adversary in thinking, perceiving and anticipating. If a fencer just reacts to a particular signal, it is usually too late.

It is critical to continually and accurately

read the pre-signals (*tells*) of what is going to happen before it actually happens. Here it is important to read the difference between false and real signals, such as a real counter-attack (with the intention to hit), and a false one (with the intention to draw the opponent's attack). Whoever does it better has the advantage, so sharp and selective perception is vital in winning hits.

EFFECTIVENESS OF ATTACKS: PREPARATION, ANSWERING AND PRESSING

In theory, the most effective attack is on preparation, as an opponent is not able to change direction so an unexpected attack gives them little chance to react.

The second most effective attack is an answering one. After finishing their attack, an opponent may be ready to make a counter-attack on the fencer's first step forward, as this step is often too fast. After an opponent's initial attack falls short, answering with one-tempo foot actions (like a single lunge or a flèche) is the best way for a fencer to avoid receiving such a counter-attack. Alternatively, if a fencer *does* wish to answer with a step, it should be slow, and small, while looking for the opponent's reaction. Italian coaches refer to this type of step as a **looking step**.

Of course, an opponent can exhibit other behaviours after their attack falls short. These include searching for the blade (it is useful to

know which way) or retreating. If an opponent retreats, and the distance is longer than can be reached with a step-lunge; it is important to recognize this as early as possible. In such a situation the best responses are to slow down or even stop before reinitiating the attack. If a fencer slows down (but does not stop) before executing a fast finish, I call this an attack of **two waves**. If a fencer stops completely, and then attacks, it will be an attack on preparation.

The riskiest attack is from pressing, particularly when an opponent has space behind them. In this case, the attacker takes a risk with every step forward while searching for the right distance from which to strike, as a good defensive adversary has many options.

Many fencers develop attacks from pressing, but sometimes give the initiative away in order to take it back again and either start an answering attack or continue pressing, often covering the full length of the piste, which requires good footwork. As they are closing in on the backline pressure is mounting on both fencers and often the initiator does not feel the right moment to attack.

Some fencers set up the timing for an attack on preparation by putting pressure while waiting for an opponent to take the initiative back and attack on the opponent's first step forward. Another option is after putting pressure on an opponent, to suddenly retreat, creating a vacuum of distance. This vacuum incites the opponent to speed up while changing direction, giving the fencer the opportunity to attack on one of the opponent's steps forward.

Effectiveness

Some fencers, like Cassara (ITA), are very effective when pressing, although others, like Baldini (ITA), have developed the defensive skills to counteract that type of attack.

CREATIVENESS

Fencing is constantly evolving, triggered by changing rules and their interpretation, equipment, innovations in training methods, developments in sports science and the creativity of coaches and fencers. In a fight, a

Innovation

Examples of innovations introduced by coaches or fencers include: German Sveshnikov's devastating **Garbushka** (fast forward preparation followed by parry second or prime and riposte on the back); Haerter's slow fleche to shoulder with flick; Pavel Warzycha and his coach Wojtyczka's **Pavlina** riposte from prime.

Jault's (FRA) riposte round the back has become known as the **Jault**. Chamley-Watson's (USA) riposte while moving the sword arm in front of the head, over the shoulder, while hitting from the side of the sword arm, is called the **Champley**.

The Champley! Chamley-Watson (USA) vs Pivovarov (RUS). This unique way of hitting at close quarters was introduced by American fencer Miles Chamley-Watson, where the sword arm goes around the neck and over the shoulder to hit the opponent. (Photo: Augusto Bizzi)

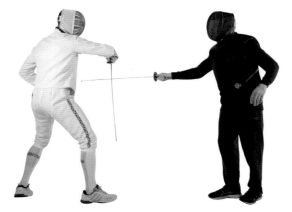

LEFT, TOP: Taking parry prime before Pavlina. First phase: stepping into the distance between an opponent's point and target, so the opponent's point is behind the fencer. (Photo: Kevin Nixon)

LEFT, MIDDLE: Second phase: the fencer releases his blade by going over the opponent's point and moving the blade behind his own back. (Photo: Kevin Nixon)

LEFT, BOTTOM: In the third phase, the hit is delivered from an unexpected position, making the Pavlina a very surprising and effective move. (Photo: Kevin Nixon)

fencer expresses their personality. In training and particularly in lessons it is important to encourage a fencer to produce their own mix of hits and practise their own actions. This approach helps develop creativity, as well as an individual style. Coaches should encourage fencers to choose the timing of actions, as well as providing different choices in lessons, as this will stimulate decision-making and contribute towards a fencer's development. Active participation by everyone in every aspect of training should be encouraged.

Make it meaningful!

Introducing names for various actions is stimulating and creates a unique culture. In Britain foilists originally called a counter-attack followed by blocking the target the **ironing board** and later the **Romanian**; hitting after defence with distance *shah-put*; and a ducking counter-attack *submarine*, as well as many others.

CLOSE THE LINE

In any position or movement, one of the lines should be closed to give a fencer additional tactile information about the position of an opponent's blade. For instance if, after an attempt to hit, a fencer closes out the sixte line

Here the line is closed in sixte taking the coach's point out of target. Developing the habit of closed line makes fencers more effective.
(Photo: Kevin Nixon)

Here the line is closed in quarte taking the coach's point out of target. (Photo: Kevin Nixon)

as they return their hand on-guard they will feel, via their sense of touch, whether or not the opponent's blade is also in sixte (6). Also, if the sixte line is closed in the on-guard position the opponent can only hit in that line with great angulation. This means the opponent has to direct their weapon to the inside or low outside line, which limits their options.

The fencer who applies this principle is more able to feel the blade and receives information early about the surrounding space, making their defence more effective. Also, an attack which closes out the opponent's blade in opposition helps the referee. Riposting with a closed line prevents an opponent from hitting with remises.

However, with simultaneous attacks where one fencer changes their line of attack, referees currently give priority to the fencer who has not changed the line. It is therefore important to understand the way a referee interprets the rules and to constantly re-assess their interpretation.

MAKE AN OPPONENT PERCEIVE A CHANGE OF LINE LATE

The later the line of an offensive action is changed, the less time an opponent has to parry. Moving the point from the outside line to the inside is easier than from inside to outside, as the arm is usually moving across. Generally, it is easier to parry an action finishing inside than outside high or low; therefore practising hitting those targets can be useful. In the case of a disengage from engagement, an action at the last moment will be more effective.

Also, a small disengage after a light beat can make the opponent see a change of line late. For example, a beat 4 disengage, if executed lightly with a partly extended arm and small movement, will cause the opponent to see the line of attack late. Keeping the hand relaxed produces a fast, hence hard-to-parry disengage, which has a very good chance of success.

KEEP AN OPPONENT OUT OF THEIR COMFORT ZONE

This can be achieved in various ways, including:

- Trying to break their rhythm (also changing speed of preparation)
- Putting them under pressure (this includes pressing with absence of the blade)
- Threatening with actions to simulate attacks, counter-attacks or parries
- Using a straight arm (the line)
- Blade actions (beat, repetitive aggressive beats, changes of engagement, pressure, engagements)
- Keeping a distance an opponent does not like (usually close or continually changing the distance), and constantly threatening their target with the point.

All these things can make an opponent uncomfortable and hinder the timing and execution of their actions.

REALISM

Often a lesson is artificial and detached from the reality of a fight. In training, a coach's signals are often construed to elicit a specific response from a fencer. Responding only to artificial signals is unhelpful to the fencer. To increase the value of a lesson, a coach should try to ensure distance, timing, presentation of the blade (threatening) and

Point-in-line position occurs when the point of the weapon is threatening the target and the foil is in a straight line with the fully extended arm. I believe teaching any action from line, and its use can pay dividends. (Photo: Kevin Nixon)

initiative are all as realistic as possible. Of course, in certain situations, a coach has to slow down and help a fencer execute a movement correctly, but should quickly revert to realistic conditions. Some coaches always have fencers responding only to their movements. They should introduce exercises where a fencer takes the initiative, as happens in a fight. Thus an additional connection between lesson and fight is created. The initiative should switch from coach to fencer and back as happens in a fight.

> ### Remember!
>
> A fencer should see a fight in their lesson and a lesson in their fight.

During a fight, a fencer *may* have the opportunity to do a particular action they have been practising. In a lesson, they can repeat the same action many more times and therefore improve the speed and accuracy of the chosen movement and embed the muscle memory. This is the most basic value of a lesson for a fencer. In a lesson a coach can also keep surprising a fencer, thereby giving them the opportunity to deal with the unexpected.

Of course, a lesson has other values: perfecting technique; efficiency of execution; feeling for distance, timing and change of rhythm; speed of reaction and execution; and speed of decision-making. Whatever the objective of the lesson, it should be executed as realistically as possible.

INTRODUCING OBSTACLES

After the initial phase of learning how and when to execute actions, coaches should gradually give fencers more obstacles to overcome. First, the coach should take genuine parries and counter-parries, then make unexpected counter-attacks or keep changing distance and speed. The target should be moved in different directions making it harder to hit. Dealing successfully with unexpected actions gives a fencer more confidence and makes a lesson more like a fight. To develop speed, coaches should give fencers very little time to hit; also, working at close-quarters should add to the level of difficulty.

Fencers themselves can create obstacles by looking to the side during a lesson (improving peripheral vision) or by closing their eyes in certain exercises with the coach's knowledge. The above principle manifests itself to a large extent in the Italian *problem-solving* lesson.

PSYCHOLOGICAL REFRACTORY PERIOD

The term **psychological refractory period** refers to a well-known phenomenon: when there are two signals close together in time (around a quarter of a second) and someone has already reacted to the first signal, their reaction to the second signal will be much slower. Sometimes there is a latent reaction to the first signal so the second signal will also induce a slower response as a result.

Fencers can take advantage of this phenomenon by making a feint counter-attack to which an opponent has been trained not to react followed by a real counter-attack against which the reaction is slower (even if the opponent reacted by stopping himself from reacting – latent response) and so has more chance to succeed.

BOW AND ARROW

Usually, a fencer should be encouraged to keep arm and body movements separate. However, sometimes it is helpful to think of the trunk and legs as a bow and the sword arm as an arrow. This can be achieved by lowering the legs while rotating the trunk and moving the head and sword arm back; when the moment comes to strike, the movement of the weapon can be accelerated considerably taking cumulative power from the legs, trunk and sword arm – like an arrow being shot from a bow.

Bow and arrow

Fencers like Chamley-Watson (USA) and Choi (KOR) sometimes use this technique while executing a flèche attack. Although it looks risky, the preparatory movements of trunk, arm and legs may invite an opponent to react in a way that makes them more vulnerable to the attack. If an opponent's reaction is to counter-attack, then doing a beat from such a position is effective or finishing the final movement still in time. Among younger fencers, we can see this principle emerging in Shikine's (JPN) fencing. This technique gives the weapon the most power and acceleration.

COACHING AGAINST LEFT- AND RIGHT-HANDEDNESS

Although right-handedness is more common, in fencing there is a relatively high percentage of left-handers. Fencing them is different because of the different relationship between blades and the curve of the target; coaches should, therefore, give lessons with both hands.

Some coaches give lessons with a weapon in each hand and randomly change hands, adding to the level of difficulty in training. Using a French grip in a lesson allows the coach to change hands more easily, which is more effective than giving one lesson left-handed and another right-handed. Of course, sometimes a coach will work on a specific left-handed opponent for the whole lesson.

COMBINING TECHNIQUE, TACTICS AND PSYCHOLOGY

The right frame of mind is critical to a fencer's performance as it can affect every aspect – technique, coordination, thinking and even muscle control. Tension, both mental and physical, affects accuracy and the ability to think clearly; being relaxed helps concentration, precision and coordination.

Power of the mind

Without doubt the mind can be a powerful tool to enhance performance and fencers must learn to control it from an early stage For example Tofalides' (CYP) mind is his greatest weapon.

Therefore correct warm-up routines are helpful to reach the right frame of mind. It is important for the coach to know a fencer well. If a fencer feels in a warm-up lesson their point is hitting correctly and they can execute actions well, such feelings have a positive effect on a fencer's mindset. Equally, if they know how to fence a particular opponent, this can boost confidence. The wrong mindset can ruin tactical thinking and coordination, and consequently timing, technique and accuracy, thus causing catastrophic results.

BALANCE

Balance is another attribute of technique. It is obvious that having good balance is an advantage as it makes a fencer able to change from one situation to another quickly, giving more power to execute any action and it offers greater control in delivering the hit. A lower and wider on-guard position gives better balance and provides optimum mobility. Generally, fencers do not sit low enough and do not use their back leg enough.

Off balance

It is also important to practise being effective while off balance, as this can happen in a fight.

EXPLOIT TACTICAL VAGUENESS

Applying this principle can create confusion in an opponent's mind as to what action to take and therefore cause a delay in reaction. The aim is to create a situation to encourage attack as much as defence. For instance, Cassara's preparation in the quarte (4) line in one sense threatens the chest but at the same time encourages a counter-attack in the sixte (6) line. Another example is a feint in the low line with little extension, so an opponent is in two minds whether to attack in the high line or take a low-line parry.

Often pressing slowly with various actions on the blade draws an opponent's attack on preparation but at the same time threatens an attack. The fencer who does this is ready to parry if an opponent attacks early but often switches to the attack if an opponent hesitates, delays or just begins to initiate.

Vagueness

Yet another example could be a partly extended sword arm which may create uncertainty in the opponent's mind as to whether this is in line or not. Peter Joppich (GER) often prepares his actions (often a parry but could be attack or even counter-attack) from such a vague hand position. Situations like this can make an opponent react more slowly and less decisively, hence there is more chance to win the hit.

INDIVIDUALITY

It is important, particularly in the later stages of development, to maximize a fencer's strengths. There are many fencers who are successful because their strong natural style has been developed. For example, those with less explosiveness will rely more on changes in timing than speed.

EFFICIENCY

Some fencers seem to score hits with ease while others use too many muscles in moving, which affects coordination and accuracy. Forcing hits is not only inefficient but also ineffective. Fencers should aim to develop efficient movements as this usually has a positive effect on timing and winning the hits as it helps with coordination, deceptiveness and overall effectiveness. Coaches should encourage fencers to focus on lightness of execution, optimal muscular involvement and of course small and accurate movements. From time to time reminders such as, 'Do not crush the bird' or 'spaghetti arm' are useful. Generally, shorter fencers have to do more work to score than fencers with a longer reach.

CENTRAL LINE – LINING UP WITH THE OPPONENT

Right of way is important, but it means nothing if you don't actually hit your opponent. The **central line** is a hypothetical line created when the fencer lines up not only their point, but also their whole body, with the middle of the opponent's target. The middle of the opponent's target is not necessarily the middle of their chest, but the centre of the target as it appears to the fencer. Usually this will be in the middle of the breast of the fencing arm, but of course, it changes as the opponent moves their body.

Fencer and coach in line. Fencers should not only line-up with opponents but should also practise this is in training. This gives fencers an accurate bearing of where the central line is and any movement out of line can be more accurate. (Photo: Kevin Nixon)

Awareness of how to create and maintain this central line with the opponent's target helps a great deal with accuracy. It also aids the fencer in defence, as it gives them a useful bearing should they wish to avoid the opponent's attack. If a fencer's point is on target, but the rest of their body is orientated elsewhere, they have a higher chance of missing. Also, any rotation in the hips may move a fencer out of line, badly affecting accuracy.

When one fencer lines up with the other, the probability of hitting on target increases, this is, therefore, a useful principle to apply. Coaches should encourage fencers to get a feel for the central line as early as possible, and to use it to their advantage. In lessons, coaches should continually check that their fencer is lining up with them correctly.

Some fencers deliberately move to the side of the piste to disrupt the feeling for the centre line. It is up to their adversary to maintain the line-up by moving accordingly.

SECOND-INTENTION

Coaches should create second-intention situations in lessons, in addition to encouraging fencers to do so in fights. The fencer who can make their opponent react and take advantage

Lining up

In the 2015 European Championships during a match for GB against Italy, Garozzo (ITA) tried to move out of line with Kruse (GBR) in between hits. Kruse continued to readjust before each hit and line up correctly with the Italian. Kruse remained accurate throughout the match.

Sometimes both fencers apply this principle and line up with each other. One example is the 1984 Olympic Men's Foil Final between Mauro Numa (ITA) and Matthias Behr (GER). Both fencers maintained perfect central lines during the entire match.

The 2018 Shanghai Grand Prix Final between Kruse (GBR) and Safin (RUS) had a particularly wide piste. The fencers appeared to be out of line as they stuck to opposite edges of the piste. However, closer inspection would reveal both of them were rotating their bodies to line up with each other diagonally. They were both respecting the principle of the central line, despite not being in line in relation to the piste.

of it is in a stronger position. Any movement making an opponent parry, attack or counter-attack should be perfected. It is of huge importance to see the difference between a false and a real action, as reacting to a false action will help an opponent to score.

ATTENTION TO DETAIL

The difference between winning and losing can often be very small, therefore small differences can mean winning the hits. Those differences may apply to many areas. For example, the way of executing certain fencing actions such as beat attack: it can be much more effective to execute a beat on an opponent's blade later, during the extension of the beating fencer's arm, rather than *before the extension*.

Other examples might be spotting the difference between the beginning of a false counter-attack and a real one, between a false beat and a real one, between the beginning of preparation and an attack, and many more.

ATHLETES' NEEDS FIRST

The nature of coaching requires the needs of athletes to always be put first. A coach should forget about ego and do everything in their power to help a fencer to develop their game. There may be situations where a coach's personal ambition can hinder a fencer's further development. This would be in conflict with the ultimate purpose of coaching which is to help a fencer get better.

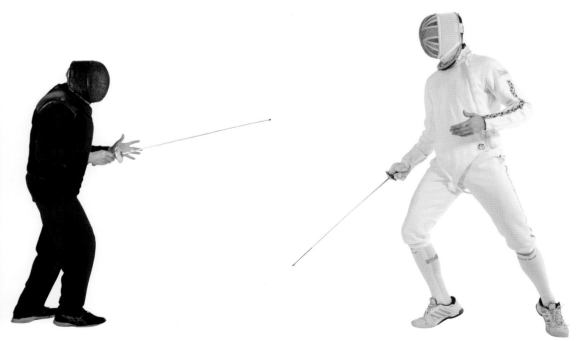

Opening the chest to invite the attack in high line. Here we see second intention by drawing the opponent's response to the opening of the target with a counter-attack, while being ready to parry and riposte. Any second intention set-up should be encouraged in training and competition. (Photo: Kevin Nixon)

2 | PRINCIPLES OF TRAINING

It is impossible to produce successful fencers without a comprehensive training programme. In this chapter, there is a list of all the principles that relate to planning the best possible programme.

PERIODIZATION

Just as in nature, every human activity is cyclical. How training is planned depends on the calendar of competitions and qualifying events but, more importantly, on the timing of the main competitions: Zonal, World Championships or Olympic Games. Periodization – the long-term cyclic structuring of training and practice to maximize performance at important competitions – is necessary, as it is simply impossible to maintain a high level of performance during the entire year.

The International Fencing Federation (FIE) calendar for the senior circuit has the World Championships finishing at the end of July with qualifying competitions every month starting in October with breaks in December and April. The obvious rest period is for four weeks

Photo opposite by Chris Turner.

immediately after the World Championships in July: ideally, one week of passive rest and three weeks of more or less active rest participating in various relaxing activities not requiring fencing movements. The four-week rest period is for healing injuries and improving health.

From the end of August, there are around eight weeks before the first qualifying competition in October followed by two further qualifiers in November. These first three competitions of the season are less important than later ones and allow fencers to continue with pre-season training, easing off for the periods of competition.

This schedule before the first competition in January allows around sixteen weeks of training. The three weeks until mid-September can be used mainly for physical preparation mixing cardiovascular and strength exercises, plus some lessons and footwork exercises (footwork with weights is advisable).

From about mid-September to the first week of October fencers should spend a lot of time fencing (lessons, footwork, learning and competitive bouts), doing physical work only as maintenance, usually at the end of fencing or on a separate day.

This activity should taper off before the first competition in October and again in November,

South East Asia pre-season fencing camp, one of the many pre-season fencing camps which takes place around the world. (Photo: Jornnawat (P'Mod) Limprasert)

after which fencers should spend two weeks in December on physical preparation with some tactical analysis of recent competitions.

From the end of December, the number of fights should increase and an international training camp arranged if possible before the January World Cup in Paris. It is good to have a five- to six-day camp finishing four or five days before the competition. The camp could be arranged to finish two weeks before the event, provided, however, that in the week after the camp there is low volume, yet high-intensity training. Low volume but high-intensity training is advisable just before a competition because it can facilitate a high quality of performance without fatiguing the fencers.

In the competitive period, post-competition micro-cycles should always include recovery

High-intensity training: sparring sessions at a pre-season training camp. (Photo: Paula Huckle)

sessions. The character of successive micro-cycles will depend on how much time there is before the next competition. The focus of the micro-cycles should be on strengths and things to be improved. In a micro-cycle when the maximum number of fights is required, a fencer should expect to do the equivalent of just under 30 × 15-hit fights over five days – depending on the standard of the opponents. (Tougher opponents then lower the number of fights.)

In building up towards the competition, it is important to remember quality; if the quality of fencing in training drops noticeably then a period of rest or stopping completely should be considered.

During the break from competition in April, there should be a return to physical preparation for about two weeks before progressing to more competitive fights. Whenever possible, before each competition, fencers should take part in an international camp of five or six days' duration finishing four or five days before the tournament. As mentioned above, such camps could be arranged earlier, provided there is high-intensity training the week after and a whole week for tapering just before the competition.

Whenever there is a longer break between competitions (at least six weeks), a similar sequence can be repeated: around 20 per cent of the time on rest and physical preparation, the next 20 per cent on more technical work (lessons and footwork) while maintaining strength and conditioning and 50 per cent on tactical and competitive fencing with a possible camp, tapering for the last 10 per cent of time before competing. Richard Kruse (GBR) often takes a whole week's rest before an international competition.

Good preparation - Richard Kruse, Grand Prix 2016, Havana. Six-week build-up. Result - 1st

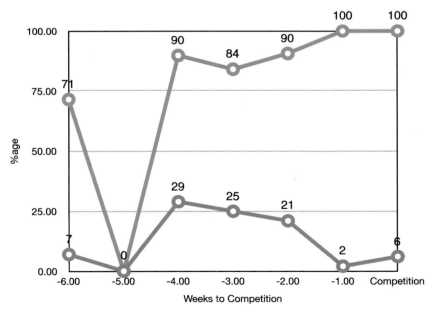

Kruse had a six-week build-up to Havana, starting with a week of strength and conditioning and a complete break from fencing. In week 5, lessons, footwork and some light fencing were initiated. Weeks 4, 3 and 2 saw competitive fights ranging from 21–29 fights per week achieving a victory rate of 90 per cent. The week immediately before the competition fights reduced dramatically. Final result - Gold.

Poor preparation — World Cup, St Petersburg, 2016. Six-week build-up. Result - L64

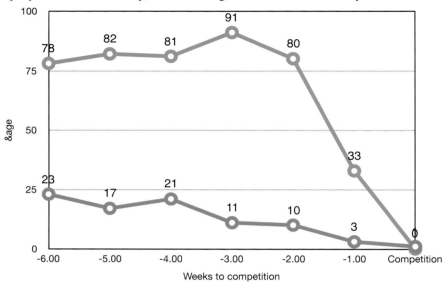

Preparation for St Petersburg was poor in comparison to Havana. Kruse was advised to start fencing from the beginning of the six-week preparation period. This was too early and, consequently, he was unable to maintain his form during the competition. Result - lost 64.

The graphs, above, show Richard Kruse's training schedule and the impact of good preparation to win the Grand Prix in Havana schedule in 2016 and, for comparison, a poor schedule before St Petersburg where Richard was out in the final 64.

In order to find the best formula, each fencer should keep a training diary detailing the content of training (lesson length, footwork, number of fights with results) and relate this to the result in the competition.

fencing and so on. Or there can be a period alternating between resting and hard training. You can hit fencers with hard training followed by several days of recovery to make them fresh, as the body will overcompensate in its recovery from hard training, before hitting them again with hard training. Or alternate periods of lessons, footwork and games with just fencing. The pendulum approach is effective and worth introducing in some periods of training, for instance in the build-up to a major event.

PENDULUM

The pendulum principle, as the name suggests, applies to contrasting changes in training content.

Physical preparation can be alternated with fencing, for instance, one week focusing on strength and conditioning, the second on

INTENSITY

Training has to be as intensive as actual fights in a competition; it brings training closer to the feeling of a real competition. It is important to remind fencers to maintain hard fencing, as there is a danger of getting into the habit of taking it easy. Fencers shouting after scoring hits in training like they would in a competition is a good sign of intense training.

Here the cooperation of both players is necessary. They have to push each other all the time and constantly create challenges. In competition, fencers must make decisions under pressure and often operate in extreme conditions. Only highly intensive training can replicate that. The fencer who does not try is wasting their time and that of their partner.

While taking a lesson, the fencer should imagine performing against the strongest opponent in the world; ideally in the lesson, they see the fight they are getting ready for, and in the fight, they see the lesson. In order to maintain intensity, the lesson should be in the region of 20–30 minutes' duration.

Squad training should also be intensive and productive, to enable fencers to do a lot in a relatively short period of time. When squad sessions are extended, intensity drops, as does speed and focus. Consequently, fencers get a sense of wasting time, which is no good for their morale. However, a fencer should never pursue intensity at the expense of quality; adequate rest between training bouts is important.

ENDURANCE, STRENGTH AND SPEED

In order to build up a fencer's form for a competition, they must first do the mileage, which means a large number of fights, long footwork sessions and lessons. Weights can be introduced during footwork (a weight jacket and wristbands or small weights, rubber bands, etc.). Also, plyometric exercises in a general session are effective in building up strength, plus weights in the gym at the end. Finally, speed drills should be introduced while fencers are fresh, with lots of maximum-frequency, short-burst movements complementing coordination and reaction drills.

While building up speed in lessons, the coach should apply short (10–20 seconds)

Building up speed. A camp where fencers are engaging in high-intensity bouts. (Photo: Chris Turner)

maximum-intensity periods of work mixed with periods of rest (around 30 seconds). Obviously, the important components of speed in fencing are sharp selective perception, anticipation and quick thinking.

WARMING UP AND WARMING DOWN

This should be habitual for every athlete to prevent injury. More advanced fencers warm themselves up very effectively and they usually develop their own personal routine. Usually, fencers who thoroughly warm up and warm down have fewer problems with injuries and their training is more effective.

CHANGING THE CONDITIONS OF TRAINING – ALTERING THE STIMULUS

It is important to regularly alter the conditions of training; every coach should introduce some changes to their pattern of lessons every year. Examples include using the opposite hand, footwork with weights or expander, shorter

Effective pair work

Sometimes two fencers can create effective changes with each other in training – what I call effective pair work. In Britain, Fiona McIntosh (GBR) worked extremely well with Linda Strachan (GBR) and Richard Kruse (GBR) was pushed hard by Laurence Halsted (GBR) and later by James Davis (GBR) and vice versa.

piste, shorter time, lower oxygen pressure, anything which is different from the norm. If the same stimulus is always applied, with time it becomes less effective.

There is a limit as to how much can be achieved simply by increasing the intensity and number of fights. There have to be other changes in order to make progress. These changes can include a new composition of exercises in lessons, new tasks in fencing, limiting time and space during practice, fencing with the opposite hand, footwork with weights, fencing new opponents and training at high altitude. Participating in international training camps brings huge stimulation to fencers.

Sometimes training can, in some ways be harder than competition. In the past fencers would be woken up at 3am to do

Legs apart against the wall: one of many stretching exercises which can be used during warming down. It is particularly important to hold this for at least a minute to achieve the maximum benefit. (Photo: Kevin Nixon)

fencing drills, or taken underwater to prac-tise decision making and tactical thinking (by Hungarian coaches Janos Kevey and Laszlo Szepesi).

PRESSURE TRAINING (WITH PENALTIES FOR FAILURE)

Pressure training is when scoring is made artificially hard and there are consequences for failure or rewards for success. In pressure training, all sorts of obstacles are created for the fencers. For example, five hits in a row or one minute at 4 metres, with three burpees for every hit against them. Fencers will become more confident by dealing with these challenges.

Pressure training is equally good for individ-uals and team matches. For instance, during the first and last 30 seconds of a 3-minute period, the opposite team scores double for every single hit. And at any stage of the match, the coach can change the score to add to the pressure, the losing team having to do some physical penalty.

Such training is linked to the principle of changing stimulus, since adaptation to such a stimulus should bring a change in the quality of performance.

SPECIFICITY

'A snooker player will not get better at snooker by running around the table.' This statement accurately reflects the principle of specificity in training: training should always have a clear and precise goal, relevant to fencing. At a senior level the correlation between the results of general fitness tests and fencing-specific fitness is rather weak (Czajkowski). There are fencers whose results in various general fitness tests are very good,

but they 'die' on the piste in direct elimi-nation (DE) matches. The closer a training session can get to the conditions a fencer will experience in competition the better. Some fencers use certain competitions for training, which are usually (but not always) better than training. However, even then there is a difference in the standard of opponents, the seriousness of their performance and the atmosphere. For example, the Olympic Games have a unique atmosphere, impossi-ble to reproduce anywhere else. Sometimes simulating the noise of a competition and the crowd can be used during a session; organizing VIP matches with foreign teams and media involvement is one such way.

Again, participation in an international camp with lots of fencers who are going to be in a real competition makes training specific.

> ## Quality
>
> Fencers need to experience as high a standard of fencing as possible. Fatigue usually decreases quality, movements become bigger, and reactions slow.

QUALITY

Fencers constantly need to push themselves beyond their boundaries to improve. Therefore the quality of their actions is important. Maintaining a solid position and balanced movements help. If one fencer raises their game, it often lifts the standard of the others so there is a chain of influence on the whole group.

In the immediate period of preparation before a major event, if there is a drop in quality during a session, it is better to take a short break. If, after the break, there is no improvement, the fencer should be advised to stop the session completely.

Of course, fencers should try all sorts of 'tricks' to bring about a better performance,

Take a break! Fencers taking time out from training. (Photo: Niki Bruckner)

as it is important to learn to win when not fencing well, but that can be practised further away from a competition date. These tricks can include focusing only on one thing, such as distance; trying to apply some relaxation techniques (including listening to inspirational music for a while); practising mindfulness – staying in the present, or visualization – mentally rehearsing a best performance.

Interestingly, some fencers perform better when they are tired, possibly because tired muscles are more relaxed and therefore coordination improves, leading to better timing and accuracy. But only in a preparatory period, when it is desirable to develop specific stamina, there is merit in fencing on 'a background of fatigue.'

Therefore, in most cases, it is better to fence when fresh, so strength and conditioning should be done after fencing or as a separate session. If strength and conditioning is done before fencing without adequate rest, it can have a negative effect on quality.

Competition preparation

Years of observation by coach and fencer lead to the creation of the most effective formula for building towards a competition.

TAPERING

This important principle is part of periodization. When approaching a competition, a fencer should significantly decrease the volume of actions and increase quality and intensity while focusing on their strengths. There has to be adequate rest in order to reach the phase of over-compensation, when the body reacts to overtraining with better recovery. The speed of mental and physical recovery varies with fencers: some need four days of complete rest and a short sharp lesson the day before a competition; some need to stop for three days and do nothing the day before; others may be happy to train every second day during a tapering period. There is no hard-and-fast rule to the amount of tapering required. The most important principle coaches and fencers should apply is individualization of training, teaching and learning.

On the last training camp before a major event, fencers should have two short, sharp sessions per day with short lessons where they perform their favourite actions. Observing and if possible monitoring an athlete's physical and mental state prevents overtraining but may sometimes lead to withdrawing them from a particular session.

A STRONG FINISH TO THE BOUT (END-GAME)

There is a tendency in all sports to work on a strong finish, as athletes who can develop this habit have more chances to win.

Coaches sometimes talk of finding another gear. Even marathon runners sprint at the end of their race. In fencing, it is more complicated, but fencers and coaches have to find a way for each individual to develop a habit of increasing the intensity of a fight towards the end. This should be practised among higher level fencers. Here, some exercises from pressure training are helpful: for example, when there is limited time and space, the task is to produce a certain number of hits or to alternate priority in the fight with a very short time limit – for example, 10 seconds per hit.

Towards the end of a fight, a fencer has more information to work with: the experi-enced fencer is aware of what to expect from an opponent, as well as a more accurate sense of timing. The last hit is the most important and the hardest; we often see a fencer who has reached 14 points receiving some hits before scoring his last one. In my opinion, we should develop fencers whose focus on the last hit is not any different than for any other hit in the fight (although they do have more information by this time). Every fencer and coach should strive to achieve an increasingly strong perfor-mance as the fight progresses.

AN INTERDISCIPLINARY APPROACH TO TRAINING

In modern sport, it is necessary to involve specialists from fields other than fencing in the training process. The services of sports psy-chologists, physiotherapists, strength and con-ditioning trainers, nutritionists, performance analysts and others, such as yoga trainers, are often used. These services should be under the guidance of the fencing coach who is in charge of a fencer's whole training process.

3 | PRINCIPLES OF PERFORMANCE

The previous chapter dealt with developing fencers' abilities. However, this is not enough. In this chapter, I outline what I believe are the major factors that will allow a fencer to perform to the best of their ability, particularly during competition.

POSITIVE THINKING

I believe in cognitive psychology. We can control, to quite a large extent, what our mind produces; to be successful we must think of ourselves as successful and therefore box away all negative thoughts and deal with them later. We must constantly develop the discipline of positive thinking, as this will affect how we feel and consequently how we perform. Coaches should encourage fencers to think of themselves as winners.

Every competition or hit should be seen as an opportunity to experience a higher level of performance. This has to be practised continually to become an ingrained habit. Fencers should see competition as the ultimate environment they want to be in, as somewhere they belong. They should see every situation

Photo opposite by Niki Bruckner.

as a positive – good to be in a competition, good to have a hard opponent, good to have the opportunity to fence well.

CONFIDENCE

Confidence is something to be practised. It is a consequence of positive experiences and thinking.

Confidence is a natural consequence of **good preparation** and a fencer has to believe in preparation in order to gain confidence from it.

Good past performances help create confidence

Examples of others doing well can also be inspirational, motivating and at the same time boost confidence ('If he/she can do it, so can I'). Also when fencers *know what to expect* from their opponents and what to do against them, they are more confident.

Success in adveristy

One of the best confidence boosters is experiencing success in dealing with difficulties in extreme conditions, such as a 5–4 victory against a former world champion from 4–0 down.

Asking fencers to *write down what they are good at* is a useful exercise. This has proved to be a helpful tool in restoring confidence.

Fencers need to think positively, they need to believe on the day of competition they will find the extra 10 per cent; they must believe they can win against a given opponent and believe in their actions. If a fencer has doubts about their performance, those doubts will drag down their performance. For instance, if for a moment they are afraid of missing the target, they are more likely to miss than otherwise. Even after losing 5–0 in a poule, a fencer should *believe* they can win the next fight. Such belief will help their performance. But this can only be achieved by believing they can score the next hit.

Physical reinforcements of success build confidence.
(Photo: Niki Bruckner)

Frame of mind

Often a lower-ranked team or fencer beats one of a higher rank because they have the *right frame of mind* (believing is an important part of it) and the *right tactics*.

Although the last hit is the most important one, it would be ideal if the fencer's belief and focus for the last hit was the same as for any other hit in the fight. One can lose a fight in spite of believing in every hit, but the fencer who believes has more chance to score and win.

Confidence can also be gained by focusing on one skill and setting oneself a small achievable improvement target; confidence should grow while achieving those targets. For example, a fencer could focus on sitting lower in their on-guard position.

HERE AND NOW

This is an old concept but it has proved to be effective. If a fencer is totally engaged in the here and now, there is no space in their mind for any negative thinking and emotions. Fencers have to be reminded to practise being in the here and now in order to develop this helpful habit.

In competitions fencers sometimes get angry with a referee who, in their opinion, has made a mistake; this rankles and consequently they are not engaged in what is actually happening, so naturally their performance diminishes. Also, when victory is close, and they need to produce the last hit, their mind shifts to the future, thus reducing their performance.

FOCUS ON THE NEXT HIT

This principle is particularly helpful and should be practised all the time. Usually, after scoring a hit, there is a tendency to relax and lose focus for a moment.

Discussions with referees often occur, and in most instances these discussions are unhelpful to the fencer. In these situations it is best to shift all your energy and power to keep your mind on fencing. (Photo: Niki Bruckner)

This tendency increases with the gap in the score. It is important to be motivated and ready for the next hit, because if an opponent starts scoring, their confidence will rise and they become harder to fence. Fencers have to be reminded to immediately focus on the next hit after scoring the last one. This must become habitual so that, while leading, a fencer does not relax but stays even *hungrier* for the next hit; this costs energy and effort but in the end, it is more efficient than getting into a long and difficult fight by losing concentration. To maintain such a level of concentration can be almost painful, but it is better to suffer a bit than relax too much and get into a messy fight that may end either way.

VISUALIZATION

A fencer tries to mentally reconstruct a fight when they performed particularly well, thus recapturing the feeling and frame of mind they had.

It does not have to take a long time. Even spending 10 minutes in a quiet corner during a competition mentally rehearsing a particular fight can be beneficial. Again, this type of activity has to be practised, so a fencer can do it at any time and their mind will engage.

A fencer visualizing a successful fight before the next round helps regain the feeling of performing well. (Photo: Niki Bruckner)

FOLLOW A ROUTINE

It is well known that athletes who follow routines tend to produce better performances than those who do not. In the relatively stressful environment of an important competition where there is a lot of uncertainty, doing something familiar can bring some sense of stability. James Davis (GBR), for instance, has a certain set of exercises he does before starting to fence and in his warm-up lesson, he always follows a chain of previously rehearsed actions. The same applies to Richard Kruse. Only in the later stages of a competition might they go into the next fight without their usual routines.

Autogenic training

I have always found autogenic training a useful method of relaxation. It takes 10 minutes and requires a quiet place.

A fencer has to find the most comfortable position and try to relax every muscle. Then focus on relaxing in turn the right arm, left arm, right leg, left leg, trunk, face and shoulders. With the feeling of relaxation, there should be a suggestion of heaviness, which means the body is *listening*. Then instruct the body to feel warmth in every limb before moving to the trunk. The final command is a sense of energy and readiness to face any opponent.

A fencer listening to music as part of his preparation before a fight. (Photo: Niki Bruckner)

RELAXATION

It is also a well-known fact that athletes focus better if they feel relaxed. Therefore any effective relaxation technique should be incorporated into routines.

Listening to music is popular and fencers are often seen getting ready wearing headphones. Having a physiotherapist is also helpful, as many fencers like a final treatment before fencing – although it is important for the coach and physiotherapist to identify if an athlete really needs help, as over-reliance on this can have a detrimental effect.

A strong warm-up to the point of fatigue relaxes muscles and mind. Relaxed muscles usually lead to a relaxed mind, and tense muscles can lead to a tense mind. Contracting and relaxing the arm and shoulder muscles for several seconds can result in lower muscular tension after contraction, which relaxes the mind.

Practising the 'here and now' or mindfulness should prove effective after a while, as the mind responds to the instruction.

PSYCHING UP BEFORE A FIGHT (RIGHT FRAME OF MIND)

The right frame of mind is an extremely important factor affecting an athlete's performance. Everyone searches for the best way to psych themselves up to perform well. Find out the most effective way to get into the right frame of mind and stick to it. Don't be afraid to try something new.

There are many different ways of achieving the right frame of mind and tried-and-tested principles of performance can be used, such as:

- Meetings and discussions
- Remembering previous victories
- Happy conversations (with jokes)
- advice (tactical advice – knowing what to do and what to expect)
- Special individual lesson or warm-up fight
- Listening to favourite music
- Visualization of one's best performance
- Positive thinking and self-talk

A group of fencers engaged in a positive and happy exchange ahead of the next round.
(Photo: Niki Bruckner)

- Engaging in the present
- Thinking what to do and when
- Relaxation
- Believing on the day one will find the extra 10 per cent

PLAYING TO ONE'S STRENGTHS

Everybody has strengths and weaknesses. In training we tend to work on both but, when it comes to competition, a fencer will have the best chance to perform well if they focus on strengths, exploit an opponent's weaknesses and prevent them using their strengths.

In competition, concentrating on strengths can lead to success. For instance, if a fencer has great mobility, they should use their legs as much as possible. If they have a strong attack on preparation, they should set up situations where an opponent might make big and fast preparations, for instance after breaking distance. Some fencers specialize in making an opponent parry and then take advantage of this with different counter-actions. Other fencers may be good at forcing an opponent to counter-attack and finishing the attack in time (winning the right of way).

STICK TO THE SIMPLE THINGS THAT WORK

As pressure increases towards the end of a fight a fencer has to be reminded to be disciplined and stick to the simple things that work. Under pressure, there is a tendency to *lose technique* when movements become bigger, so a strong foundation supported by simplicity should work well.

Keep it simple

Sticking to the simple things that work has produced results for me many times.

A fencer achieving his performance goal. (Photo: Niki Bruckner)

The enjoyment, camaraderie and fun of fencing leads to success if there is hard work. (Photo: Chris Turner)

If one particular action works, a fencer should draw their opponent's attention to another action and only return to the effective one after a while, giving the opponent a chance to forget it.

FOCUS ON PROCESS AND PERFORMANCE GOALS

In sport, we can differentiate between outcome, process and performance goals. A fencer should bear in mind outcome goals but try to achieve them by focusing on process and performance goals during a competition.

An *outcome goal* is the final position (gold, podium, top eight, top sixteen). Whilst the outcome is important, it is dangerous to focus solely on this as it takes the mind out of the present, which will lead to a poorer performance. *Process goals* can be to control the dis-

tance, change the rhythm, have a loose arm. *Performance goals* can be an accuracy of over 70 per cent, hitting with four flicks to shoulder, using more ripostes than counter-attacks, hitting with answering attacks.

ENJOYMENT

Apart from considering the outcome goal and engaging one's intellectual powers, it is essential to develop positive emotions and a feeling of enjoyment. Enjoyment stimulates creativeness and contributes towards relaxation, leading to better concentration, quicker thinking and sharper responses. A fencer must have fun fencing!

4 | SETTING GOALS

It takes many years of hard and systematic training to achieve the goal of being a complete and successful fencer. Here, I try to analyse specific areas that contribute to achieving this broader goal. I give many examples of fencing-related goals for athletes to work towards.

Goal-setting strategies clearly focus a fencer's mind on particular areas and have great motivational value. Generally, there are three types of goal in sport: *process*, *performance* and *outcome* goals.

PROCESS, PERFORMANCE AND OUTCOME GOALS

Process goals

Process goals specify the processes in which the performer engages, such as keeping the sword arm loose, moving smoothly, moving

the feet, keeping the right distance, keeping the point on target, changing the rhythm, small preparations, starting slowly, developing patience and eliminating rushing.

Performance goals

Performance goals specify an end product, for example achieving an indicator of plus 15 or over in a poule of 7, increasing accuracy to 80 per cent, hitting with more ripostes than counter-attacks, or hitting the outside sectors of the target.

Outcome goals

Outcome goals concern the final position in a competition, such as gold, podium, top eight, etc.

It is possible to create an almost endless list of goals to work on. Below are some examples of the most useful goals in the areas of footwork, technique, tactics and fighting skills, which can be of a performance or process nature. Of course, there are other areas where goals can be set, such as frequency of training, effort, intensity, duration and quality.

Photo opposite by Tom Jenkins.

Focus on process and performance goals

It is easy to focus too much on outcome goals. In terms of maximizing performance, it is best to bear outcome goals in mind but concentrate on process and performance goals. If one looks after the process and performance goals, then the outcome goals will take care of them-

The assessment of process goals is usually made by subjective observations by the coach and the fencer. Sometimes feedback from other coaches and fencers is helpful. Working on various goals can be done in individual lessons, footwork, pairs exercises, sparring and, finally, competition. The typical progression in the fulfilment of goals is from individual lesson to sparring and ultimately competition.

Performance goals are easier to measure than process goals in fencing. The most objective measures of performance include, for example, the score achieved in a particular fight or session, the percentage of on-target hits and the percentage of ripostes. Video analysis can give more objective information regarding the particular goal a fencer is working on. It is useful to conduct performance reviews after different periods of training and competition, to evaluate progress on previously set goals.

DEVELOPMENT OF FOOTWORK

Precision in controlling distance

Precision is essential while moving backwards and forwards, and when breaking distance.

The winners of the 2016 GB Team Championships. (Photo: Chris Turner)

There is a tendency for fencers to be too far away while moving backwards and too close while moving forwards. Judging distance is subjective and both fencer and coach should be involved in this assessment during sparring, competitions and lessons. Exercises in pairs using foils, rubber ropes and balls are also useful, as it is easy to get feedback about how well a particular distance is kept.

Improving preparations of attack

The preparation of an attack can involve smaller and slower steps, with the back leg ready to respond, Avola steps, and breaking distance while advancing. Preparation also concerns the blade movements, which should be optimal (rather small) and before the legs.

There are three types of attack:

- On preparation
- Answering attacks
- Attacks from pressing

Many fencers have a tendency to make their preparations too big and too fast and consequently receive attacks on preparation or counter-attacks. Working on improving the preparation of attacks requires the constant attention of both fencer and coach. The simplest way of measuring improvement is to look at the number of successful attacks on preparation and counter-attacks received; reducing this number means better preparation. We can also include the number of ripostes against; however, in the initial stages, I would only focus on the number of attacks-on-preparation and counter-attacks received. The ideal timing to prepare an attack ensures it is too late for any counteraction against it.

To obtain meaningful figures, it is necessary to take a representative sample of hits from a variety of opponents. Combining attacks on preparation with counter-attacks is useful as it is often difficult to separate them; interpretation varies and if a counter-attack succeeds it usually means the preparation of the attack was not right. Constant observation of a fencer during training and paying attention to the way they prepare attacks can be enough to notice an improvement.

Improving the preparation of attacks is a continuous and perpetual process. If a particular fencer has an ineffective attack from pressing, I advise spending more time perfecting attacks on preparation or answering attacks which are from an opponent's initiative. Then, once attacking from the opponent's initiative is well established, it can be used as a basis to work on an attack from pressing. When developing a pressing style, there are other options apart from continuous pressing, such as a stop-start approach (stuttering preparation), each time assessing how the opponent responds after each stop. For example, Safin (RUS), and Avola (ITA) employ this technique to great effect. Repeatedly breaking distance backwards while still preparing forward is another option. Many Korean fencers use this method of preparation, and in the 1970s the famous Carlo Montano (ITA) – who was the last fencer using an Italian grip – also used this technique.

Two-tempo attacks after taking a step back

After a step back by the fencer there is less chance that an opponent will attack on the fencer's first step forward, as the fencer stepping back creates a bit of space. However, the step forward still has to be executed carefully.

Step-lunge attacks prepared by stepping back should be practised as they are safer than step-lunges initiated by moving forward. On the other hand, one-tempo attacks should be practised at the beginning of an opponent's step forward from slightly further than lunging distance. A coach could register all hits during particular fights and give the fencer feedback about how many overall attacks succeeded and how many were by step-lunge or step-flèche after a step back.

Working on changing the rhythm (fast–slow–fast, deceptiveness)

Although it is difficult to measure, this area is important and should be addressed continuously, using a subjective scale of 1–10, for instance. It is particularly necessary to try to break one's own rhythm pattern as everybody tends to follow a particular pattern. Slowing down after a fast start is very important, as a fencer needs to create the illusion the attack is about to peter out, before reinitiating with a fast finish. In fencing, deceleration can be just as important as acceleration.

Periodically during a lesson, a coach needs to increase the distance to make a fencer slow down before picking up speed again (in a 'second wave'). Then the coach can assess how well the fencer changed their rhythm (two waves) and how deceptive the action was. While working on the goal of changing rhythm, the fencer can speed up if he wants to prepare a parry and riposte as on a fast signal we should expect a fast reaction. Changing the rhythm also applies to blade movements. For example, when executing a 1-2-3 compound offensive action, a fencer could use a slow 1, and fast 2-3 or with a **double engagement**, a shorter first contact and then a longer second one.

Looking for the opportunity to shah-put

Both fencer and coach can identify how many times a hit is won after defending with distance. This skill can take a while to develop as it requires very responsive and powerful legs. If the goal of improving defence with distance is proving difficult to achieve, an alternative goal can be set: defence with distance *or* parry-riposte at the last moment.

Fencers should try to keep a tight distance in defence, since it is easier to defend with distance when an opponent does not have space to speed up. In most fencing lessons there should be an exercise which involves this skill as an effective way of improving footwork and a feeling for distance.

Holding opponents with good footwork

Often fencers stop moving their feet too early and as a result are hit by good opponents, who force them to counter-attack out of time. Follow the classic advice: keep your distance. When they cannot keep up with an adversary, some fencers develop an effective sweeping parry while stepping forward, often in high prime. The more positively they do it, the more likely they are to score a hit or at least avoid being hit. In recent years sweeping parries with a step forward have been partly replaced by the so-called Romanian counter-attack which, after hitting, involves immediately closing the threatened line, resulting in a single light.

The fencer with the better footwork has more chance of causing an adversary to make mistakes in preparation and consequently creates more opportunities to hit. Coaches should remind fencers in training and in competition to keep their feet moving. One incentive is to develop a physical penalty for every counter-attack out of time caused by poor footwork. Fencers know when their legs stop. A reasonable indicator of how responsive legs are and how well a fencer holds an opponent with good footwork is the number of counter-attacks out of time. Again, it is necessary to look at a representative number of hits and a variety of opponents.

Starting slowly

This goal is part of developing good preparation and is mentioned here separately as it is hugely important in developing more effective fencing. While preparing attacks, a fencer should move slowly, giving themselves more time to see what an opponent is doing and allowing themselves a greater change of speed when committing to the attack. This should happen during pressing and when reclaiming the initiative.

This goal is difficult because a fencer has to deal with controlling speed in a competitive environment, high adrenalin levels and a strong desire to hit. It is not easy to measure, but reducing the number of successful attacks on preparation and counter-attacks by an opponent can be an indication of starting slowly. Coaches often shout 'Start slowly!' When taking the initiative from an opponent, apart from a slower first step, it is sometimes useful to jump on the spot, to see whether the opponent will counter-attack, provided the fencer is ready to parry or to slowly initiate the preparation of an attack afterwards.

Distance

Here it is important for a fencer who is taking back the initiative to be at the distance they want rather than the distance an opponent wants. If a fencer starts from the distance their opponent dictates it is more likely they will be unable to cope with counter-attacks.

Working on improving the ability to change direction

The ability to change direction (agility) is an important skill in all sports requiring mobility, and fencers who can do it quickly and unnoticed by opponents have more chance of scoring hits.

An exercise to develop such a skill is to try hitting the target after defending with distance, while being attacked by an opponent using different footwork at the beginning of a fencer's step forward. During footwork sessions, coaches can use their hands to show the direction of movement, turning the hand to indicate a change of direction, back of the

Exercises in pairs can be used to help improve speed and agility. (Photo: Niki Bruckner)

hand indicating steps forward, front of the hand steps backwards (one hand slow steps, two hands fast). Sometimes coaches use clapping to indicate changes of direction. In a lesson, a coach can naturally tell how well a fencer is keeping distance. Some fencers make an additional step in the same direction before changing direction and are consequently late. This has to be worked on and corrected.

Also, any exercises which involve attacks with lunges followed by a fast recovery and another attack with a lunge or flèche are very useful in developing agility. Footwork in pairs, when one dictates the distance and the other follows, can involve lots of changes of direction.

Although it is possible to measure agility, in practice the coaches rely on observation and knowledge of the fencer.

DEVELOPMENT OF TECHNICAL AND TACTICAL SKILLS

Selective timing of counter-attacks

This involves working towards setting up a situation – proactive fencing rather than reactive fencing. In training, one exercise for this goal is to penalize a fencer for counter-attacking out of time, or being counter-attacked in time. In a lesson, a coach may require a fencer to differentiate between the beginning of an opponent's fast attack (preparation) with the point not threatening the target, when the fencer can counter-attack, and a slower movement with a non-threatening point, when the fencer can react with a point in line.

In a bout, a fencer needs to use distance and **false parries** to encourage their opponent to start an attack (preparation) quickly with a non-threatening point. The way to measure this can be the ratio of successful to unsuccessful counter-attacks; the higher it is,

the better the timing. Peter Joppich (GER) is well known for using false parries, where he pretends to search for an opponent's blade, who in an attempt to avoid the search, takes his point outside the opponent's target area.

Development of attacks with the blade to prevent being hit on preparation

There are two main actions on the blade: taking and beating. Taking the blade takes longer, as it allows for feeling the opponent's blade and changing the movement if necessary; whereas beating is short and crisp, creating an active blade movement with more energy. The opponent's blade is not always available but, if there is an opportunity to attack by taking the blade, it is also possible to control it, thus preventing the opponent from hitting the fencer on preparation. If the blade is not available, a fencer can offer their blade to be taken and when it is, they have access to their opponent's blade.

The ratio of successful attacks with the blade to the total number of attacks can be an indicator of fulfilling this goal. Usually, shorter fencers are more likely to attack by taking the blade, as it can be controlled for a longer time, whereas **beating the blade** can leave a timing gap in which the taller opponent can hit after the beat. Generally, it is advisable for shorter fencers to attack taller fencers by taking the blade.

Whenever possible, the taking and beating of the blade should be initiated with point movements while extending the arm – the reason being that it is harder for the opponent to see the point movement.

If the blade is available, beat attacks are particularly effective on preparation, as they give right of way. Taking the blade causes a reaction from an opponent and provides the attacker with tactile, in addition to visual information.

Making an opponent react by parrying. This is a potential 'gold mine' for many hits. (Photo: Niki Bruckner)

Choosing the moment for one-tempo or one-and-a-half-tempo attacks

In footwork, one tempo is a lunge or flèche, one-and-a-half is a half-lunge-lunge, half-step-flèche, patinando, flunge or hop-lunge.

Many fencers tend to do a step and lunge. This creates more opportunities for gaps in timing thus allowing counter-attacks. Therefore coaches should work on their fencers' ability to do one-tempo or one-and-a-half-tempo attacks, where there is less time for an opponent's counter-attacks. Recording hits will help to have more objective estimates when pursuing this goal.

In a lesson, a coach should practise more one-tempo foot actions than two-tempo, as a step-lunge is easy to absorb and is often over-used due to the lack of explosiveness. In addition to steps, I would encourage half-steps or half-lunge-lunges and any development from them. Also the so-called hop-lunge, which is similar to a sabre flèche without crossing the legs; this has a different rhythm to a step-lunge and can be used mainly as a preparation.

Looking for the opportunity to hit after making an opponent react by parrying

Anything to make an opponent react by parrying is good. Being parried should be considered a new opportunity to hit, rather than the end of an action. This is particularly important since deliberately creating a situation in which one is parried can be a gold mine of second-intention hits. There are a number of options.

Making a counter-parry and riposte
The difficulty here is in making the attack deep enough to force an opponent to parry, yet shallow enough to give time and space for a counter-parry. The depth of attack can be disguised by more visible and rapid movements. Making an opponent react by parrying is an example of one of the many challenges in fencing. Another challenge is to recognize the difference between a real parry and a false one. Often a counter-parry is not planned but occurs spontaneously as a result of an unexpected counteraction. This is fine but it is better to omit such actions from any

assessment as they are not second-intention. Taking a counter-parry with a step forward and riposting at close quarters is also effective and developing this skill can be a separate goal.

Making a renewal (remise or redouble)

A remise and counter-attack while blocking can be effective, particularly when an opponent delays the riposte (redouble) or makes a wide riposting movement (remise). In many cases, the approach can be premeditated, based on an assumption as to how an opponent will react, or dictated by the character of an opponent's response.

Attacking deep in order to follow up with a premeditated remise while closing the distance rapidly and hitting with angulations

A deep attack can put an opponent off balance, and also bring the fencer's target to a very close distance; both these factors increase the likelihood that the opponent will miss their riposte, giving the fencer an opportunity to hit with a remise.

Stop hit against a riposte (simply outreaching an opponent, or if a riposte is slow, hesitant or compound)

We can see fencers with a longer reach often score with renewal at maximum distance while moving back quickly. Choupenitch (CZE) can often be seen scoring this hit in international competitions.

In a lesson, following a stop hit and a false or real parry, the coach should attack or defend. This helps prolong a fencer's concentration and sequence with the intention of scoring again.

Shah-put against a riposte

Defending with distance requires great agility. Training such a skill will develop another way of dealing with the riposte.

The fencer's actions will depend on how an opponent parry-ripostes. They can be off-balance, indecisive about how to riposte, holding the parry, delaying the riposte, making a beating parry or using a wide riposte. To some extent, the character of an attack determines the way an opponent parries. For example, it may be possible to make an opponent take a parry while being off balance, but usually, they will parry by force of habit; always responding with beating parries, always holding or always riposting wide or indirect.

It is critical to recognize the difference between a false parry and real one. If an opponent bluffs, then the fencer must also bluff otherwise the opponent will be in control. The ability to recognize the difference will come with experience; however, encouraging a fencer to focus on reading their opponent's intentions can accelerate this learning process.

Learning to deal with pressing opponents

As previously mentioned, pressing, particularly with absence of the blade, is a style of fencing becoming more common and therefore learning to deal with such fencers is an important goal. There are numerous options to work on and implement in a real fight:

- Simultaneous actions: while hitting, avoid colliding with the blade.
- Lifting the point up on the first action and either finishing straight (down) if the opponent hesitates or closing in low octave (**spike of the cactus**) if they attack first.
- A premeditated chain of searching for the blade (false counter-sixte (c6) followed by real octave (8) and real sixte (6)) executed forward while coordinating with distance. The fencer avoids the blade while taking false counter-sixte (c6) but tries to find it with octave and sixte. A fencer will execute both real parries, regardless of which one finds the blade.

- Fast beginning (feint of attack) and parry-riposte (this includes parries with a step forward).
- Holding an opponent with good footwork and:
  - if they stop then take over preparing forward
  - if they continue, then at the end of the piste ether parry at the last moment or make some kind of counter-attack, if the moment is right.
- Repeatedly breaking distance in defence, provoking the opponent to commit to an attack or an over-preparation. Against an attack, responding with a parry-riposte and against an over-preparation, with counter-attack.
- Using the line for derobement, parry-riposte, attack, counter-attack, or even just to regain the initiative to start preparing a new offensive action.
- Feint counter-attack and, if the opponent reacts, any appropriate action, depending on the character of the opponent's reaction.
- Premeditated feint with **half-lunge** and disengage with lunge or flèche ending with the Romanian deflecting the opponent's blade (if there are two lights, the referee may give the opponent the hit). These actions could work against the opponent who is searching for the blade.
- Feint attack followed by defence with distance and reply using appropriate footwork (using a direct reply against a committed attack with a lunge; using a beat attack against an uncommitted attack finishing with a straight arm; using a last moment parry-riposte against a flèche attack, while retreating so as to allow space for the riposte).
- After feint of attack, premeditated Romanian or counter-attack with opposition.
- Any combination of false parries, false counter-attacks, dropping the guard (pretending one is not ready) and beat

attacks if distance is shorter and the blade accessible.
- A chain of premeditated actions based on previous actions and, most probably, the opponent's next action.
- And, of course, keep pressing to prevent being pressed.

Observation of a fight and review with the fencer can provide information about how the fencer is dealing with a situation while being pressed by an opponent. Fencers should be advised to have two fights in which only one fencer is pressing with absence of blade. A victory for the fencer who was being pressed can be a measure of fulfilling the above goal. In an effort to prevent an opponent from pressing in the first place, fencers can be asked to practise near-simultaneous attacks.

Controlling the rhythm of the fight and hindering

This goal can be achieved by increasing preparatory actions, such as false attacks, false beats and various other actions on the blade, using the line, breaking the distance, preventing the opponent from imposing their rhythm and at the same time breaking their rhythm while imposing initiative. This is an important skill coaches and fencers should pay attention to, but it is difficult to measure, although the subjective 1–10 scale of assessment is useful.

Development from an opponent's initiative (from mistakes)

To work on this goal, a fencer will try to attack mainly on preparation or make an answering attack. They can make answering attacks using good footwork to hold an opponent when they stop or after finding the blade, in addition to parries, counter-attacks, stop hits and using the line. When the opponent initiates their movement, there is a chance they will make a mistake by starting too fast or finishing too early; thus giving the fencer a chance to use the opponent's energy against himself. Additionally, when an opponent finishes short they are more vulnerable to an answering attack as they are at least partly developed and possibly off balance. However, in this instance, the first step of an answering attack has to be rather careful, as this is the classic moment, on the first step, when an adversary will attack or counter-attack.

Developing a feeling for where an opponent's target is going to be at the end of a fencer's action (tochka)

This goal is important as distance is always changing and it is just as important to feel where the target is going to be as it is to know where it is now.

This is a dynamic concept of the distance between point and target; it requires adapting footwork to changeable distance and hitting in time. This is a continuous process goal for one's whole fencing career and every fencer works on it, often subconsciously. For instance, it applies to a fencer's feeling for the distance from which they should attack on preparation, as well to the reflex of lunging with the riposte, should the distance suddenly change. This feeling is also used to determine the maximum distance from which a fencer can hit the target with a stop hit, and the moment when a fencer finishes the attack from pressing.

Both fencers usually move continuously and therefore it is necessary to anticipate the distance at the end of a particular movement. Sometimes the target can be too close in relation to the end of the movement and some-

times too far away. If, at the end of an action, a fencer finds themselves at riposting distance or longer, their point should reach the target just before a full extension of their arm. Obviously, if at close quarters then the arm has to be bent while hitting.

Adapting the best tactics against a particular opponent and, if necessary, changing

The right tactics can be defined as the most efficient way of using one's skills in order to win a fight or achieve the best possible score. Tactical planning, therefore, has to consider using the strengths of a fencer against the weaknesses of an opponent, as well as prohibiting an opponent from developing their strengths. This is an interesting and educational exercise in training and very useful in competition. Fencer (and coach) should prepare plan A and plan B before a fight and then evaluate them afterwards.

Working on improving the efficiency of hits (eliminating off-targets)

Valid hit efficiency is often overlooked as a goal; however, it is extremely important. Efficiency should be around 70 per cent as a benchmark, but some fencers still only achieve 40–50 per cent. One way of measuring efficiency is to register all scoring hits, as well as those off-target hits that otherwise would be winners. Two or three fights for fifteen hits should be enough to indicate how efficient a fencer is, providing they score at least thirty hits. Converting correctly timed off-target hits into valid hits is a permanent goal of foil fencers. Fencers should work continuously on improving the feeling of their point in relation to the target. This can be achieved through a combination of optimal grip strength, a relaxed arm, balanced movements of the body, correctly lining up with the opponent, and leading with the point. All fencers should practise hitting a target every day at home.

Working towards improving energy efficiency in fights

Here a fencer focuses on cutting down unnecessary movements and tries to execute all others as efficiently as possible, using only those muscles needed and eliminating extra tension, particularly at the end of movements. Some fencers remark, the day after an especially good performance in a competition, they do not feel fatigued because their muscles were so relaxed and this is why they performed well. (Carlos Llavador (ESP) said this about his third place in European Championships in 2015.)

Although it seems possible to measure how many steps and lunges or flèches on average were needed to produce one hit or win the fight for a particular number of hits, in practice this goal can be assessed by observation and possibly using a scale from 1–10.

Measure efficiency of hits by recording the number of off-target hits. (Photo: Niki Bruckner)

Working towards increasing parries and ripostes

Confidence in parry-ripostes significantly improves the effectiveness of attacks and counter-attacks. This is because if the opponent is concerned about being parried, the fencer will have more time to prepare an attack, and more chance of finding the right time for a counter-attack.

It is important to develop the ability to riposte automatically with a lunge if the distance increases. Such automatic responses can be developed during lessons. In a fight, a coach can often see when their fencer has an opportunity to hit with an immediate lunge after finding the blade, but this is wasted if a fencer does not respond straight away or is not quite in the right position. I have noticed improvements in this area with my fencers during bouts after several months of working on it in lessons.

There is also merit in working on open-eyes ripostes after holding parries, when there is time to change, and working on any other situation where a fencer can improve their ability to parry and riposte.

Mashing grapes

In the old days, all Soviet fencers could be easily recognized, even from a long distance, by the way they kept their legs moving, as if mashing grapes. The purpose of this action was to relax all muscles, particularly those of the upper body, in order to have the most efficient and best-coordinated movement, as well as being ready to react quickly to any changes in direction and disguise the beginning of a real action.

73

Developing counter-time actions or second-intention parry-ripostes

A fencer or coach should try and determine how effective a second-intention parry-riposte is in training or (after analysing footage) in competition. An important ability is to draw an opponent's counter-attack or attack-on-preparation and then vary one's parries. There are many ways to draw an action and a fencer will develop the most effective way for them. Coaches may suggest any of the following: make circular movements while beating the opponent's blade and taking their blade away; slowly pressing with absence of blade or while making openings in different lines, shake the weapon while moving forward, constantly beating the opponent's blade; or make so-called false engagements in which movements simulate engagement while actually moving over the opponent's blade. In order to be more successful at drawing an opponent's action, it is useful to keep altering the speed of preparation and expect a reaction to the faster movement.

Improving control of holding parries and counter-parries

This can be done easily in a lesson but in a real fight it is much harder to implement as a fencer's mind is preoccupied with the 'what and when' rather than 'how'. Nevertheless, in learning and non-scoring bouts, it is certainly possible. The coach should observe and monitor or, if not possible, then the fencer should let the coach know how holding parries are working.

Perfecting instant beat-parries and beat-attacks on preparation

Work on perfecting instant beat-parries and beat-attacks on preparation at such a distance and in such a way that if the opponent is caught, there should be no time for them to parry. Beat-attacks and beat-parries are effective strokes if done correctly and in time.

Instant parry-ripostes have to meet the opposing blade, moving forward right at the beginning of the opponent's attack. The meeting of the blades (medium-part against weak-part, or medium-part against medium-part) has to happen while the fencer's arm is extending with the wrist in pronation to beat the blade and then in supination when hitting the target. Although the beat consists of two movements, a coach's intention should be to teach this as one motion.

A newly-introduced rule states that when both fencers hit simultaneously and both lights come on, if one fencer who makes a beat attack with the weak part of their blade against the strong part of the opponent's blade, the hit will be given to the opponent as a parry riposte. However, weak against strong moves the point closer to the target, increasing the chances of a single light.

Developing ripostes with opposition (closing the line)

This technique combats remises and should be included in lessons, with fencers encouraged to perform it in bouts.

In case of an opponent's second-intention attack for renewal, an effective approach is to react to a false attack with a **false parry**, opening a line to draw an opponent's response. Here it is important to see the difference between a second-intention/false attack and a real one. Against a real attack, there should be a real parry and riposte.

Eliminating being hit with attack-renewals, a frequent way of scoring

This can be achieved by developing holding parries, second-intention parries (false parries) involving drawing the renewal followed by real parries and ripostes, riposting with a step back, riposting with opposition and premeditated riposting in time while allowing the renewal to arrive. Again, monitoring hits can help estimate how effectively a fencer deals with attack-renewals. In training, a referee can award an extra hit for any successful attack-renewal as well as for any successful riposte against renewal.

Developing alternating first- and second-intention premeditated actions

A fencer must decide what to do and when – for example, mixing first-intention attacks against particular parries with second-intention attacks for renewal, counter-parries or defence with distance.

In a lesson, the fencer and coach can agree in advance what parries the coach is going to take, for instance, circular sixte-quarte (c6–4), with the fencer planning a mixture of first- and second-intention attacks against that defence. In a fight, this is more difficult, but still possible, as a fencer can learn which parries an opponent habitually takes.

Second-intention attacks give a fencer information about what the first-intention attack should be. For example, if a fencer prepares a second-intention counter-riposte, they will learn which parry their opponent takes, and could then deceive this parry with a first-intention attack later in the fight.

Perfecting the ability to hit the target correctly

Hitting correctly means a simple movement in line with the target without leaning on the point and holding the foil lightly with the fingers ('Do not crush the bird,' as the famous nineteenth-century French fencing master Lafaugère used to say). This ability has to be perfected throughout a fencer's career. This goal can be realized through exercises on lunging pads, in pairs and during lessons. There is always a tendency to grip the foil too tightly and use more muscles than necessary.

Hitting the target after finding the blade

This goal is important for beginners who tend to find the opponent's blade but do not hit. This is because with the blade the fencer feels safe, whereas trying to hit the target would mean opening up their own target to a possible hit. This instinctive behaviour has to be changed.

DEVELOPMENT OF FIGHTING SKILLS

Pausing the match if getting hit too often

Coaches need to remind fencers to interrupt the match with a short pause after receiving two or a maximum of three hits in a row. This could be as simple pacing to the back of the piste, or removing the mask to wipe one's face, or even taking time to re-straighten a blade or re-tie one's shoelace.

During this break, the fencer should try to relax and find a way of at least stopping the opponent from hitting again with the same move. Usually, but not always, a referee will allow a break to be taken. Pausing a match is an important way of dealing with a situation

Pausing a match to re-straighten a blade is a good opportunity to regain composure if the match isn't going well. (Photo: Niki Bruckner)

where the opponent has the advantage and a fencer does not have a clear idea of how to deal with it. This tactic can be practised in training as well as in competition.

Developing patience and eliminating rushing (good preparation)

This is also something coaches need to remind fencers about. During a fight, a coach should immediately tell a fencer if actions are rushed and badly timed. Footwork here is of major importance because with good footwork a fencer can hold their opponent for longer without feeling that they need to rush. Younger fencers are more likely to rush than more experienced ones. Also, there are often more rushed actions at the beginning of a competition than during the later stages.

Showing an ability to improve at the end of a fight – strong endgame

In other words, developing a strong finish. A fencer gathers information during the whole fight. It is useful to strive to build up a habit of improving towards the end by using this information, increasing the intensity of the fight as time progresses and generally trying to be more effective while sticking to simple things that work. This goal is hard to achieve, but striving to have a strong finish should always be on a fencer's mind.

Developing an ability to come back from a losing position

This is a difficult and challenging skill to acquire, often requiring a change in tactics, rhythm or intensity. The more often a fencer experiences the ability to turn a fight their way during training, the more likely they will be able to do it in competition. To try this in training, start a fight from 3–0 down.

Reading an opponent's intention – developing the ability of anticipation

Coaches should remind fencers of the importance of reading pre-signals, or tells, for what an opponent is about to do; I call this anticipation. If a fencer reacts only to what is already happening, it is often too late. In order to be in time, one has to keep developing anticipation. Being able to differentiate between false and real signals is of huge importance, as is being aware of one's own tells.

Making sure an opponent is uncertain what action a fencer will make (keeping the opponent guessing)

Coaches should encourage fencers to have a broader repertoire in order to be able to vary their actions. Fencers should be able to alternate different actions in the same tactical situation. Realizing this goal adds a different dimension to a fencer's decisiveness. For example, in a lesson the coach can ask the fencer to alternate his ripostes between direct, disengage and compound from parries 4 and 6, or to alternate first-intention and second-intention attacks, etc. Evaluation of this goal in a fight has to be based on the subjective opinion of both fencer and coach.

However, in some cases, it is possible to hit an opponent with the same final action many times. To be successful with this, it is necessary to make an opponent think another action is coming and then return to the successful one. Many top fencers disguise the same final action with different preparations throughout a bout.

Prediction

Prediction is when a fencer calculates an opponent's future actions from their previous ones.

Coaches can encourage fencers after each hit to think about what the opponent is most likely to try next based on the history of the fight. For example, if an opponent has been more successful in attack, it is likely they will continue attacking. Here it is important that a fencer remembers what has happened during a match. A fencer should also assume that his opponent is capable of making intelligent predictions about his own actions.

Using a loud voice to produce a more decisive finish

Using a loud voice after scoring hits increases a fencer's performance and speeds up reaction time and execution. It also increases adrenaline and helps a fencer fight with more authority.

Using the voice increases adrenaline, speeds reaction time, can influence a referee's decision and can intimidate the opponent. (Photo: Niki Bruckner)

Developing an ability to hold the score or not be hit

Although it may sound negative, this skill is very useful in team competitions. Some fencers are more effective in defence. Their role is to hold the score or make small gains and, if an opponent is strong, to lose by a narrow margin. Numerous scenarios can be created to practise such a skill. For example, in three-minute bouts, at the end of time for every hit difference, some physical penalty is imposed on the loser. Another way is to double received hits, so winning 5–4 means losing 5–8 and the only positive result is to win at least 5–2, which will be interpreted as 5–4.

Know your strengths

Jamie Kenber (GBR) is an expert in predicting his opponent's next move.

Marcus Mepstead (GBR) is well known for his impenetrable defence, which makes him especially useful in team matches when it is necessary to hold the score.

Improving fighting at close quarters

This skill is important, as fighting at close quarters happens often in competition. To improve close-quarters fencing it is useful to practise this fighting for a pre-arranged number of hits. Each action starts from close quarters and fencers take it in turns to initiate an action from a parry position of their choice. Fencers are not allowed to move out of close-quarters distance.

In every lesson there should be exercises involving close-quarters fencing. While exercising on lunging pads, fencers can practise hitting with a second action at a close distance with the arm bent in different positions. In general, left-handers are stronger at close-quarters fighting; they collapse distance more often and so have more experience in this situation.

Results in fights at close quarters will be a reasonable indicator of realizing this goal. However, monitoring success rates at close quarters in a real fight would be the ultimate way of evaluating this goal.

Increasing effectiveness in near-simultaneous actions

There are many fencers who are more effective while pressing and attacking. To fence them well it is important to develop near-simultaneous actions, as such confrontational tactics usually take them out of their comfort zone. Here we can practise a number of actions and ways of fencing, as discussed in Chapter 6 (Training Methods and Exercises).

Fencing with limited space

The goal here is to develop the ability to keep a short distance and fence with small distance changes and not to give ground. A good exercise for this goal is for two fencers to fence only within the central 4 metres of the piste. This excellent exercise develops the skill of fencing in a limited space and should prove useful when forced to the end of the piste and when under pressure from an opponent who presses continuously.

Developing the ability to score hits when time is running out

This is an important skill as time pressure is typical in fencing. A useful exercise to develop this skill is to alternate priority for each hit between two fencers using a 10-second time limit. Whoever scores before the end of 10 seconds wins, but if there is no score then the fencer with priority is the winner. Another exercise is to arrange a fight with a coach or fellow fencer for a particular number of hits while trying to hit as quickly as possible. The time taken to complete the task indicates the level of skill. For instance, how long it takes a particular fencer to score with ten attacks, or five ripostes, or twenty hits.

This skill is particularly important for female fencers, as bouts in women's foil very often go to time. Top female fencers have a noticeable ability to keep their cool while closing a deficit with very little time left.

Using a flèche attack can be very useful when there are only a few seconds left and a hit is needed. Based on my research there is a chance of hitting an opponent with a flèche if there are at least 2 seconds left; 1 second is not enough if there is space for the opponent to retreat.

No time!

One exercise for developing techniques under pressure is to execute twenty flèche attacks as fast as possible from both on-guard lines while changing direction. The record held by Jamie Kenber (GBR) is 30 seconds for twenty flèches.

Fencing at close quarters is a common situation in every match, so improving this skill is a key performance goal for every successful fencer. (Photo: Shutterstock)

5 | PHYSICAL PREPARATION

Physical preparation in fencing, as in any sport, is always very important. In recent decades there has been a rapid development of science-based study in sport, resulting in changes in methods and exercises for physical fitness, together with the establishment of professional trainers for physical preparation.

This is a rather brief chapter as so much information is available in the public domain on this subject. However, the content of this chapter focuses on the best physical preparation for fencing in particular.

Every world-class fencing programme includes a professional Strength and Conditioning (S&C) coach who designs and monitors the details of an individual fitness programme for each fencer.

Full-time fencers spend several sessions per week (2–4) just in the gym in addition to specific fencing sessions, which, in a non-competitive week, take place every day.

Physical preparation for fencers has following benefits: it increases confidence (stronger body = stronger mind); increases the range of speeds and its control (footwork and blade

Photo opposite by Niki Bruckner.

work); helps to fence with high intensity for longer; makes their body more supple; and speeds up recovery, preventing injury.

THE MAIN ELEMENTS OF GENERAL FITNESS

There is much information available about the main elements of general fitness; however, I consider the following to be the five main elements of fitness: speed, strength, endurance, flexibility and coordination.

All of these elements are important. However, as fencing requires very fine coordination and neuromuscular control it is prudent to avoid exercises with bodybuilding effects. All these elements can be developed by using general physical, semi-specific or specific exercises for fencing. Ultimately, fencing requires all these elements.

Exercises to develop general fitness should play a significant role during the preparatory period and play a secondary role in the competitive period where the general exercises are used to maintain an already developed level of fitness. However, speed, flexibility and coordination components should be included every day in the warm-up period before fencing and flexibility in the warm-down afterwards. Younger fencers will benefit from more physical exercises, often in the form of various games, whereas older, more experienced fencers require more sport-specific exercises.

To prevent a fencer becoming stale, it is sometimes good to switch to general exercises for a few days; they stimulate recovery from mental fatigue and can allow for a faster return to fencing afterwards, as opposed to passive rest. To combat jet-lag, light general conditioning combined with footwork and flexibility can have a positive effect.

SPEED

There are three components to speed: reaction speed (simple and complex); frequency of movements; and single movement speed.

It is particularly important to control speed – this is critical in executing compound actions and where adaptability to changing conditions is required. Since the ability to *change the rhythm* is important, a fencer has to possess superb speed control. However, in executing simple and premeditated actions, maximum speed is needed. Changing direction (*agility*) is also of huge importance as many hits can be won by sheer speed.

In general exercises, speed can be developed by making fencers carry out short sprints from various positions and preparations, using lines, ladders and cones on the floor for frequency and agility. Here a coach's creativeness has no limits. Obviously, football or basketball are great but there is always a risk of injury. Since speed is correlated with strength, exercises which develop both are highly beneficial.

During footwork sessions, it is possible to measure the time taken to make several changes of direction over short distances.

General footwork exercises to develop speed and agility are helpful in developing specific fencing footwork.
(Photo: Niki Bruckner)

Other exercises can be used to develop reaction, change of direction and frequency times. Again, there is much scope for a coach to demonstrate creativeness.

To improve reaction speed, a useful exercise during a lesson is for the coach to ask a fencer to hit direct from engagement with a lunge or flèche during the time it takes the coach to hit the floor with their point and return to on-guard, the fencer having to hit before the coach can close the line. At any time the coach can change the speed and direction of legs, hand and point.

To develop changes of speed while working on any answering attack, from time to time the coach breaks the distance and the fencer has to slow down, pretending they are not going to develop the final attack, but actually they are finding the right distance to execute a beat lunge with maximum speed – the 'two waves' principle.

To develop changes of direction while working on attacks from pressing, the coach may develop different lengths of attack on a fencer's preparation, the fencer's task being to defend with distance and hit back with a lunge or flèche.

To develop point speed the coach tries to take a real parry towards the end of a fencer's movement so the fencer has to accelerate or be parried. Another way to increase speed at the end of an action, is to move the target back and ask the fencer to hit it. The fencer has to recognize when they can reach the target and when they cannot, in which case they should slow down or stop completely. Also, speed of point can be developed through practising various combinations of beats, change beats, and double engagements followed by feints and deceptions. Introducing any combination of beat cut-over helps with getting a feeling for the speed of point. Of course, finishing with a flick should give the fencer a sensation of speed.

The coach can work on speed, changes of tempo, agility and reactions in any exercise.

> **Remember!**
>
> In fencing, deceleration is just as important as acceleration.

STRENGTH

In general exercises, strength can be developed with resistance training, jumps, squats, planks, push-ups and small weights. As far as squats with heavy weights are concerned, fencers should consult their S&C coach. Not everyone will feel the benefit of heavy weights for their fencing and also they may inflict some back problems.

In the following images, James-Andrew Davis demonstrates some general strength exercises which fencers can undertake in the gym.

In footwork sessions, rubber bands, weight jackets, small weights in each hand and expanders can all be used. Lessons and bouts should not be taken with resistance or weights, as they give an unrealistic feeling of timing, thus affecting speed of movement.

ENDURANCE

Endurance can be built up in general exercises by running. For example, fartlek (Swedish for 'speed play') is a training method blending continuous training with interval training – mixed sessions of jogging and sprints. Ball games are another good way of building endurance; however, be aware of the risk of injury. Local muscular endurance can be developed by carrying out various exercises and increasing the number of repetitions or going for as long as possible, such as sit-ups, plank, press-ups, etc. In footwork training, use long sessions like three to five sets of 5 minutes, or simply extended footwork exercises. In lessons of 45 minutes' duration or more, extend the normal length of exercises.

Leg lift/raise: this strength exercise works the abs as the main muscle group and also builds strength in the upper and lower legs.
(Photo: Jornnawat (P'Mod) Limprasert)

Dumbbell lunges: a single-leg strength exercise to increase strength in the quads, hamstrings and glutes. The exercise also improves core stability and develops lower body speed.
(Photo: Jornnawat (P'Mod) Limprasert)

Dumbbell bench press: to help increase push strength in the upper body and also help build a greater range of motion in the shoulder. (Photo: Jornnawat (P'Mod) Limprasert)

Dumbbell fly exercise: this strengthens the upper body muscles. It targets the chest muscles and strengthens the arm muscles. The key benefit of this exercise is that it works several muscles concurrently.
(Photo: Jornnawat (P'Mod) Limprasert)

Single arm bent-over row: this exercise helps build the muscles on the upper, middle and lower back. It strengthens the chest muscles and triceps. (Photo: Jornnawat (P'Mod) Limprasert)

FLEXIBILITY

Flexibility can be developed during warm-up and warm-down exercises, in addition to separate yoga sessions. Yoga and pilates can be particularly useful for older fencers where tendons and ligaments become stiffer with age. Hip mobility is important, as is the length of hamstrings and abductors. Progressively pushing already stretched muscles against resistance is particularly effective.

Exercises to improve flexibility should occur during both warm-up and warm-down. During the warm-up passive stretching exercises should be held for up to 20 seconds but during the warm-down phase up to 60 seconds. However, the duration these exercises are held for will depend upon the individual and when they feel they have achieved an optimal stretch.

In addition to passive stretching, active stretching exercises which involve various bouncing and swinging movements such as jump squats, high kicks and jump lunges, in my opinion, better prepare the body for a vigorous fencing session and should play an important role in any warm-up routine. Some

Research has shown there is no correlation between competition results and **VO₂ max**, which suggests fencing is a strongly anaerobic exercise (Płocharski). The most effective method for training fencing endurance is actual fencing for timed periods at high intensity without scoring, such as 5 or 10 minutes without a break or changing partners. The pyramid exercise is excellent for developing endurance – fencing in nine separate fights for 1, 3, 5, 7, 9, 7, 5, 3 and 1 hits without a break. Also, having the winner stay on for a prearranged number of hits with a queue of fresh people to fence will help develop endurance.

Another exercise which can provide huge benefits to stamina is fencing for three or more hits in a row without any time limit. Some bouts of this kind can be as long as 30 minutes. I believe that for sports-specific stamina the best exercises are sport-specific.

Fencers warming up with a hip mobility exercise. (Photo: Niki Bruckner)

Right hip flexor (leaning to other side helps). This exercise strengthens and increases hip flexor flexibility. It is useful for fencers as the hip flexor on the dominant side often gets tight.
(Photo: Kevin Nixon)

Right leg hamstring, left leg adductor. This position stretches both the right leg hamstring and the adductor muscles helping with hip flexibility and rotation. This can be an excellent dynamic stretching exercise if the fencer changes the position of the hips from above one foot to the other while pushing them down. Note: The adductor on the dominant side of a fencer can often be tighter. (Photo: Kevin Nixon)

examples of stretching exercises are demonstrated here by Richard Kruse.

Hamstring stretches are important for the flexibility and range of motion of the hip and hamstring muscles. Good hamstring flexibility allows for unrestricted, pain-free movement of the hip and upper leg.

COORDINATION

Coordination is an important fitness attribute in most sports. Exercises to develop coordination should be a permanent feature in warm-up exercises. Examples include moving the arms and legs together in a random order, catching gloves or tennis balls while moving the legs, turning, introducing additional positions and movements from which the exercise is executed or any combination of foot movements on a ladder or cones on the floor, and jumping over a skipping rope. Don't forget there is value in developing the non-dominant side of the body too.

In footwork, examples include smoothly extending the sword arm while moving the feet and changing direction or moving the arm quickly and the feet slowly. From the lunging position, partly recover while balancing on the back leg with a fast and independent extension of the arm before pushing off from the back leg to develop a full lunge.

As balance is a vital part of coordination, any exercise utilizing the Beemat balance beam will be of great benefit. Additionally, some balance positions from yoga or pilates can also be carried out on the Beemat balance beam. Balance can also be improved by correct landing following various airborne spins. Landings can be in on-guard position or on one leg.

Further examples of footwork exercises can be found in Chapter 7.

Left hamstring and right side of the back. A good exercise for stretching adductor muscles in the groin. (Photo: Kevin Nixon)

Left hamstring stretch. This exercise helps improve flexiblity and range of motion of the hip and hamstring muscles (keep pelvis square). Note: fencers should pay more attention to stretch the hamstring on their dominant side. (Photo: Kevin Nixon)

Lats and lower back stretch. This exercise in addition to stretching lats and lower back, opens the groin and touches the hamstring (push right knee to the floor). (Photo: Kevin Nixon)

Double quad stretch. This position provides a deep stretch for the quads and hip flexors. Rotate the pelvis; do not arch the lower back upwards. (Photo: Kevin Nixon)

6 | TRAINING METHODS AND EXERCISES

There are endless ways to organize and implement training sessions. In this chapter, I list the methods and exercises I have personally found most helpful.

FREE PLAY

The first and most obvious training exercise is free play, in which fencers do not count the score but work on individual goals set by themselves or their coaches. The advantage of this method is by taking risks and trying different actions in different situations, fencers have more opportunities to improve technique and tactics. They usually arrange to fence for a prearranged time, for instance, 10 minutes, or with high intensity until fatigue starts affecting quality.

The moment players start counting hits, their fencing becomes more risk-averse, thus limiting the opportunity to try different techniques and tactics. However, competitive matches contribute towards the development of the psychological qualities necessary to win hits and fights in competition.

Photo opposite by Chris Turner.

A popular way of training is to ask fencers to complete a poule unique for a prearranged number of hits or to fence a prearranged number of fights, for example 4 × 15 hits with a chosen opponent. Players often arrange this between themselves (booking each other), deciding whom they are going to fence in advance of the session.

Ideally, the coach would be involved in piste coaching during the fencing session and would give lessons either outside of those sessions or when there are more coaches available. In such cases, a fencer knows they are being observed by the coach, who may give feedback during the bout and discuss tactics afterwards. I believe strip coaching during training provides the coach with another useful and effective addition to one-on-one lessons. However, in a club situation, the coach usually provides lessons and is unable to have a significant impact on sparring matches.

LEARNING BOUTS

In order to enhance the development of various skills, coaches can give fencers different tasks; these fights can be called **learning bouts** and they allow the coach to exercise some creativity.

The choice of exercise will depend on what is most relevant to the group, or for particular fencers based on analysis from recent competitions. For example, a coach may decide counter-attacks do not count during a particular session, or certain fencers receive double points for parry-ripostes. Another option could be to reward and target different fencers' strengths. For instance: Fencer A loves to score with attack-remise. Any riposte against this remise is worth double, while if fencer A scores with their attack-remise they also receive double points.

A good form of group coaching is to organize a session ensuring all or most of the fencers work at the same time on given tasks for a given time. For example, 5-minute bouts before changing partners in an organized manner and repeating the task. The coach times each period of 5 minutes, and assigns a new task every few periods. One task could be to see who can score the highest number of consecutive hits in 5 minutes.

This form of training requires all fencers to be ready at the same time and is therefore, more suited to training camps than club sessions (where fencers tend to arrive and depart at random). However, I have managed to implement such sessions during club time. If there are more fencers than spools, a *resting station system* can be introduced whereby non-active players wait until there is a change, and then join the exercise while some fencers leave to take their turn at waiting. This achieves focused intensity and engagement, as players have a limited time to rest.

For more competitive fencing, some clubs organize a ladder, or various forms of training competition, sometimes with prizes. Some fencers like to combine fencing without scoring (i.e. working on a particular technique) with several five-hit bouts (good for first-round or team matches) and fifteen-hit bouts. It is always good if fencer and coach can review training matches throughout the session.

The forms and methods above can be combined with the following specific exercises (tasks) to create rich and enjoyable learning bouts. The exercises marked with an asterisk* are strongly recommended.

Footwork, distance and change of rhythm improvement

Vigorous footwork
The coach asks fencers to *use the entire piste at high intensity for the entire period* (e.g. 5 minutes), pointing out when they see a fencer has stopped using their legs too soon, not bending their legs enough, or is generally too static. Here, vigorous footwork is appropriate.

Defence with distance
For every defence with distance (*shah-put*) and hit after, a fencer gets some sort of reward, perhaps an extra hit if they count hits or something of value. Equally, one can introduce some physical penalty for the fencer who is hit by *shah-put*.

Queuing

Another useful form of training is to use a queue system. This involves some fencers waiting while others fence. Players may have a specific task, such as: fencing at 4 metres; fencing in a progressive way; fencing for either four hits in a row or in 2 minutes; or fencing for five to ten hits at close quarters.

Losers move to the end of the queue and are replaced by the fencers at the front. Usually, after three wins both loser and winner move to the end of the queue and are replaced by the next two fencers in the queue.

Shah-put game *

Best of three fights to five hits. The game has the following rules:

- Taking and giving back the initiative in the form of false attacks with a maximum of three foot actions forward.
- From time to time one player decides to commit to hitting with a lunge and the task of their opponent is to try to defend with distance and hit them back. One point is awarded to the fencer who hits successfully.
- Fencers are not allowed to parry; if they do, a point is awarded to the opponent.

Later on, it is possible to introduce flèches and parry-ripostes: if a fencer attacks with a flèche, only then is the opponent allowed to parry and riposte. The key here is for the defender to differentiate between the lunge and flèche attacks of their opponent.

Direct lunge hits

Both players can hit each other only with one direct lunge from manoeuvring back and forward (not continued pressing) – no parries allowed. In this exercise, players may choose the same moment to attack, in which case the referee will call it simultaneous and no hit is awarded. This exercise can also be modified by adding a direct step and lunge with no parries.

Regulating distance

The coach reminds fencers to focus on a shorter distance in defence and a longer distance in offence. Here the coach observes and reacts if the distance is not right. Fencers will feel they are being observed and should keep distance control.

Changing rhythm

The coach asks fencers to focus on changing rhythm and explains various situations. For example, the coach could ask fencers to use stuttering preparation while pressing, or to apply the principle of two waves when an opponent retreats. There is no score, and the fencers try to work on changing their rhythm. Some fencers have a predictable rhythm of footwork, so the coach will ask them to break the pattern. A robotic and repetitive step-lunge rhythm is a particularly common bad habit. This is a difficult exercise to measure as it is a subjective observation of the coach. The principle of changing rhythm also applies to blade work, but this can be a separate focus.

The next few exercises are ideal for group footwork lessons.

Keeping distance in pairs *

Fencers pair up and play the game of rock, paper, scissors. The winner dictates the distance and the loser tries to hold the same distance for twelve sets of 15 seconds.

Holding the distance

Fencers in groups of three use the whole length of the piste: one advances, one retreats and the third, who is on the edge of the piste, runs alongside the other two. They rotate their roles each time they reach the end of the piste, so the fencer who retreats always becomes the runner, while the runner becomes the one who advances, and the one who was advancing then retreats. The aim of the exercise is to hold the distance up and down the whole length of the piste. Usually 3 × 30 seconds, with a minimum break of 45 seconds between each set.

Fixing the point/straight arm

In pairs, with one fencer fixing the point on their partner's chest or glove while keeping the sword arm straight. The partner moves in both directions at variable speed and the task of the fencer with the straight arm is to keep it straight while maintaining contact with the target. Again, roles are usually changed after 30 seconds.

Technique improvement

Hitting different sectors of the target

Fight for 21 points (or some other number) with hits counting as follows:

- One point for hits scoring into the inside sector (quarte line).
- Two points for hits scoring into the high outside sector (sixte line).
- Three points for hits scoring into the low outside sector (octave-seconde line).

This exercise develops the skill of hitting into the outside low and high lines which are generally harder to defend than the inside line. Most beginners finish mainly in the inside line. There is merit in practising hitting in the low inside line, but this is not included in the exercise as there is no clear distinction between high inside and low inside.

Changing technique

Five or more hits scored with a different technique. This kind of exercise develops a fencer's technical versatility. For example, after hitting with a direct thrust, a fencer cannot repeat the same move, but has to change to a different technical action. They can perform any technical action only once throughout the match; if they have done a beat quarte (4) direct attack, they cannot do a parry quarte (4) direct riposte, since from a technical point of view they are the same action.

Hitting with and without the blade

A match to 21 points (or some other number) scored in the following way:

- One point for any hit without touching the opponent's blade.
- Two points for any direct hit after contact with (beat/parry or engagement) the opponent's blade.
- Three points for every indirect hit after contact with (beat/parry or engagement) the blade.

Hitting inside low line on an opposite hander. A competent fencer should be able to hit any line of the target.

This exercise encourages hitting after contact with the blade, which is technically more complex. Taking the blade gives priority as well as preventing being hit by a counter-attack. Situations where there is longer contact with the blade or when the fencer delivers their hit with opposition make it particularly difficult for the opponent to counter-attack.

No off-target

In a 5-point bout, any off-target hit is penalized with one press-up or a minus point. These exercises focus on accuracy, which is an essential part of technique. No matter how clever the tactics and how great the state of mind, if a fencer cannot hit on-target, then all effort is wasted. I believe fencers could and should pay more attention to minimizing off-target lights.

Only single lights count for 5 points

It is useful to be able to hit with a single light, as even at top-level tournaments unreliable refereeing can occur.

Tight preparations and keeping the point on target while closing distance

Fencers fence to a given number of points or amount of time, focusing on the above task. There is always a tendency for preparations to be bigger and faster than necessary and this is one of the reasons for being hit on preparation. Tension also negatively affects coordination, as well as the size and speed of preparation. Therefore, fencers should be reminded to make good, small, balanced and controlled preparations when they are preparing to attack. Bringing the point on target as they close the distance is an important habit to develop as it improves accuracy.

Fencers try to fence as technically as possible

Coaches observe and mark the fencers' technical skills, assessing footwork and blade work. Coaches should select the best technician or

An example of hitting direct in quarte opposition against same hander. (Photo: Kevin Nixon)

even rank fencers based on their subjective assessment of technique. After this review, the coach watches again, for who moves with the most control, how controlled the movements of the weapon are and what variety of actions are performed, in addition to how small and accurate point movements are, and announces any improvements. This exercise can be performed with less experienced or younger fencers.

Specific technical tasks

The coach can give a specific technical task, e.g. holding parries, whereby a session can focus on hits after a holding parry, with successful fencers receiving a reward, such as an extra point.

Beginners tend to hold the blade too long and not riposte, then later in their development they tend to habitually riposte after a short (beating) contact with the blade. The disadvantage of always riposting immediately is a fencer has no time to adjust to any change in circumstances (it is too late to turn back). Also, as the fencer's blade leaves the opponent's blade there is a gap in space and time for a counter-action by the opponent. Holding parries open up many other ways of hitting, hence making fencing richer and more interesting.

In my opinion, beating parries are usually more effective at the beginning of an opponent's attack, whereas holding parries (closed line) are better right at the end.

Technical–tactical tasks

No counter-attacks out of time*

If any fencer counter-attacks out of time they do three burpees (or any other exercise). However, if a fencer should receive a counter-attack *in* time they also perform an exercise penalty. Here both players learn to improve the preparations of their attacks, as well as how to find gaps in the timing of an opponent's preparation for a successful counter-attack or attack on preparation.

Attack and defence – opposite tasks

One fencer can only attack while the other can only defend (the attacker can score with a counter-riposte or renewal, but the defender can parry-riposte, defend with distance, counter-attack, stop hit or attack on preparation with one lunge).

Fight at close quarters*

An excellent exercise to improve this important skill. Close-quarters fencing happens in a fight all the time. Sometimes it is set up by a fencer and expected, but at other times it might be unexpected.

In this exercise fencer A and fencer B must start and remain with their front feet touching one another. To begin each phrase, one fencer chooses a parry position in which to hold the opponent's blade, and the referee or opponent says 'play'. So, fencer A holds parry quarte (4), before the referee or fencer B says 'play'; if there are two lights straight away, fencer A wins the hit as they began the phrase with priority. For the next hit, fencer B holds a parry of their choice. They fence for a prearranged number of hits, usually 5 or 10. Fencers are penalized 1 point if they move their front foot.

In a competitive match, when closing the distance to an opponent, there is a point at which it becomes more advisable to force a close-quarters situation rather than to retreat. This is because a retreat from such a distance gives the opponent an easy opportunity to attack. Fencers should continually develop a feel for this distance. Frequently when fencers get to this distance, they react by retreating, and get hit by the opponent's answering attack. This tendency seems to be an instinctive response to run away from danger rather than confront it. In my experience, left-handers have a better feel for this distance than right-handers, and are generally stronger at close-quarters fighting.

Fighting on the backline

One fencer has their front foot on the backline (they cannot step back) and their adversary has to initiate an action from step-lunge distance. The fencer on the backline can only do one lunge, with their back leg remaining behind the backline at all times. Fencers fence to a prearranged number of hits.

Backline situations happen frequently in a real fight. Theoretically, the fencer who is on the backline is in a worse position than their adversary, as they cannot retreat any further. The fencer on the backline, in addition to parry riposte or counter-attack, should try to do an attack *with the blade*, false attack with second intention to draw a counter-attack or riposte, or they should attempt a simple one-tempo counter-time action.

Garozzo (ITA) vs Imboden (USA) close quarters. This encounter illustrates two different common arm positions while hitting at close quarters, which often happens in combat. Garozzo is holding his arm behind his target (on the right) and Imboden has his arm well above his target. (Photo: Dawn Uhalley)

The opposing fencer should do the same, as their opponent has nowhere to retreat. Some fencers who have a pressing style are reluctant to finish their attack when an opponent is on the backline, and often give them back the initiative. They would rather wait for a counterattack before the end of the piste is reached than risk being parried if they finish their attack at the end of the piste.

Against such players, it pays to stay at the right distance while retreating – *hold them with the legs*. On the other hand, there are players who will attack only after pushing their opponent to the backline. Against such fencers, it is better to try and keep them away from your backline.

Backline

Fencing on the backline is almost unavoidable in competitive matches. There are some fencers, for instance, Peter Joppich (GER), who look very comfortable and are very effective on their backline. By practising backline situations in training, a fencer can turn their backline from a weak position into an area of strength.

Turn a position of weakness into a strength; practise backline situations in club training sessions.
(Photo: Niki Bruckner)

Five hits but counter-attacks do not score

This exercise clearly focuses a fencer's mind on developing attacks and parry-ripostes or defence with distance. While there is a risk of over-preparing, this exercise can help fencers to be more courageous in their attacks, as they are not afraid of counter-attacks. However, the main purpose of this exercise is to help those fencers who counter-attack too much, and at the wrong time. They should try to develop their attacks and parries and move their legs more to hold an opponent while retreating.

Second-intention ripostes/attack on preparation

A bout to 15 points with 3 points awarded for any second-intention riposte or attack on preparation (referee judges whether an action was indeed second-intention).

Fencers must focus their minds on two opposing areas: attack on an opponent's preparation and second-intention parry-ripostes. Both fencers engage in a normal fight. The referee decides when a hit is scored by an attack on preparation or by a second-intention parry-riposte and then awards 3 points. This psychological-tactical exercise helps to develop a fencer's ability to switch their attention quickly between attacking and defending.

Dealing with flèche attacks

A match to 5 points; in attack fencers can only score by direct or broken time flèche attacks, but in defence, they are free to score from any action (ripostes, counter-attacks, stops hits). The flèche attack is common, particularly in men's foil (in my opinion, it is under-used in women's foil); however if a flèche isn't carried out with enough speed, the adversary has more time to parry.

There are two major types of flèche attack: direct and broken time. Some fencers find it difficult to deal with such an attack, hence the need for this exercise. The ideal defence against a direct flèche is the parry-riposte, but against broken time it could be a stop hit, Romanian or general sweeping parry (often with a step forward).

Attack renewals or ripostes against renewals

A match to 15 points but a fencer is rewarded with double points for any successful attack-renewal or riposte against an unsuccessful renewal.

Hits scored by attack-renewals happen often in competitive bouts. This exercise helps develop both offence and defence. An attacking fencer tries to use a false attack to make their opponent react with a parry, then surprises them with a renewal afterwards. On the other hand, the defending fencer will have the opportunity to improve their skill in dealing with renewals after having parried.

Attack-renewal

The best way to set up an attack-renewal is to get the opponent off-balance and taking a reactive parry. Another opportunity for attack-renewal is when an opponent's riposte opens up the line that had been closed by their parry (this case requires the fencer to block the opponent's blade after their renewal).

Dealing with pressing with absence of blade

Two matches to 10 points; fencer A scores only from pressing without the blade while fencer B scores with any action from retreating. Change roles for the second fight. A similar exercise could be dealing with a pressing fencer who continuously carries out actions against the blade (**blade bully**).

Handling pressing with absence of blade

Pressing with absence of blade is one of the most difficult situations to deal with in a conventional weapon such as foil. Fencers should be encouraged to try the following:

- Hindering actions: simulating attacks, counter-attacks, false parries and breaking the distance.
- Use **point-in-line** or threaten the target with the point.
- Parry after a feint counter-attack (if an opponent reacts).
- Invite the opponent to finish into an opening line.
- Attack on preparation after a feint.
- Feint counter-attack, counter-attack and block (Romanian).
- Keep a tight distance and wait until the opponent decides to commit to an attack and parry at the last moment (difficult but still a possible and realistic alternative).

In this exercise, one fencer is asked to press and the other to retreat. In reality, going for **near-simultaneous actions** may be more effective, but the exercise is to improve performance while already retreating against an opponent who presses with absence of blade.

A 10-point bout with any parry-riposte scoring double

A parry-riposte is usually more difficult to teach than an attack or counter-attack. It consists of two movements, one defensive (the parry) and the other offensive (the riposte). A fencer who is confident with parry-ripostes will feel under less pressure to attack, and so their attacks are generally better prepared. Furthermore, their counter-attack becomes more effective as the opponent is concerned about being parried, and thus is more likely to make a compound or broken time attack. The uncertainty of whether to expect a parry or counter-attack puts the defender in a stronger position.

Alternate two periods of 5 minutes or more where one fencer can only score from point-in-line

Most fencers do not like it when their opponent uses point-in-line. It is a position that still has an important place in foil. Therefore the point-in-line should be practised often and widely used. Firstly, it can deter an attack, and secondly, any hit can be executed from point-in-line.

Point-in-line

The most obvious hitting option from point-in-line is the derobement. Parries and attacks from point-in-line can be a surprise, as the opponent will expect a derobement. Point-in-line is considered 'in time' if it is established before the start of a final step-lunge or step-flèche; however, this interpretation varies amongst referees, so a fencer needs to bear this in mind and constantly check a referee's interpretation. Even if a fencer feels that they have presented their point-in-line too late, they could use it to set up another way of defending (distance, parry, counter-attack). A fencer who has successfully established point-in-line can deliberately allow their blade to be found by the opponent, and then perform a parry-riposte. In some cases, a stop hit or a counter-attack from point-in-line can also be effective. An attack from point-in-line can be a surprise as the opponent usually expects more defensive actions.

Fencing for 5–10 minutes without scoring* (practising strokes and situations without pressure)

This exercise is often neglected as fencers are naturally competitive and like to score points. However, there are great benefits to such an exercise as fencers can practise intensively with much less concern for being hit. To some extent, the exercise develops courage, intensity and opportunities to practise actions one is yet to master. I would strongly recommend fighting without scoring for fencers at any level.

Near-simultaneous actions for a prearranged number of hits or period of time

Someone referees two fencers who try to hit while initially both moving forward and scoring within a relatively short time. The objective here is to not allow the opponent to press continuously. Continuous defence defeats the objective of the exercise. Simultaneous actions should happen frequently in this exercise – tactically resulting in a draw. An easier exercise to follow, which tackles a similar problem, is described in the next section (Fight at 4 metres*).

While practising near-simultaneous situations, players may experiment with a premeditated approach (actions most likely to succeed in the light of previous actions) and anticipate what an opponent is most likely to do next. When using a premeditated action against an expected move by the opponent, if the fencer's prediction turns out to be wrong, they will still have some chance to adapt. One can also adopt an 'either... or...' approach, where a fencer gives themselves two options, for example finishing an attack in one particular way or making a parry-riposte. Trying more options is less advisable, as making more complex decisions under time pressure is difficult and players may not be able to react adequately or in time. A fencer could also opt for a premeditated parry-riposte by deliberately starting a bit later than their opponent, encouraging them to finish.

Parries with a step forward, ripostes at close quarters

The coach may ask fencers to use parries with a step forward and riposte at close quarters, rewarding a successful manoeuvre with an extra hit and also rewarding an opponent's ability to hit after deceiving a parry with a step forward.

Developing fighting skills (pressure training)

Holding the score

Two periods of 3 minutes with one fencer tasked with holding the score, and receiving no extra reward for a hit scored, but a physical penalty for each hit lost. The coach may note how much time has elapsed before a fencer was hit, as well as the final result. The ability to hold the score is particularly useful during team matches when one bout lasts 3 minutes. One fencer must try to maintain the score while the other tries to increase their score. There are fencers who are hard to hit but do not have great *fire power*. They should be good at this exercise. However, more attacking fencers should play to their strength, which is attack, and hold the score by scoring.

Three hits behind

Two periods of 3 minutes as above, but one fencer starts three hits behind and tries to level the score while the other tries to maintain the advantage. In theory, the score should not have an impact on the exercise but, in reality, fencers do feel different when the score is 0–0 rather than 3–0. At 3–0 down a fencer has a clearer objective and feels a greater pressure than when simply maintaining a score of 0–0.

The longest holder and the fastest scorer

No time limit. Both fencers have the task of not receiving hits for as long as possible and, at the same time to score as soon as possible. After the first hit, the time of scoring (of the scorer) in addition to the holding time (of the fencer who received the hit) is registered. The fight continues until both fencers have scored, giving a scoring and holding time for both fencers. The fight finishes at this stage. After everybody has fenced each other the coach identifies the average time of the longest holder, the fastest scorer and indicates the holder of the record time of individual hits.

Fight with alternating priority* for a prearranged number of hits (ten or fifteen)

Priority alternates between fencers, for periods of 10 seconds or longer. One fencer always has priority (change after each hit scored) and, if there is no hit by the end of the 10-second period, the fencer with priority scores. This is typical pressure training and 10 seconds is probably the right length of time. This exercise is strongly recommended, as it develops decisiveness and courage – important personality traits.

Fight at 4 metres*

This exercise puts both players under pressure to hold ground and force them into a continuously confrontational game. Hits are scored quickly, and often fencers have to decide what to do beforehand. There is little time to make decisions and a fencer should not give themselves more than two options after the initial step forward. This is an excellent tool for developing the skill of dealing with a permanently attacking fencer. The exercise has similar characteristics to 'near-simultaneous actions' previously mentioned.

Five hits in a row or 3 minutes, whichever comes first*

A fencer can win the match by scoring five hits in a row, or by being the last to score at the end of time. This is an excellent exercise for developing the ability to score several hits in a row and is also great for concentration. This is highly recommended.

Five in a row

Practising five hits in a row also prepares a fencer for a good indicator, after the first round poules. In this exercise, the incentive is based on the score. The fencer who is leading will lose all their points every time their opponent scores a hit. Some fencers are good at scoring a particular number of hits, for example three, after which they usually lose concentration and receive at least one hit. For them trying to achieve the more difficult five in a row is the right task and success will give them greater self-belief in the future.

Five hits in a row or one minute, whatever comes first, at 4 metres*

Queuing exercise. For every hit against, the coach imposes a different physical penalty. This is a harder version of the above as hits are scored more quickly and at a shorter distance, with greater pressure.

Hits scored in a particular period of time count double

For example in the last 30 seconds of a fight for 3 minutes or in a team event. Some fencers have difficulty maintaining intensity and focus during the whole 3 minutes and they tend to lose hits at certain times, hence the selection of a particular period of time for the exercise. This exercise adds to the pressure, particularly in team training.

Winning from a losing position

Fifteen hits, with the score starting at 3–0 in favour of one fencer. This exercise develops the ability to win from a losing position. Fencers who can come back and win will have more confidence when they find themselves in a similar position in competition. Of course, for the other fencer, this exercise also develops the important ability of winning from a winning position – closing the deal.

There can be many other handicap exercises such as starting from 0–2 down for five hits and if there is a victory then the next fight starts from 0–3.

Winning from a losing position with a time limit

For example with the score at 13–9 with one minute to go, the task is to win. This is a much harder version of the above and the time limit creates more pressure; therefore the fencer has to take greater risks while choosing the moment and strike.

Poule or direct elimination for one hit only* (the loser receives a physical penalty)

'One hit' is fundamental in fencing. Fencers should concentrate on one hit at a time. When the scores are tied, for example at 14–14 or 4–4, one hit is all that is needed. It is good if a fencer can rely on a favourite action in such a situation. Focusing on one hit at a time should help concentrate the mind and improve performance. This exercise is particularly effective at the end of a camp when everybody is tired; it will get the most out of the players.

Fight for one hit, the victor being the first to win ten fights, with a maximum of three victories in a row before moving to the end of the queue

This is a queuing exercise: another way of fencing competitively for one hit only. Depending on the number of players, they can fence on one or more boxes. After three victories in a row both winner and loser move to the end of the queue. Everybody remembers how many victories they have. The winner is the player who first achieves ten victories.

Poule for five hits but every hit received counts double

For example if a fencer wins a fight 5–4, they will record it as losing 5–8, as 4 counts as double. This exercise strongly discourages being hit. It is an interesting exercise and most score indicators are negative at the end of it.

Progressive fencing*

Fencers begin fencing a match needing one hit to win; after each victory they will require an additional hit to win their next match (one, then two, then three...). So, one fencer could need five hits to win the match, while their opponent needs only one. This exercise gradually equalizes the difference in ability between the players, so there is no need to create a handicap beforehand (highly recommended, particularly in a mixed ability group). It also has an element of pressure which grows with the number of hits that have to be scored. The winner is the fencer with the highest number of hits at the end of the session.

First hits/taking the lead

Fight for fifteen hits: who scores the first hit gets two hits, and whoever retakes a lead also gets a bonus hit. Here the stress is on the importance of the first hit, as well as on overtaking from behind.

Pressure testing

Fight for a greater number of hits within the same time or in a shorter time (intensity). For instance, instead of five hits within 3 minutes, fence for seven hits in 2 minutes; instead of fifteen hits in three periods of 3 minutes, fence for twenty hits in three periods of 2 minutes – or anything similar. Such changes prepare fencers for poor refereeing (often, to win a five-hit fight it is necessary to hit seven times). The time limit will also add extra pressure.

Pyramid*

A pyramid is a good exercise when fencers have to prepare for endurance against a background of fatigue. Two fencers fence several matches against each other, steadily increasing the required hits for each bout. A small pyramid has two fencers fencing five separate bouts to 1, 3, 5, 3 and then 1 hit. A medium pyramid would be separate fights to 1, 3, 5, 7, 5, 3, 1; a large pyramid would be 1, 3, 5, 7, 9, 7, 5, 3, 1. A particularly large pyramid takes a long time and will cause tiredness. It is a very useful exercise to prepare fencers for two key challenges: the opponent and fatigue.

Five hits with two hits in a row to confirm the last hit

Every fencer has to hit twice in a row at the end to win – this shows extra concentration.

Tactics and control

Poule: fight for one hit with the referee being told how each fencer is planning to hit. Fencers mark their victories scored with and without their pre-planned action. The coach identifies the fencer with the highest percentage of victories from pre-planned actions. This is a good exercise for developing tactical thinking and control, encouraging premeditated fencing under pressure.

Winner stays on in a queue fencing matches for five hits

This is a good way of developing stamina under pressure while dealing with fresh opponents.

7 | FOOTWORK TRAINING

In this chapter, I emphasize the importance of footwork training. I suggest some specific areas of focus, and also give several examples of different footwork programmes for different levels of fencers.

Everyone who has achieved a good international result would agree that it would not have been possible without good footwork. If you want to be a good fencer you have to be a master of mobility. Good footwork means always being in the right position, ready to attack or defend. It means keeping your distance, changing direction without delay, reacting in time, and being able to change speed and rhythm. One of the great things about footwork training is that a positive effect can be felt quickly.

Photo opposite by Chris Turner.

Club warm-up session in the form of station training. (Photo: Chris Turner)

Fencers warming up. Skipping is a great warm-up exercise and excellent for improving foot dexterity. (Photo: Chris Turner)

At club level, after a group warm-up, it is advisable to keep repeating a particular footwork programme for a duration of 15–20 minutes so fencers get used to the required quality and intensity before changing exercises. In every training session, a fencer should spend some time perfecting their mobility. Often fencers practise extra footwork in separate sessions. In addition to performing a prepared footwork programme, the fencer or coach can develop their creativity.

In footwork training, special attention should be paid to the following areas:

- Small steps
- Change of rhythm
- Change of direction
- Controlling speed while moving forward (forward slower, back any speed)
- Various degrees of bending the legs (using numbers)
- Independent foot actions (tactical steps, appels, **Vezzali** steps, Avola steps)
- Drums (frequency)
- Skipping
- Turns and semi-turns
- Lunge and flèche after moving back

- Flèche from lunging position
- Intensity
- Distance
- Timing
  Bouncing, hopping
- Ability to make a fast attack from a fast retreat
- Independent arm (while moving and from a lunge)
- Efficiency
- Responsive legs
- Using the fencing squat position (as in the well-known Italian video *La Gimnastica per la Schema* by Elio Malena)
- Reactions (different types)
- Any development from a half-lunge
- Mixing any combinations of footwork (short with long attacks)
- Deception

Below are examples of exercises, dependent on the ability of the fencer.

FOOTWORK FOR BEGINNERS

Come on-guard from standing still

- Begin with the feet at right angles, with the front foot directed towards the instructor and the heel touching the heel of the back foot.
- Move the front foot forward to shoulder width while extending one arm forward and the other back.
- Bend the knees so the bulk of the weight is on the balls of the feet, and bend the elbows so they are both at the same level, with the sword arm elbow a hand's width away from the hip bone, avoiding the 'chicken syndrome' where there is a tendency for both elbows to stick out.
- Keep the trunk somewhere between a profile and square position, with the head turned towards the opponent.

Step forward

Move the front foot forward comfortably and land on the heel. As the sole of the foot lands on the floor, bring the back foot the same distance as the front one, landing on the balls of the foot first, which is the opposite movement to the front foot where the heel lands first.

Step backwards

Move the back foot first followed by the front, keeping the same distance between them. In the step back movement, the balls of the feet land first before the heels. *While moving, keep your knees bent and avoid any movements of the trunk, keeping the upper body relaxed.*

Two steps forward followed by two steps back

Make sure while moving in one direction the two steps consist of four movements, completing the last step before changing direction. With this exercise, it is often the case the fencer only makes three foot movements as it is an easier option, and not what has been asked.

Lunging

At the beginning of the lunge, extend the arm first and, when it is about half extended, start moving the front foot forward, landing on the heel first and throwing the back arm back in the final stage. It is helpful to give beginners some coins to kick out with their front foot while lunging. The main problem is the tendency for the front foot not to land far enough forward, so the back hip moves up and causes the heel of the back leg to stick up, making the fencer unbalanced.

At the end of the lunge, the back leg should be straight with the back hip low and the back foot flat on the floor. The shoulders should be parallel to the floor, and the back arm should be parallel to the back leg.

To recover from the lunge, push back from the front leg while at the same time bending the back leg, so in one movement the fencer is back in the on-guard position.

Lunging after completing a step forward or step back, fencers should hold their final position for some time to memorize it.

Lunging practice. Fencing has to be based on a strong attacking movement and fencers should always aim to perfect their lunge. Lunging practice is an essential warm-up exercise regardless of ability. (Photo: Jornnawat (P'Mod) Limprasert)

MORE SESSIONS FOR BEGINNERS

- From running on the spot, come on-guard on the coach's signal (check correctness).
- From lying on the floor, come on-guard on the coach's signal (check correctness).
- From jogging backwards and forwards while keeping distance with the coach, come on-guard on the coach's signal.
- From squat jumps while swinging arms, come on-guard alternating right with left side (this is quite a hard movement to coordinate so some fencers will find it difficult).
- From the on-guard position moving forwards and back, change from right side to left on the coach's signal (each time checking correctness).
- Different sizes of steps forwards and back (coach calls the number and whether small, medium or long).
- Different speeds of steps (slow, medium, fast).
- Stepping along one line with eyes closed (for example, five steps backwards); open eyes and check position at the end in relation to the floor line. (This is a simple exercise to prevent fencers 'crabbing'.)

A group warm-up session involving sprinting creates a sense of enjoyment and camaraderie.
(Photo: Chris Turner)

- Keep distance with the coach and on their signal lunge (check correctness).
- Step lunge: initiate by extending the arm then step forward while the arm is still extending followed by a lunge.
- Jump forward: start by tapping with the front foot, then hopping on the back foot, then try to synchronize both movements to land on both feet simultaneously.
- From moving, lunge or step lunge on the coach's signal.

INTERMEDIATE FOOTWORK

- After each step, squat and return to the on-guard position (to build up leg strength).
- Bouncing in the on-guard position while keeping hands on hips, each time landing in a lower on-guard position until reaching a squat (with feet still in the on-guard position), and the same jumping upwards eventually coming back to the normal on-guard position (another good exercise for developing leg strength, but not suitable for fencers with knee problems).
- While moving frequently with small steps in both directions, slowly extend the sword arm and bend it back to form the on-guard position (coordination exercise for developing an independent sword arm).
- The coach moves their hand forwards and the fencers execute two short steps forward while partly extending the sword arm. When the coach's hand moves back, they take two short steps back while moving the sword arm back to the on-guard position. From time to time the coach, while initiating these steps, drops their hand whereupon the fencers lunge by changing their second step into a lunge.
- Lunge and step-lunge from the fencing squat position executed from left and right (when step lunging from this position, fencers should rise gradually and stay low).

- Execute a flèche attack from standing still in the on-guard position. The hand starts moving first, then the back leg pushes the body onto the front leg which turns into a flèche with the force from the front leg at 45 degrees. A typical error is to rise too much or lift the back hip up while flèching, consequently dropping the hand and head and losing control. While executing the flèche, a fencer should feel a loss of balance when pushing off from the front leg, regaining it when landing on the back foot which crosses the front one (forbidden in sabre).
- Flèche from fencing squat.
- A partner throws a glove for the fencer to catch with a lunge or a flèche.
- Keeping distance in pairs (a good game is 'rock, paper, scissors', where the winner dictates the distance).

ADVANCED FOOTWORK

The duration and intensity of each exercise depends on the stage the training has reached. During the preparatory period, exercises should be longer and more extensive, whereas in a competitive period they should be shorter with maximum intensity.

- Tactical steps (feint moving forwards (with half-step) – step back; feint moving backwards – step forwards).
- Alternating: 'drums' (tapping the floor as quickly as possible with the sole of one foot and then the other) with small steps and fencing skips (lifting the knee as high as possible without raising the hips and moving forwards or backwards). These three exercises should be changed every 5 seconds for at least 45 seconds (3 × 5 seconds for each exercise).
- Steps while sitting lower than usual.
- Intensive footwork while breaking distance and moving forwards or backwards.

- Vezzali steps, mixing slow and fast periods. In this exercise the fencer stands still while their feet constantly move independently from each other in the following order:
    - front foot forwards
    - back foot backwards
    - front foot backwards
    - back foot forwards
- Avola steps are steps forward executed by initiating a movement forward with the back foot first followed by the front foot, ready either to move back or change to an attack with a lunge after gaining the appropriate distance with the back foot.
- While manoeuvring and making half-lunge preparations, practise the following combinations from the half-lunge position in any order:
    - moving back starting with the back leg
    - developing a full lunge
    - developing a step-lunge starting with the back leg
    - developing a step-lunge starting with the front leg
    - developing a flèche.
- Shadow fencing and disguising a one-tempo attack with a lunge or flèche by initiating it from a backwards movement.
- Working on a hop-lunge action which starts like a step forward but without using the back leg, hopping on the front foot and landing in the lunging position. This action is used more and more in competition. It covers more than lunging distance in a different rhythm than a step lunge. Numerous fencers use this footwork, including Massialas (USA) and Meinhardt (USA). In sabre, this movement is known as the 'flunge'.
- Patinando – a combination of step and lunge executed in such a way the fencer lunges as soon as the back leg lands and does not pause as they might when doing a step-lunge.
- Jump-lunge from 'drums'.

A half-lunge is in itself an uncommitted offensive action which can be used to provoke a response from the opponent. From this position there are numerous continuations to progress into attacking or defending, depending on the opponent's response.
(Photo: Kevin Nixon)

- Twelve sessions of keeping distance for 15 seconds using the 'rock, paper, scissors' game – the winner dictating the distance.
- In groups of three, one advances, one retreats and one runs alongside covering the whole length of the piste. The purpose of this exercise is to keep the same distance while moving back. Players move from one role to another in turn, so everyone retreats after advancing and sprints after retreating. Due to the high intensity of this exercise, each set should not last longer than 30 seconds with a 1-minute break between sets.
- Shadow fencing with all steps forward executed slowly and all steps back executed at any speed while alternating committed and uncommitted attacks.

MORE ADVANCED FOOTWORK

- Jog loosely forwards for 2–4 metres, then execute a lunge on your dominant side. Recover and jog back to where you started. Then jog and lunge on your non-dominant side. Change sides and try to gradually increase the length of your lunge. After a while, stay in the lunge and move your hips as low as possible from one leg to the other (fencing gymnastics). The purpose of this exercise is to relax all muscles and lunge using just the muscles needed in addition to stretching. Continue for 2 minutes.
- From lying on the floor, on a signal from the coach come on-guard, take five steps forward, lunge and recover followed by five steps back and then lie down again.
- Normal steps but on the coach's signal change to maximum intensity, jumping forwards and backwards in the on-guard position.
- Alternate short steps forward followed by 'drums' on your dominant side with the same actions on your non-dominant side. Keep doing this in both directions with the duration of steps and 'drums' about 5 seconds each. The whole exercise should take a minimum of 30 seconds.
- Alternate bouncing footwork with smooth steps.
- From the fencing squat position, lunge and recover by leaving the front leg where it landed and straightening it, then hop forward off the back leg to a new fencing

squat position and repeat the exercise for a total of five squat lunges. After a short rest, repeat the exercise five times. This develops dynamic stretching and leg power.

- Slowly and carefully press forward towards the coach. If the coach moves forward without any hand actions, retreat quickly starting with the back leg; if the coach starts moving while bending the arm upwards or backwards, lunge direct; if the coach moves forward extending the arm, execute a beat direct lunge. An alternative is on a slow movement forward by the coach, the fencer retreats, but a fast movement triggers a lunge direct with the arm leading.
- Hopping from one leg to the other while keeping balance.
- From Vezzali footwork, look for the best positions from which to initiate a lunge or a flèche, alternating those actions.
- From moving, practise initiating attacks with the back leg. Fencers should vary the distance gained with the back leg to confuse the opponent and, of course, not always develop the attack but sometimes just step forward to make the eventual attack more unexpected.
- Lunge after a dynamic movement backwards with the whole weight on the back leg.
- While manoeuvring, prepare a flèche from a lunge. Options include:
  - flèche from the half-lunge position
  - flèche from the full lunge position
  - flèche after a full recovery from the lunging position
  - flèche after recovery with a jump back
  - flèche after a jump to the on-guard position in the middle of a lunge, so the back leg moves forward and the front leg moves back together to reach the on-guard position.

GADGETS IN FOOTWORK TRAINING

The most common items used in footwork training are foils, gloves, rubber bands, diving belts, weight jackets, rubber expanders, weight bands on ankles, tennis balls and lunging pads.

Foils

First, foils can be used to add the feeling of a fight (shadow fencing) and also for distance training, one exercise being to hold the point on target with a straight arm while moving.

This is an excellent fencing-specific stretching exercise, executed from a lunge position. It prepares the fencer for lunging by stretching the hamstrings. (Photo: Kevin Nixon)

Second, they can be used to build up finger strength and coordination. For example, a fencer holds their foil blade at the tip between thumb and forefinger and then between the last two fingers and moves the thumb and forefinger down to pull up the blade, at the same time moving their feet forwards and back while repeatedly extending the arm fully and bending it back to the on-guard position, still holding the foil. The blade is gradually pulled up until the guard reaches the hand.

Third, foils can be used for floor exercises – moving the front foot over a foil while lunging, flèching or both, practising hop-lunges and stepping over them on the floor.

While exercising with foils, fencers can reproduce movements from a lesson and rehearse fragments of a fight or shadow fencing. They can also try hitting lunging pads or gloves while practising footwork.

Gloves

Glove exercises mainly involve pairs catching while standing still, or with a lunge or flèche where the partner throws a glove with random timing. These exercises develop coordination and good habits (arm first), and they allow the coach's creativity to blossom.

An interesting exercise is for one fencer to hold two gloves while their partner is on-guard, following their foot movements with proper fencing steps. The fencer with the gloves first throws an easy catch and their partner collects it with a short flèche before returning to on-guard and advancing, whereupon the fencer throws a challenging glove which can only be caught with a really competitive flèche.

Another is the shah-put game where two fencers face each other, each holding a glove in their weapon hand. One fencer is allowed up to three leg movements while making preparatory actions and when they decide to commit to an attack, should try to touch their partner's glove (each other's glove). The task of the retreating fencer is to defend with distance and touch their partner's glove back with their own attack. Moving the glove away sideways is not allowed.

An excellent exercise for accuracy and coordination involves one fencer holding a foil and the other wearing a glove. The foilist continuously moves over a range of 2 metres while changing direction and the position of their weapon. Randomly, the other fencer opens their gloved hand at various distances and heights. The task of the fencer with the foil is to hit the palm of the hand as quickly as possible with optimum strength and fully extended arm using footwork appropriate to the distance.

The use of fingers is imperative in fencing; here is one of the ways to build up strength in the finger muscles. Carry out this exercise while moving both sword arm and feet backwards and forwards to develop fencing-specific coordination. (Photo: Kevin Nixon)

Lunging on a balance beam is particularly difficult as the movements have to be perfectly aligned both during the execution of the lunge and the recovery. (Photo: Niki Bruckner)

Weight jacket

A weighted jacket worn during footwork sessions will contribute to an increase in the strength of specific muscle groups used in fencing actions. Using a jacket weighing between 8 and 12 kg for a minimum of 10 minutes' footwork three times a week in a preparatory period has been shown to produce a positive experience as soon as it is removed, but also provides a long-term benefit. Fencers improve the acceleration of attacks and speed of retreat considerably. But it is not advisable to have a lesson or a fight with a weighted jacket, as it causes actions to be executed with a different timing and leads to incorrect learning. A rubber band, which helps with resistance, and rubber expanders are also good for improving footwork.

Beemat balance beam

Using a balance beam for practising footwork helps in perfecting technique or movements, builds up strength in the legs and core, and of course helps develop a sense of balance.

OTHER FOOTWORK PROGRAMMES

- Any combination of shadow fencing using at least two speeds in periods of 3 × 3 minutes, 3 × 4 minutes and 2 × 4 minutes, with the coach giving the signal for the speed (slow, fast, medium).
- Six periods of 1.5 minutes, each period consisting of 30 seconds of slow steps, 30 seconds of fast steps and 30 seconds of rest.
- The coach in front of a class indicates footwork speed by using one hand (slow) or both (fast) and indicates a change of direction by turning the palms out. A lunge is shown by extending one arm and a step lunge by extending both. The most common intervals are 3 × 3 minutes and 2 × 4 minutes.
- 2 × 3 minutes: for the first 3 minutes the fencer reproduces movements from a lesson at 60 per cent speed; in the second period 90–100 per cent speed shadow fencing (with the exception of steps forward). In normal shadow fencing, steps forward are much slower and rather short.
- For competitive period shadow fencing, maximum intensity for 10 seconds followed by 10 seconds of slow pace.

A coach's imagination is the only limit here!

8 | ASPECTS OF AN INDIVIDUAL LESSON

The individual lesson will always be an essential part of a fencer's training. During the lesson, fencers develop helpful habits and learn new actions and their application in particular situations.

This chapter endeavours to cover general aspects of an individual lesson with specific exercises providing a useful source of ideas when tailoring lessons for individual fencers.

GENERAL REMARKS

There is no other sport where a coach's direct involvement with an athlete is so intense and absorbing as in an individual fencing lesson. International fencers usually take four or five 20–30 minute lessons per week. Some coaches give longer lessons; for instance, Mark Midler's lessons were often 90 minutes long, and Oleg Matseychuk's 40–50 minutes. The length of a lesson depends on its character and when it is given in relation to a competition. Warm-up lessons are always short.

Photo opposite by Chris Turner.

In an individual lesson both coach and fencer develop the following areas:

- Point control (this includes speed and change of speed of the point and accuracy) and correct hitting with a loose, independent spaghetti arm.
- Footwork.
- A feeling for distance and blade.
- Technique (positions and movements).
- Timing (paying attention to initiating and finishing actions in time).
- Decision making (sharp perception – senso-motor level; fast thinking – prognostic level).
- Tactics.
- Coordination.
- Change in rhythm and acceleration.
- Stamina, strength and speed of footwork and blade work; the most important quality of speed is its change and control.
- Quickness of reaction and ability to change (adaptability).
- Efficiency of execution of various strokes.
- Qualities of character, such as decisiveness, punctuality, concentration, initiative, creativeness, tenacity, emotional control, determination, courage, positive thinking and confidence.

Types of lesson

Various aspects of a lesson can be identified as follows: warm-up; learning; training; checking-up; correcting; bouting (coach and fencer rehearse fragments of particular situations from matches); and opponent tactics (specific actions for specific opponents).

The role of the coach

A coach should facilitate the relaxed, well-coordinated and smooth execution of an action and only gradually increase the level of difficulty, eventually leading to highly intensive practice.

Presentation of the blade by the coach should be precise and realistic. Movements should gradually become more and more realistic with real attempts to hit the fencer and allowing only well-timed actions to succeed. Ultimately, a coach should not allow actions that would not have much chance of success in a real fight. Presentation of the blade should be into all sectors of the target, if possible at random to develop an equal readiness to defend against each of them. The aim is to achieve a highly intensive lesson, strong on training stimulus, lasting around 20–30 minutes.

Just before a fencer makes a hit, the coach can introduce various behaviours:

- Stop hit or counter-attack out of time.
- Delay a parry with the purpose of encouraging acceleration.

Slow down!

'Chasing the rabbit' is an atavistic behaviour to run as fast as possible to catch fleeing prey. In foil fencing, such behaviour is not effective and should be replaced with a slowing down (two waves) or a complete stop.

- Duck or evade.
- Make a real parry and require a counter-parry-riposte or renewal.
- Suddenly increase the distance so the fencer can practise many responses but not 'chasing the rabbit'.

It is helpful if the coach can move at different speeds and change direction, as this is good training for a fencer's footwork and feeling for distance. The backwards steps of a coach should be short as they help develop a fencer's habit of short steps forward.

A coach should alternate exercises against right- and left-handed opponents during the same lesson. This is more beneficial than giving a whole lesson using the left or right hand, as is it more challenging for the fencer.

Encourage fencers to use their fingers and elbow, but not the shoulder. To further help, the fencer should sometimes hold the weapon with only two fingers, in addition to doing exercises from a low hand position combined with exercises where the point is 'busy', stimulating the use of the fingers and developing a spaghetti arm.

Also pay attention to changing their rhythm and distance (realism – avoid working on repeated executing actions with the same timing and distance).

Perfect hit

It is very important to consider the quality of hitting. Confidence in hitting is an important part of a fencer's preparation for competition. Be a perfectionist when it comes to the *quality of hitting* (perpendicular, optimal strength, using fingers, balanced), as it leads to long-term benefits in accuracy and confidence. It also helps if the fencer slightly lowers their position while hitting, as this will increase the readiness to lunge immediately, take a counter-parry or any other subsequent action.

If working on preparing attacks from pressing, a coach should make sure the fencer is making small and slow steps (here, it is helpful if a coach develops a habit of small steps backwards), or changing rhythm (two waves, stuttering preparation). It is particularly important when taking back the initiative, the first step of a fencer's preparation is slow and cautious (Italian looking step).

To maintain a high level of concentration and develop a resistance to being surprised, a coach should introduce something unexpected from time to time, for example:

- Sudden attack, including instant beat attack (early parry or beat attack to develop resistance against such actions – the fencer should make a return beat or change beat in time and usually hit direct).
- Sudden renewal.
- Duck.
- Sudden defence with distance.
- Sudden stop hit moving back.
- Sudden flèche.
- Sudden counter-attack.
- Change of timing and speed of parries and ripostes.
- Parries with step forward.
- Change of distance in both directions.

An individual lesson with the coach is a very important method of developing fencing skills and perfecting techniques. (Photo: Paula Huckle)

Surprise the coach

Equally a coach should encourage the fencer to carry out an unexpected action now and again in a lesson to develop their own ability to surprise. Mastering this skill will be of benefit in competitive fights.

Taking the initiative should also be varied. In some exercises, only the coach takes the initiative and the fencer follows and vice versa in others. Then there are exercises where the initiative changes from coach to fencer and back, and some exercises where both try to initiate at the same time (near-simultaneous actions).

It is important for the coach to tailor coaching to a particular fencer's needs – working on the most relevant areas. Falling into certain habits and patterns in a lesson is a perpetual danger for the coach – for example, always changing the distance on the third riposte or always presenting the blade in the sixte (6) line after an attack. All patterns should be changed randomly. Accepting feedback from an observant fencer is always useful.

When practising parries a coach should also offer some degree of resistance to a fencer's blade in order to help give the fencer a sense of closing the line correctly; if a fencer's parry is too shallow they risk being hit with a continuation, and if it is too wide they become vulnerable to a disengage.

Unhelpful habits

One of the most common but unhelpful habits is hitting a fencer's blade quite hard upwards after a hit and helping to fix the point on target. The fencer should place the point by themselves. Also when practising parries, a coach should be sure to present the blade so it threatens a valid target. Otherwise, the fencer is learning to respond to the wrong signal and their parry will become too large.

I advocate a democratic approach to coaching, which includes actively encouraging the fencer's participation in a lesson to help develop creativity and initiative. Coaches can learn new things from experienced, inquisitive and observant fencers and even young fencers can provide eye-opening observations. We are never too old to learn!

Although the classic principles of fencing are eternal, the sport is constantly evolving and a good coach should never stop searching for new developments and, if possible, even try to anticipate them. Inevitably, coaching is affected by changes in equipment, the rules and the interpretation of them.

In developing a fencer's creativity and tactical diversity, the coach should require the fencer to vary their actions when faced with the same tactical situation. For instance, against a direct attack from the coach, the fencer should try using various parries (instant and delayed); defence with distance; and various counter-attacks including ducking.

In developing tactical thinking and confidence it is helpful to develop a series of pre-meditated actions to various situations based on the most probable action of an opponent. This approach is especially useful in high-pressure situations when it is difficult to think. In near-simultaneous actions a chain of six actions can be used in the following order:

1. Attack direct going for simultaneous.
2. Attack by feint disengage, assuming that the opponent will take a parry.
3. Feint attack, followed by a prearranged parry-riposte, assuming the opponent will go direct.
4. Feint attack, followed by a counter-attack (Romanian), assuming the opponent will go for a compound or broken time attack.
5. Second-intention attack for a counter-parry-riposte, assuming the opponent will go for a parry.
6. Feint attack, defence with distance and prearranged answering attack, assuming the opponent will attack again.

Adaptability is a key requirement for a coach, especially the ability to switch from a beginner's lesson to a one-on-one lesson with an experienced international fencer. This is not easy but must be mastered.

Good habits

- Slow beginning
- Keeping the point on target
- Reacting to an opponent's blade contact with change beats or a change of engagement (**referee-friendly parry**)
- Acceleration of the point independently from the legs
- Staying loose (coordination)
- Quality of hitting
- Reacting with actions in time
- Changing rhythm
- Riposting immediately with a lunge should the distance increase
- Small preparations
- Correct position of hand and body
- Independent foot actions (half steps, tactical steps)

Whether an international fencer or a beginner, a coach must be able to adapt to their student and instil good habits. (Photo: Chris Turner)

Different focus

- Feeling for distance
- Timing
- Feeling for the blade
- Technical precision
- Change of rhythm
- Accuracy and speed
- Coordination
- Concentration
- Decision-making
- Anticipation
- Efficiency
- Strength

Generally, in lessons, the coach should develop good basic fencing habits in their fencers. An invaluable approach is to categorize actions, as detailed below, as this will provide a good lesson structure and help develop good muscle memory. All these actions could be first- or second-intention. Introducing third-intention is very rare.

Premeditated actions

These are planned reactions to particular actions by an opponent.

Partly premeditated actions

Part of the action is premeditated and part is not: either the action starts as premeditated but changes because something unexpected occurs, or it is open-eyes (when the beginning is known, but the ending still depends on the reaction of the opponent). Some choice reaction exercises could also be partly premeditated if there is a premeditated beginning.

Off-hand actions

Off-hand is when the whole action from the beginning is completely spontaneous, when fencer or coach does something unexpected.

In lessons, coaches should introduce exercises to develop a fencer's sharp eye, where they must differentiate between subtle changes to their signals. Often similar signals will require a different response. In particular, a fencer should be required to spot the difference between false and real signals such as between false and real counter-attacks, between an uncommitted and committed attack, between the beginning of real and preparatory beats, and the difference between the beginning of an attack and the beginning of preparation.

These exercises should help to develop a sharp eye, which is so important in sports where every situation is different and conditions are constantly changing. This ability to read signals leads to a faster anticipation, which is what separates many top athletes from the rest of their field.

Equally, subtle changes from a coach can require only subtle changes from the fencer. Even if a fencer practises parry 4 many times, there will never be two identical situations in terms of distance, speed, changing rhythm and other parameters of engagement. Every repetition will be different depending on the immediate circumstances and the tiny nuances of movement, which have to be recognized and differentiated.

In foil, a fencer's sense of touch plays an important role after their sense of vision. Developing exercises based on feeling for the blade are useful and include exercises with closed eyes.

It is vitally important for a coach to maintain a high level of fitness. In some lessons a coach will need to recreate fight situations, where they will need speed and agility. A fencer will always benefit when a coach's hand is fast and accurate.

Creating an ideal 30-minute lesson

Aim to include most of following themes:
- **Knitting**
- One of the systems for searching for the blade
- Attacks on preparation
- First- and last-moment parries
- Various ways of dealing with counter-attacks
- Dealing with counter-time
- Near-simultaneous actions
- Answering attacks
- Change beats
- Attacks from pressing
- Mixing first- and second-intention attacks, correct and non-correct attacks, attacks on preparation with answering, etc.
- Actions from line
- Backline defence
- Defence after false actions
- Defence with distance
- Choice between attack and parry
- **Mincemeat**

MATERIAL FOR INDIVIDUAL LESSONS – EXAMPLES OF EXERCISES

Lessons provide the opportunity to teach more than just technique or tactics; it's also about broader skills and anticipating an opponent's actions. Whilst every exercise can develop many areas, I find it helpful to divide exercises into three groups: technique, coordination and timing; reading an opponent's intention; and tactics. Unless specified, all exercises below are for same-handers.

Exercises for developing technique, coordination and timing

Direct thrust or any action executed with pre-arranged footwork

Standing still, step forward, two-steps forward, lunge, step-lunge and half-step flèche. The coach creates the appropriate distance and calls for the appropriate foot action. Later the fencer can be responsible for deciding the distance. The coach's role is to give feedback about the technical execution of a stroke.

As above, while the coach moves backwards and forwards

The fencer chooses the right moment to hit and coordinates their steps, while the coach sometimes increases the distance so the fencer has to finish with a lunge. Virtually any action can be practised. For example, hitting with any beat, two beats, any engagement, *double engagement* followed by a change beat cut-over, feint disengage, two deceptions, one-two-three, etc.

Deceive and parry

- After hitting with a disengage or two deceptions, parry-riposte standing still and while moving. This can be prearranged to start with, so the fencer knows exactly which parries to deceive and which to take afterwards. If the exercise is going well, the coach can build in more and more choices. For example:

  - There is a choice between any two deceptions depending on the parries the coach takes or any parry-riposte

A fencer working on his direct lunge. (Photo: Chris Turner)

depending on the sector of target the coach threatens.

- As above, with an additional choice of riposte depending on the coach's response to the fencer's parry.
- As above, with the exercise starting at lunging distance with the coach changing the distance as well as deceiving parries and parrying the fencer's ripostes and requiring them to take counter-parries.
- Similar to above, with a choice after the first deception of making a second deception or moving to take any parry.

- If in an exercise there is a choice of riposte, then the fencer should take a holding parry, as this gives them adequate time to see, feel and decide on the appropriate riposte. If after one riposte the coach presents the blade again for another parry, then it is useful to ask the fencer to lower his on-guard position while taking the next parry, to combat the generic tendency to straighten one's legs. In general, lowering the on-guard position increases balance, power and concentration.
- The fencer constantly deceives at a slightly longer than riposting distance, hitting only if the coach moves closer or parrying if the coach presents the blade in any sector of the target. In this exercise, the coach can introduce various movements of his target requiring different perpendicular hits. The signal for hitting can also be a wider movement of the coach's foil which clearly gives a fencer more time to hit.
- Similar to above, but at lunging distance with fencer and coach standing still. In this exercise the fencer should choose the moment to attack into an opening sector of the target (the coach can help with wider openings if necessary); the signal to parry is given when the coach presents the blade in a particular sector of the target.
- To progress further, fencer and coach

both manoeuvre at greater than lunging distance; the signal to attack can be when the coach stops while opening a particular sector of target or simply when the fencer feels it is a good moment to attack. Here the coach should gradually vary the distance and speed and the fencer will have to feel when the moment is right to hit. They have to both watch and feel.

This exercise develops an instinctive feeling for distance, timing and what action to do in the moment, which is the basis for intuitive and creative fencing. The coach must help the fencer eliminate their pre-signals before attacking, so the attack is disguised as much as possible.

Mincemeat

'Mincemeat' is the name I gave to a close-quarters exercise where the coach takes constantly varying parries, slightly varying the distance, angle and body position with each parry. The fencer tries to avoid each parry and hit continuously. Each hit should be perpendicular to the target with optimum strength at various degrees of arm extension. The coach stops when the fencer's hand gets tired or too tense. A further variation of this exercise is for the coach to alternate attempts to take the blade with attempts to hit different sectors of the target at a distance varying from riposting to close-quarters. The fencer practises parries and ripostes at those distances.

Envelopments and binds from basic hand positions

This is a technical exercise where the fencer transports the coach's blade by doing envelopments and binds, stopping from time to time in a particular position for the coach to check if the line is closed and the point is in position, ready to riposte. Periodically, the fencer hits in a particular line. It is important for the coach to provide slight blade resistance to help the fencer get a better feel for keeping the line

Envelopment and bind

Envelopment is the transportation of the opponent's blade with a circular movement back to the same position, while a bind is a diagonal transportation of the blade to a different position, for example from 4 to 8 or from 8 to 4.

closed, with the coach's blade in the strong part of their own blade.

Systems of searching for the blade, practising standing still

- Octave, counter-octave, sixte, counter-sixte (8, c8, 6, c6)
- Quarte, counter-quarte, sixte, counter-sixte (4, c4, 6, c6)
- Septime, counter-septime, quarte, counter-quarte (7, c7, 4, c4)
- Counter-sixte, quarte, counter-quarte, sixte (c6, 4, c4, 6)
- Counter-sixte, counter-sixte, quarte, counter-quarte (c6, c6, 4, c4)
- Quarte, counter-quarte, septime, counter-septime (4, c4, 7, c7)

Here a fencer goes through all the positions in order and, when they do it well, the coach can ask them to riposte at any stage if the blade is found.

The next stage is to do this exercise while moving backwards and forwards, hitting after the blade is found while coordinating with distance. The parry should be held for long enough so the fencer has ample time to decide on a response depending on the coach's next action. The coach should also encourage only point movements and reduce any movements of the guard parallel to the target. The guard should move along a straight line unless the exercise involves practising closing the opposite line while hitting.

In the later stages, the coach may change from deceiving the fencer's blade to searching for the blade, requiring the fencer to change immediately to deceiving the coach's blade while feeling for the right moment to hit the target.

Deceiving three prearranged parries with different footwork

The most typical distances from which a fencer should hit during the exercise are riposting, lunging and step-lunge. The coach initiates the exercise by taking the first of the three parries and decides the distance at the end of the movement. Here, common parries are two circular sixtes (6) and quarte (4). In order to develop acceleration, the coach tries to parry the fencer's blade with a fourth parry, which in this case will be sixte (6) taken from quarte (4), the fencer's task being to hit the target before this fourth parry can be taken.

Flèche attacks

From a standing position, starting when the fencer is ready. The focus of this exercise should be on execution. Possibilities include a flèche on the coach's step forward, from pressing when the coach stops, after defending with distance, or as a riposte.

Knitting

This is a technical exercise, which I compare to a musician practising their scales. The coach engages the fencer's blade, then the fencer changes the coach's engagement before sliding along the blade while waiting for a reaction. Depending on the reaction, the fencer can choose from disengages or counter-disengages, hitting directly or with up to two deceptions and a lunge if the coach increases the distance and takes an extra parry. The coach may also deceive the fencer's attempt to re-engage the blade; in this case, the fencer should first make a step back before taking successive parries (usually circular). This exercise develops the *referee-friendly* habit of reacting with a change of engagement to the blade being found, as well as training change of rhythm, coordination and responsive legs.

Hot and cold

While moving, the fencer constantly deceives the coach's parries with cut-overs, without hitting, at slightly greater than lunging distance and, if the coach stops, the fencer chooses the moment to hit with a cut-over lunge or, if the coach attacks, they take the appropriate parry.

Hitting with one or two cut-overs from a stationary lunging position

The fencer decides whether to make one or two, but the coach always takes two parries.

Two hits in the same place while moving using mainly steps

The second hit must be faster so there is a clear change of speed. The arm reaches full extension both times to achieve maximum distance, giving the fencer immediate feedback about accuracy. The objectives of this exercise are:

- To hit the same spot.
- To coordinate with distance.
- To change the rhythm (the first hit slow, the second fast).
- To hit twice correctly with the arm fully extended using mainly fingers.

Blocking the entrance

With the fencer keeping the point on target and the arm fully extended, the coach steps forward threatening any sector and the fencer practises blocking the entrance to that sector while closing the distance. Unlike a Romanian where there is a choice between leaving the point on target or taking it away, in this exercise the fencer should *always* leave the point on the target when they block out a line, as this will require them to differentiate between lines more precisely. Similarly, after any successful parry-riposte by the fencer, the coach can try to hit in any sector – the fencer should block immediately and close the distance (some fencers find it more effective to take the point away while blocking).

Training of counter-attacks (Romanian)

This action combines hitting the opponent's target and immediately blocking the opponent's blade in all lines. In this exercise a fencer learns to distinguish between the fast or slow beginnings of an opponent's initiation: if the movement of the opponent (coach) is fast then the blocking movement of the fencer should be forward; against a slow movement of the opponent (coach) the blocking movement should be backwards after hitting at maximum distance.

The conditions for a Romanian should be as follows:

- Relatively short distance (if the distance is too long the opponent has space to finish or time to parry).
- The point of the opponent's weapon moving away from the target area.
- The opponent's blade movement is relatively wide.
- If the opponent's movement is fast, block forward, if slow, hit at maximum distance and block the line backwards holding the closed line while moving back.

To progressively increase the level of difficulty:

1. From standing still at a slightly further then riposting distance, the coach takes his point away from the prearranged line (inside, high outside or low outside) while moving forward fast. The fencer tries to hit the coach and immediately takes the point off the target to block the coach's blade, whilst at the same time moving forward using a step, lunge or flèche (start with step).
2. As above, with the coach moving slowly and the fencer doing a stop hit at maximum distance, holding the closed line while moving back.
3. As above, except the fencer initiates with a half-lunge preparation when the coach stops. The coach will then take their point away in one of the prearranged lines.

Here we see a stop hit at maximum distance which has a good chance of success. The hit arrives on target with the full extension of the arm, and the opponent's (coach) point is furthest away from the target area. The movement of the coach's blade is relatively slow. (Photo: Kevin Nixon)

4. As in 3, with a choice of lines to block.
5. As in 4, adding the choice between a parry if the coach is initiating his movement while directing his point towards the target area or a Romanian if the coach takes his point away from the target while moving forward.
6. With the coach pressing, the fencer does a half-lunge preparation on one of the coach's forward steps. The coach does not respond so the fencer moves back and tries again. The coach directs their point to one of the lines, and the fencer takes an appropriate parry or the coach takes their point away in one of the lines, and the fencer does a Romanian.
7. Fencer and coach manoeuvre at slightly further than lunging distance. On one of the coach's steps forward, the fencer executes a beat quart (4) direct lunge, then a fast remise while recovering from the lunge and increasing the distance. At this point, the coach either presents the blade in one of three basic lines and the fencer

does a parry-riposte or the coach takes the point away and moves fast into one of the lines and the fencer carries out a Romanian in the appropriate line.

Simple attack from pressing

The fencer chooses the moment to attack from pressing with a simple lunge when the coach stops and is about to start a counter-attack or take a parry. However, if the coach attempts an attack on preparation, the fencer switches to a parry. To make the exercise harder, the coach can sometimes retake the initiative from the fencer who, rather than finishing immediately, retreats while maintaining distance, waiting to take back the initiative again. Another option could be to ask the fencer to defend with distance should the coach attack, before replying with a lunge.

Attack with one feint from pressing

Here instead of making a simple attack, when the coach stops, the fencer does a sudden feint as their back foot lands, before deceiving a prearranged parry. Such an attack is essentially a premeditated action. However, a coach may develop it into a **choice reaction** exercise by introducing one of four options:

- No reaction – then direct attack.
- Reaction to one of two parries – feint disengage or counter-disengage.
- Step back – no attack.
- If the coach takes two parries, whether prearranged or not, the fencer must make two deceptions after the feint. The fencer must also switch to a parry if the coach attacks. The parry can be taken on the back foot and the riposte will depend on the depth of the coach's attack.

Alternating attacks on preparation with answering attacks against prearranged parries

The fencer follows the coach stepping forwards and backwards and either: attacks with a lunge as the coach begins a step forward (the fencer chooses which attack to make, but knowing which parries the coach is allowed to take); or steps back engaging the coach's blade as the coach steps forward. After this, the coach can react by moving backwards and the fencer can follow the coach's step back with a step forward and execute an answering attack (knowing which parries the coach is allowed to take).

The answering attack for example, could be:

- While making the step back, engage in circular sixte (6), step forward with the same engagement and lunge with a one-two.
- Step back in quarte (4) followed by a step forward in quarte (4) and late disengage on the lunge, one-two, direct attack with opposition, transfer to octave (8) with opposition and many other options.

These attacks are premeditated by the fencer who perfects the timing and execution of them.

This exercise allows for many more combinations of actions. For example, instead of taking the blade, the fencer could beat and take the blade away before restarting their answering attack. Equally, the coach could prepare without giving the blade, inviting the fencer to start an answering attack when they stop or give up priority. The coach's response to these attacks can be pre-arranged.

Beat attack against final phase of uncommitted attacks

The fencer retreats, holding the distance, and just before the end of the coach's uncommitted attack chooses the moment for a beat direct with a flèche or a lunge. This exercise has the element of breaking the opponent's rhythm and limits their opportunity to parry. The fencer should beat *while* extending the arm and start their direct thrust before the coach is able to start their parry.

Choosing a direct attack or feint disengage with a lunge on preparation

This exercise helps to choose the moment to hit with a direct attack or feint-disengage with a lunge on one of the coach's steps forward. The fencer keeps distance with the coach at slightly greater then lunging distance. The coach is allowed to take one prearranged parry. The fencer tries to alternate a direct attack with an attack by feint-disengage. In this exercise, it is better if the fencer premeditates his attack and just chooses the right moment to hit. The coach tries to take a prearranged parry. If the action and moment are good, the fencer should hit. To make this exercise more tactical the fencer can also make a short attack for a counter-parry and riposte. Also, the coach can attack the fencer on one of their steps forward and require a parry-riposte.

Hitting in 'spike of the cactus' position. The merit of this position lies in accessing the target from underneath, which is hard to parry and has potential to achieve strong opposition to the opponent's blade. The nature of the movement can be related to an uppercut in boxing. (Photo: Kevin Nixon)

Exchange of beats

The coach presents the blade while moving, and the fencer makes a beat and presents their blade, which the coach then beats back again; the fencer responds with another prearranged beat before they hit, adapting their footwork to the changing distance. This prearranged beat can be in the same line, or it can be a change beat. The simplest example is a beat quarte (4) direct followed by a beat quarte (4) direct by the fencer. This is a good opportunity to work on changing the speed of the blade.

Another combination is a beat quarte (4) followed by a change beat sixte (6) flick to shoulder. Here the emphasis should be on a change of rhythm from the hand and accurate flicking; at the end, it could be useful to add a choice between a renewal in the sixte (6) line while closing the distance or a renewal in low octave (8) opposition ('spike of the cactus'), depending on the coach's presentation of the blade. This is a good habit while practising flicks, as they do not always register.

Yet another is a beat quarte (4) with the coach taking quarte (4) and the fencer responding with a change beat or change engagement and one of the following touches: direct hit, disengage, one-two, double-disengage, cutover or any other option.

Double engagement

The fencer, in their own time, executes a double engagement – change beat one-two-three. The fencer does this while moving backwards and forwards; here it is important to perfect a change of the *rhythm of the point*, accelerating on either the last disengage, or the last two disengages. For example, hitting either: one-*two-three*, or one-two-*three*.

Magic of direct thrust

Both fencer and coach keep manoeuvring and the fencer's task is to disguise the beginning of a direct thrust so the coach sees it as late as possible. The fencer can do various body-feints, such as moving backwards before moving forwards and the coach genuinely tries to parry. The fencer obtains positive feedback about the deceptiveness of their action if the hit succeeds. In addition to the body-feint while moving backwards, the fencer can make a direct thrust after a feint. This has a good chance of succeeding if the coach reacts to the feint, due to the psychological refractory period.

Hitting from prime position

The fencer engages the coach's blade, which is in low line, to low prime with either a step back (legs before hand) or step forward (hand before legs), while closing the line. The fencer then hits various targets with a cut-over (releasing the blade) while adapting footwork as the coach varies the distance.

Here it is important to:

- close the line before making a cut-over and hit
- have the hand moving before the legs when engaging forward, but have the legs moving first while engaging backwards
- change the rhythm (slower engagement and faster hit)
- mix hitting with the point with flicking.

If this is going well the coach can introduce a deception of the fencer's engagement, to which the fencer reacts with a very fast circular prime (1) and hits with a flick to shoulder or wherever originally planned. So a relatively slow engagement in low prime changes into a fast successive beat prime cut-over and hit.

Back foot practice

Practising beats, parries and feints on the back foot. Examples:

- The fencer prepares with a half-lunge and, if the coach moves back, they do not attack, but if the coach stays still, the fencer recovers forward and executes a beat direct as the back foot lands, developing a full lunge. This type of action could be more useful for fencers with a shorter reach.

- Step-lunge attack executed from a step-lunge distance with a feint on the back foot and a disengage of a prearranged parry.
- As above but from pressing, with the fencer attacking when the coach stops. The coach starts moving forwards and stops at some stage; at that moment the fencer takes the initiative and starts slowly pressing and the coach responds by stepping back while keeping the distance. When the coach stops or delays moving backwards, the fencer commits to an attack with a feint on the back foot and disengages.
- While moving the fencer does two beats and a disengage on the coach's presentation of the blade. The fencer can vary the rhythm of these beats if they choose, but the first beat should be on the front foot and the second on the back foot. The fencer aims to hit with a step-lunge, but if the coach decreases the distance the fencer must adapt their footwork to two steps of varying length.
- When the fencer prepares with a half-lunge, the coach reacts with a direct thrust. The fencer parries as they bring up their back foot and then ripostes while standing still or with a lunge, depending on the distance.

From pressing, the fencer executes a prearranged attack when the coach stops

Sometimes the coach stops and immediately moves back again, so the fencer does not commit and carries on pressing, but sometimes the coach executes a surprise attack, forcing the fencer to parry or defend with distance. Eventually, the fencer will find the timing to commit to the attack.

Practise taking parry 5 (quinte) * with a step forward and riposting at close quarters

There are various options for hitting: moving the hand back low and hitting upwards into the low line in supination; moving the hand back

126

Miyake hit. Miyake is the way of hitting mainly opposite-handed opponents, usually at close quarters. Named after Japanese Olympic medallist Ryo Miyake who used this action often and very effectively. (Photo: Niki Bruckner)

in the same line and supinating while throwing the point forward like Japanese fencer Miyake; moving hand up to a high prime position; **scorpion** – hitting the shoulder from above the head; **Jault** – hitting behind one's back usually into the opponent's flank. An element of choice can be introduced by either hitting low target in supination or using Jault, depending on the coach's behaviour.

This exercise can be executed more mechanically if the coach attacks from a medium distance, or can be set up by the fencer in several situations. For instance, while moving and keeping a short distance: when the coach stops, the fencer invites with a half step and opening to tierce (3) whereupon the coach attacks and the fencer parries with a step forward. This can be adapted to near-simultaneous actions by using a feint of attack instead of the half step and opening.

*Note: some people might call this parry 4 (quarte), but it is technically 5 (quinte) as the blade is taken forward and down to cover the whole space in front.

Fencer decides how to riposte

The coach continuously simulates attacks into the sixte (6) and quarte (4) lines, and the fencer decides how to hit the coach with a riposte. The coach also changes the distance, so the fencer sometimes has to riposte standing still and sometimes with a lunge. The fencer can hit direct (but must start the riposte before the coach's defensive action has begun), with a disengage (but must start *after* the coach's defensive action), or make a compound riposte by starting to disengage after the coach starts a defensive action but waiting for the coach to take another parry before completing the riposte. After simulating an attack the coach always tries to take a simple parry first.

Taking parry quinte (5) with step forward. Parries with a step forward are always difficult for an opponent to deal with. Parry quinte takes the entire space in front of the target, and proves to be particularly effective when moving forward. (Photo: Dawn Uhalley)

This exercise develops decisiveness, as the fencer constantly has to decide how to hit the coach, and how to time various ripostes. Anything out of time should be parried by the coach, and most importantly, the fencer has to be ready to lunge immediately if the distance increases.

A fencer's own composition of hits

The fencer changes the distance and plays with the coach's blade, from time to time prac-tising hitting as deceptively and efficiently as possible. The coach may gradually change the distance and blade position, making the fencer adjust accordingly. This exercise develops crea-tivity for both the fencer and the coach, who can gradually introduce obstacles.

Beat cut-overs

This is similar to the exercise above, with the fencer practising any combination of two (or more) beat cut-overs in the high line,

Riposting with Jault. Jault is riposting after taking a parry with a step forward at close quarters. It is named after a French fencer who used this often; it is a surprising way of reaching the target as the sword arm goes behind the fencer's back. (Photo: Dawn Uhalley)

using the first beat as a preparation to build up momentum for the speed of the point on the second beat. A fencer can hit with a flick or place the point, coordinating with the distance after the second movement. The coach moves forwards and backwards while the fencer initiates in his own time. The fencer tries to make his movements as natural as possible and should feel the first movement helps with the acceleration of the second one. The fencer also varies the target area for hitting.

Direct thrust on lack of touch
From standing still, with blades engaged in such a way the coach's line is closed, the coach drops their weapon to touch the floor and up again to parry as quickly as possible. The fencer's task is to hit the target as soon as the coach drops their weapon, thereby avoiding being parried. This exercise is mainly a tactile reaction, so if the fencer applies light pressure on the coach's blade it usually helps the fencer perform better.

The next progression is the same exercise but moving with the fencer doing extremely short steps. It is harder to do it from retreating as there is a change of direction.

129

Reading an opponent's intentions (differentiated reactions)

In fencing, the development of fast and selective perception is crucial. Fencers need to be able to make the right decision quickly. Exercises where a fencer has little time to recognize small differences between signals helps to achieve this goal.

Recognizing the difference between real and false attacks

One of the most common situations in a fight is when the opponent mixes real attacks with false attacks, in other words, committed attacks with uncommitted ones. Fencers have to quickly recognize the difference between these two. There are numerous possibilities for useful exercises in lessons. A *real attack* should be executed with the same conditions as if the coach were genuinely trying to touch his student (deep with the point threatening the target), while a *false attack* would usually fall short, often with the arm still bent.

1. Against a real attack, the fencer does a parry-riposte direct, while against a false one the fencer takes a real parry, but ripostes indirect with a lunge. It is always good if the fencer mixes parries, for example quarte (4) with circular sixte (c6).

2. Against a real attack, the fencer takes a real parry and riposte, while against a false attack they take a false parry, before opening up in another line in order to draw the opponent's response, usually with a step back. After a false parry and opening there are numerous situations to practise: the coach does a remise of attack and the fencer responds with a real parry-riposte; the coach searches for the blade while at medium distance and the fencer chooses the moment to lunge into an opening sector of the target; the coach moves back while searching for the blade

and the fencer presses slowly and feels the best moment to finish his attack.

3. Against a real attack, the fencer takes a last moment parry and riposte. Against a false attack the fencer executes a beat direct towards the end of the coach's movement. The fencer does this while the coach is still moving forward, in this way they can use the momentum of the opponent to speed up their own attack. Such attacks characterize the breaking of an opponent's rhythm, as they interrupt in an unexpected way.

4. Recognize whether the attack is committed or uncommitted while defending with distance. If committed, answer with a direct attack, but if uncommitted, answer with a feint-disengage attack. The coach may sometimes finish an uncommitted attack with a straight arm (establishing point-in-line), whereupon the fencer after defending with distance does a *beat* attack. The coach may sometimes do a committed attack with a flèche and the fencer has to parry-riposte as it is hard to defend with distance against a flèche attack. Against a flèche it is often better to hold the parry and continue moving backwards to riposte, keeping the line closed against a possible remise. The above exercise is also good practice in near-simultaneous situations.

Recognizing the difference between false and real counter-attacks while attacking

The fencer ignores false counter-attacks and deceives the anticipated parry; against real counter-attacks just finish or execute a real parry-riposte. The coach starts the counter-attack on the fencer's feint or on a step forward with absence of blade. A false counter-attack is usually short with some foot movement but without full extension, whereas a real counter-attack is deeper and more genuinely threatening.

Choosing between counter-attack and parry-riposte

It is important to recognize the difference between good and bad preparation of an attack from a bent arm position with the intention of hitting and the same attack with the mistake of preparing too close or too wide. In other words, there is a choice between a counter-attack and a parry-riposte, but the signals are not clear. So both fencer and coach manoeuvre and the coach starts preparing an attack by moving their point away from the fencer's target but not too quickly and still keeping a good distance; or the coach does the same thing but faster and wider, giving a clear gap in timing for a counter-attack. If the fencer chooses to do a stop-hit, they should close the line to show their ability to find and control the blade quickly; afterwards, there can be a continuation with a choice between a real parry and an answering attack.

The coach can make a subtle addition to this exercise by sometimes opening up in order to draw the fencer's counter-attack for counter-time. The fencer must spot the difference between this second-intention preparation and a real over-preparation. The fencer can mix the following responses against attempted counter-time: ignore such preparation and keep the distance; make a feint in tempo and disengage; or offer the blade and take a counter-parry-riposte at the first or last moment.

Defence against two types of flèche attack: single burst and broken time

In terms of progression of teaching, a coach should be careful to introduce the flèche only after a fencer has a strong foundation of lunging. Otherwise, there is a danger they will overuse the flèche at the expense of their lunge.

The advantages of a flèche are as follows: it is the fastest offensive action; and the fencer who does it, even unsuccessfully, is harder to hit as they quickly run past the defender.

Against a single burst flèche the obvious defence is a parry-riposte, but against broken time, if the defender is tall and at the right distance, a stop hit followed by a false parry can be a solution. Another option is the Romanian counter-attack with blocking while closing distance. Such a defence can be used more effectively by shorter fencers. Also, closing distance with a sweeping general parry might work well if the broken time flèche is executed quickly as the defender is suddenly close enough to find the blade and the attacker has less time to avoid it.

Recognizing the difference between the beginning of a preparative beat and a real one

Here the coach mixes preparative beats with real beat-attacks. If anticipating the beginning of a preparative beat the fencer either steps back and does not react, or attacks immediately (almost at the same time) but without any action against the coach's blade. Such an attack is counter-intuitive as one naturally wants to beat back to regain the right of way. But in my experience, a direct attack after a preparatory beat is very effective as the fencer who has just made contact with the blade feels completely secure (for a moment), and reacts rather late – hence there is a good chance of the fencer's attack-on-preparation succeeding. Against a real beat attack the fencer obviously takes a prearranged parry-riposte. The coach can also introduce some subtle changes, such as doing second-intention beats to draw the fencer's counter-attack, against which the fencer should not react, but instead go for some second-intention action.

Recognizing the differences between an opponent's fast engagement, normal parry-riposte and holding parry without a riposte after offering them the blade

The fencer offers their blade to the coach who does one of the above actions: against a fast engagement, the fencer disengages while stepping forward and hits the coach with a bent arm and opposition; against a normal parry-riposte, the fencer does a circular counter-parry and indirect riposte; against a holding parry without a riposte the fencer redoubles at maximum distance while going backwards before closing the line.

This exercise can be performed after the fencer offers the blade with a half-lunge from retreating.

Recognizing the character of the coach's blade movement – differentiating between thrust, beat and parry

The fencer follows the coach's steps forwards and back at medium distance. When the coach attacks with a thrust, the fencer responds with a circular sixte (6) parry and direct riposte. If the coach deceives the parry, the fencer takes another circular sixte (6).

Against a beat, the fencer responds by a change of engagement and disengage hit. Here, it is a good idea to try and finish in the outside sector. So against a beat quarte (4), the fencer responds with a change engagement one-two (finishing in the sixte line). Against a beat circular sixte (6) the fencer responds by a change of engagement and single disengage (still finishing in the sixte line).

Against a parry, the fencer attacks using one or two deceptions. Here the coach usually takes two parries and it is the fencer's choice whether to hit after the first or the second one.

Recognizing the difference between an immediate and delayed riposte

The fencer does a second-intention attack and the coach either parries and ripostes immediately or delays the riposte by holding the parry. After an immediate parry-riposte, the fencer can take a variety of counter-parries or use shah-put, or respond with a Romanian if the riposte is wide; if the riposte is delayed, the fencer does a renewal.

Recognizing the differences between a proper attack, a badly prepared attack and a second-intention preparation for counter-time

- Faced with a proper attack, the fencer parries and ripostes.
- Against a badly prepared attack, the fencer executes a counter-attack.
- Faced with a second-intention preparation for counter-time, the fencer can make a feint disengage in tempo, make a false counter-attack and counter-parry-riposte or ignore the invitation.

The whole exercise can be done from manoeuvring or pressing, with the fencer doing a half-lunge preparation.

Recognizing the difference between a lunge and a flèche

The fencer defends with distance against a lunge, but parries against a flèche. This exercise can be done in many situations, for instance after the fencer's attack, feint counter-attack, stop hit, and drawing counter-attack.

Tactics

Actions against a counter-attack

Draw the opponent's counter-attack before a parry-riposte with immediate renewal, defending with distance or finishing in time, maintaining right of way. The fencer can draw a counter-attack or attack on preparation by doing several preparations, either with or without the blade. The immediate renewal is a useful safety habit, particularly after a riposte to shoulder, which sometimes does not register. The fencer can mix these three options against the coach's various counter-attacks.

Second-intention attacks for various counter-parry-ripostes

This exercise can be performed as follows: when the coach stops, the fencer makes a short second-intention beat quarte (4) direct attack with half-lunge. The coach parries in quarte (4) and ripostes direct, whereupon the fencer takes a circular counter-sixte (c6) parry while recovering from the half-lunge with the back foot first to gain extra distance. The fencer then ripostes direct while standing still or with a one-two lunge depending on how deep the coach's riposte is.

There is one more situation: when the fencer feels unable to reach the coach with a lunge (perhaps because the coach has moved back to help develop a feeling for distance), they can switch to a second-intention disengage riposte (falling deliberately short) and then there are numerous options:

- If the coach takes the initiative without any hand movements, the fencer recovers, keeps distance and waits for the opportunity to make a parry-riposte if the coach finishes the attack, or makes a prearranged answering attack if the coach stops.
- If the coach takes the initiative with the blade moving forward, the fencer executes a fast beat direct attack.
- If the coach takes the initiative slowly with a bent arm, the fencer establishes point-in-line, leading to various scenarios, such as a prearranged answering attack if the coach stops, a derobement or a parry. This is yet another exercise where the fencer can develop anticipation of distance and the opponent's intentions.

Actions against counter-time: dummy counter-attack and counter-parry-riposte

The coach provokes a counter attack. The fencer does a false counter attack. If the coach reacts to this by finishing their action (counter-time attack), the fencer takes an appropriate parry. The distance at which the fencer makes the false counter-attack is important; it has to be close enough to make the opponent believe they can hit yet still far enough to give the fencer time to parry.

Another action against counter-time is the feint in tempo and disengage as the coach may take a parry. The fencer can alternate a counter-parry-riposte with a feint disengage. The fencer decides whether to deceive the coach's parry after a false counter-attack (feint in tempo-disengage) or to take a counter-parry. In the case of no response to the fencer's false counter-attack, there is another alternative: to make a beat attack direct or indirect if distance and blade position permit.

Second-intention attack for the Romanian or counter-parry-riposte

When the coach stops, the fencer does a beat direct with a half-lunge. If the coach's parry-riposte is direct, the fencer moves back for a counter-parry-riposte, but if the riposte is executed with the point moving away from the target, the fencer can make a counter-attack forward and block with the Romanian.

Here the coach can introduce some changes: if their parry is made with a long step back and the riposte is with the point moving away, the fencer should not do the Romanian as the distance is too great and the opponent has too much time to deal with it. If the coach's parry is made with a long step back, holding the blade without riposting, the fencer can renew their attack by making a small advance in the closed line followed by a fast disengage.

Chain of preparations

First, the fencer makes various openings to draw a counter-attack or attack on preparation and, if the coach attacks, takes a prearranged parry-riposte. However, if the coach does not attack, the fencer continues with a different preparation – for instance, a beat circular sixte (6) cutover with a half-lunge, then being ready for the following responses from the coach:

- If the coach moves back, the fencer continues with the first type of preparation.
- If the coach does not react and is within striking distance, the fencer does a circular sixte (6) opposition attack with a full lunge.
- If the coach attacks, the fencer takes a quarte (4) parry and ripostes direct with opposition.
- If the coach parries successfully, the fencer recovers (back foot first) taking a counter-sixte (c6) counter-parry. The fencer ripostes direct or indirect depending on the commitment of the coach's riposte.
- If the coach *attempts* to take a parry, the fencer attacks with an appropriate disengage.
- If the coach is relatively close and starts moving the point away from the target, the fencer can do the Romanian.
- If the coach moves carefully forward with a bent arm but the point on target, the fencer keeps distance and parries at the last moment. If the coach stops before finishing the fencer can make an answering attack.

- If the coach moves back slightly with no weapon reaction, the fencer executes a broken time flèche attack from the half lunge position, suddenly taking the blade away.

Near-simultaneous attacks

Against fencers who constantly attack there are various options and it is good to practise all of them, although usually, a fencer will specialize in the one that suits them best.

- From slightly longer than lunging distance, the coach steps forward and the fencer simultaneously confronts them with a half-lunge: if the coach attacks, the fencer parries with a small step back; if the coach searches for a parry, the fencer makes a disengage attack; if the coach hesitates, the fencer attacks direct; if the coach moves back, the fencer prepares forward waiting for the coach to change direction, whereupon the fencer can once again confront them with a half-lunge preparation or simply attack.

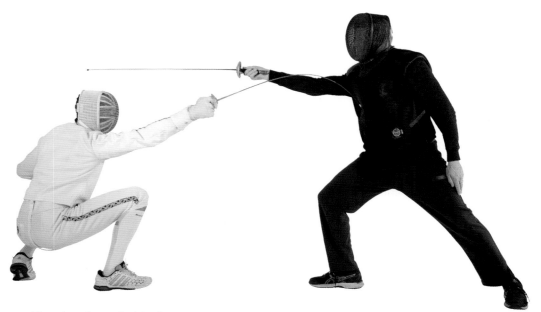

The submarine or duck is a last-moment hit from a squat position, used against an offensive action from an opponent. It is a surprising move, as it is used only sporadically. (Photo: Kevin Nixon)

- From **fencing distance**, the fencer steps forward and reacts according to the coach's response (open-eyes).
- A premeditated chain of parries, for example, false counter-sixte (c6) followed by real octave (8) before hitting in sixte (6) so that if the coach deceives the octave (8) parry, their blade will be collected as the fencer hits in sixte (6) opposition.
- The fencer steps forward raising the point to invite an attack on preparation or counter-attack in quarte (4). If the coach responds to the invitation, the fencer hits with quarte (4) opposition or octave (8) opposition depending on the line of the coach's offensive action. But if the coach hesitates or searches for a parry, the fencer does a direct lunge. The fencer makes a decision as the back foot lands at the end of the step forward. After the fencer's invitation, a third option is for the coach to respond with their own invitation against which the fencer does one feint disengage.
- The coach always attacks direct with a step lunge but the fencer can react in various ways against this direct thrust: a simultaneous direct attack; a feint of attack followed by parry quinte (5) with a step forward and riposte in low line or from high prime position; after a feint attack, the fencer can also step back and take a circular parry sixte (6); counter-attack with opposition; defend with distance and reply direct; or practise counter-attacking and ducking – *submarine*.
- The coach either attacks direct or takes a circular sixte (6) parry after a step forward, whereupon the fencer, after a feint attack, closes with a direct thrust in octave (8) opposition against the direct thrust or, against a circular parry, closes the coach's blade in circular quarte (4) opposition.
- The coach does various attacks: a committed step-lunge, an uncommitted step-lunge ending with a straight arm, an uncommitted step-lunge ending in a position that draws the blade, or an attack with a flèche. The fencer, after a feint attack, defends with distance against the committed step-lunge and ripostes direct with any appropriate footwork. After an uncommitted step-lunge with a straight arm, the fencer defends with distance and replies with a beat direct attack flèche. After a coach ends in a position that draws the blade (bent arm), the fencer does a feint disengage attack. But against the coach's flèche attack the fencer should take a parry, continuing their retreat in order to maintain a closed line.
- The coach either attacks direct or takes parry quarte (4). The fencer does a premeditated feint disengage attack with two steps or a step lunge. This action should be done in such a way that, if the coach goes direct, the fencer takes the coach's blade and closes the line in sixte (6); if the coach takes a quarte (4) parry, the fencer hits with the same disengage. From time to time the coach may take a sixte (6) parry and the fencer should counter-parry with a seeding high prime (1) and riposte at close quarters, or do a simple sixte (6) parry and riposte to flank with bent arm.
- If the coach attacks direct, after a feint attack the fencer alternates taking parries prime (1), and quinte (5), before stepping forward to riposte in sixte (6) at close quarters (with bent arm).
- If the coach always does a feint attack followed by a counter-sixte (c6) parry, the fencer either does a premeditated feint counter-disengage or lets the coach take the parry and delivers a counter-parry counter-sixte (c6) direct riposte.
- In this exercise, the coach can assign various numbers to the above exercises, and trigger a specific response from the fencer by calling out these numbers.
- Also, the coach and fencer can agree a probable and realistic chain of

premeditated actions to be done in a row, for instance: they both go for simultaneous attack; the coach parries quarte, the fencer does feint-disengage; the coach parries sixte, the fencer does feint-counter-disengage; after the coach attacks direct the fencer takes a prearranged parry; the coach moves back and takes two parries counter-sixte–quarte, the fencer makes a compound attack; the coach pulls their arm back, the fencer does a Romanian.

Second-intention attack for various counter-parry-ripostes or renewals

This exercise develops quick perception in changing situations.

Both fencer and coach manoeuvre. The fencer chooses the moment for a second-intention attack in order to draw the coach's parry-riposte. The coach can riposte with a step forward, upon which the fencer recovers from their lunge and responds with a counter-riposte. The coach can also parry with a step back and make a shallow riposte (like a second-intention action), whereupon the fencer takes a counter-parry (with recovery) and ripostes indirectly with a lunge.

Another option is for the coach to parry with a deep retreat and not riposte (as the distance is too great), after which the fencer *slows down* but still continues to advance with their blade resting in the coach's closed line parry (thus giving a false sense of security) before *suddenly* disengaging or doing a one-two (depending on which parry the coach takes) ending in the outside sector of the target. This response is rather counter-intuitive as the fencer's blade has been found by the coach, but it should work, as the opponent feels more secure having found the blade, and the fencer advancing in a closed line should not feel threatening to them. It is therefore, more likely that the fencer will be in a good position to attack. If executed correctly, the fencer should actually regain right of way through the combination of slowing down for a period before attacking suddenly, and the coach's lack of an immediate riposte.

Practising stepping forward with a parry-riposte at close quarters

Various situations can be set up, for example:

- The coach does an uncommitted attack and the fencer, after holding the distance, starts with a half-step and opening to tierce (3) upon which the coach makes a direct attack. The fencer parries with a step forward and practises a prearranged riposte at close quarters.
- In near-simultaneous actions, the fencer, after a feint attack, takes any prearranged parry-prime, counter-sixte, quinte (1, c6, 5) – with a step forward and practises a prearranged riposte at close quarters.
- The coach elicits a regular parry-riposte from the fencer; if the coach parries the first riposte, the fencer takes a prearranged counter-parry with a step forward before riposting at close quarters. In contemporary fencing, the counter-parry-riposte at close quarters has been largely overtaken by the remise at close quarters. However, I still believe it to be a very useful and effective weapon.
- In near-simultaneous actions, the fencer does three premeditated parries: false circular sixte (6) followed by real octave and sixte (8, 6). If the coach goes direct, the fencer parries octave (8) and ripostes with a disengage. If the coach deceives the octave (8) parry, the fencer closes in sixte (6). However, if the coach counter-parries, the fencer has to take another counter-parry and hit at close quarters as the distance is rapidly closing.

There are many more situations where this exercise can be incorporated.

Various counter-actions after a feint counter-attack

The fencer does a feint counter-attack and:

- If the coach takes two parries standing still, the fencer decides which of them to deceive, or both, and lunges (when the coach takes two parries, the fencer can hit while deceiving only one of them, but has to execute more quickly or use different timing to deceive both).
- If the coach parries while stepping forward, the fencer deceives the parry, while doing the Romanian with a lunge or flèche.
- If the coach moves backwards and takes three parries, the fencer deceives them and hits – usually with a double-disengage two counter-sixte-quarte (c6, c6–4).
- If the coach does not react, the fencer moves back and tries again or attacks direct.
- If the coach attacks in different sectors of the target, the fencer takes the appropriate parry. It is always good to encourage the fencer to mix different parries against in the same line. However, in order to consciously mix different parries against similar attacks, it is necessary to expect the attack to be in a specific line.

Open-eyes response after invitation with a beat cut-over and step back in any line; the fencer responds with open-eyes depending on the coach's counter-action

As the coach steps forward, the fencer does an aggressive beat cut-over with a step back, inviting the coach to react. During their action, the fencer's hand should move quickly to start with, and then considerably slower after going over the coach's point.

This deceleration of the fencer's hand stimulates the coach's reaction and gives the fencer adequate time to respond to that reaction. In order to maintain right of way, it is important that the fencer's hand movement be continuous and they take no more than one step back during the entire action. For example, Chamley-Watson (USA) scored America's twelfth hit during his match with Avola (ITA) during the final of Men's Team Foil at the World Championships in Leipzig 2017.

- If the coach attacks in spite of the beat, the fencer simply finishes, ensuring the movement is continuous.
- If the coach stops and looks for the blade using a rapid side-to-side motion ('*windscreen wiper*'), the fencer hits into an opening sector of the target.
- If the coach starts moving back while searching for the blade, the fencer follows while developing an open-eyes attack – just feeling the right time to finish. The coach can stop hit, counter-attack, break the distance, duck or move out of line, and the fencer must react accordingly. This exercise stresses the timing of the finish of an answering attack or riposte. I believe this timing illustrates the 'unique spirit' of foil fencing.

The fencer constantly breaks distance (in-and-out) in defence and either parries with a step forward or does a Romanian with a flèche

This is possible if the coach presses slowly with absence of blade (which most fencers find difficult to cope with). At some point when the fencer closes distance, the coach tries to hit direct, and the fencer parries with a step forward. At another time when the fencer increases distance, the coach can speed up their preparation with wide point movement (giving the conditions for a Romanian), upon which the fencer can counter-attack with the Romanian. The fencer has to be patient and only respond when the coach reacts to the fencer's change of distance.

Muhammad Ali – any action from a low hand position (parry, defence with distance, attack on preparation direct or indirect, second-intention attack for any possible counter-action)

Both fencer and coach manoeuvre as in a fight and the initiative passes from one to the other. The fencer takes a low comfortable hand position, which naturally relaxes the shoulder. This absence of blade positioning helps give almost any action a character of suddenness and considerable acceleration.

The Muhammad Ali position, named after the famous boxer who often fought with dropped arms. The merit of this position in fencing lies in the fact it relaxes the arm, from which the fencer can generate a hit with considerable speed. It also creates an absence of blade, which many opponents find uncomfortable. (Photo: Kevin Nixon)

For example, the coach can give the fencer a choice between alternating any defensive action if the coach attacks. Otherwise, on the coach's step forward the fencer can alternate first-intention direct and indirect attacks with a second-intention attack for any counter-action afterwards. This could be a counter-parry-riposte, defence with distance, a counter-attack or a stop hit (particularly if the fencer has a long reach). When the fencer is performing a first-intention attack, it is better they know in advance which parry the coach is going to take.

In defence, the fencer can alternate quarte (4) and sixte (6) parries with defence with distance. Another option is to mix various counter-attacks: counter-attack with ducking (submarine), counter-attacks in opposition, any Romanian or a deceptive stop hit moving back. The coach gives feedback and tries to be as realistic as possible so the fencer learns the correct timing.

Training of Romanian counter-attacks and stop-hits followed by closing the line

When the coach stops, the fencer does a second-intention beat attack in order to draw a parry-riposte from the coach. Here, the character of the coach's riposte is key, it can be either fast or slow while opening line. The fencer alternates the stop-hit followed immediately by closing of the line (going backwards) with the Romanian (going forwards). Remember the Romanian forwards has more chance against a fast movement and the stop-hit is better against a slower movement. With the stop-hit the fencer closes the line immediately after the hit, while keeping distance and waiting for a response from the coach – the coach may respond in any of the following ways:

- Makes a disengage attack upon which the fencer takes a real parry circular and riposte.
- If the coach stops moving and parries standing still, the fencer answers with an appropriate disengage attack.

- If the coach starts moving backwards, the fencer advances with the blade and makes any prearranged answering attack, this could involve binding the coach's blade from quarte (4) to octave (8), before hitting the flank with angulations. Hitting with disengages to the high line or simple opposition in the low line are also possible.

The fencer performs a beating parry in the first moment while retreating, followed by a false parry holding the blade and keeping the distance, inviting a response from the coach

If the coach attacks, the fencer takes a circular parry; if the coach stops, the fencer makes an invitation by opening to tierce (3). If the coach attacks, the fencer then takes a deep parry quinte (5) with a step forward followed by a prearranged riposte; if the coach starts to retreat the fencer follows with a step forward and prearranged attack.

Against someone who is aggressive and favours counter-time: after 'Allez!' the fencer steps forward with a sudden feint direct (the opponent has to believe it is a genuine direct attack), and disengages the opponent's counter-time parry

The fencer has to know which parry the opponent is likely to take, if presented with a sudden feint. The suddenness of the feint is increased by synchronizing it with the landing of the back foot.

Backline situation – the fencer cannot move backwards

This is a defensive exercise where the coach attacks into various sectors of the target from different distances between lunging and close-quarters, while the fencer defends appropriately. This exercise helps the fencer deal with an uncomfortable distance, which is inevitable in a fight.

Here the coach sometimes makes a wide movement with his weapon to which the fencer should respond with a Romanian. The coach could also make a counter-parry-riposte against the fencer's action, whereupon the fencer should take another counter-parry-riposte. Additionally, the coach should try to cover with the mask or introduce any other obstacle (parry with back arm, twisting of the target) which could help the fencer learn to deal with an uncomfortable situation.

Simple choice between attacking and defending

There are numerous options for the fencer in this exercise, but the most important aspect, is being able to spot the difference between the beginning of an attack and the beginning of a preparation. In general, the fencer should attack against the beginning of a preparation, while against the beginning of a real attack they should prepare to defend, reacting as late as possible. The fencer's choices can be:

- Between a direct attack and a quarte (4) parry-riposte.
- Between a direct attack and feint disengage in offence and a quarte (4) parry-riposte in defence.
- Between a direct attack and feint counter-disengage in offence and a circular sixte (6) parry in defence.
- Between a beat disengage lunge on preparation and a circular sixte (6) parry.

Study in attacks on preparation and a choice between answering attacks and parry-ripostes

The fencer does one of the possible attacks on preparation, then redoubles at their maximum distance while recovering from the attack, before keeping distance as the coach advances. Here the fencer has the choice between making an answering attack if the coach stops, and making a parry-riposte at the last moment if the coach develops their attack.

The fencer follows the coach's steps forward and backwards at a slightly greater than lunging distance and chooses the moment to make a prearranged attack with a lunge at the beginning of a step forward. The attack can be:

- Beat quarte (4) direct in the high line
- Beat quarte (4) direct in the low line with the hand in supination
- Beat quarte (4) disengage
- Beat sixte (6) direct
- Beat sixte (6) cut-over
- Beat sixte (6) disengage
- Beat sixte (6) one-two
- Beat quarte (4) to flank with the hand in pronation (supination against opposite-handers)

Practising a redouble at full distance while recovering from the lunge teaches the fencer good coordination – being able to reach the target at maximum distance while recovering from the attack is useful because not every attack is successful.

Then comes the important skill of holding an opponent using good footwork, which the coach teaches by gradually making it more difficult to achieve this. The coach can develop an attack, which the fencer parries at the last moment or the coach can stop, whereupon the fencer begins an answering attack. Since an opponent will often stop in order to set up a counter-attack or an attack on preparation, it is always safer to start slowly (looking step) or with the blade. If attacking with the blade, the simplest action is an engagement to quarte (4), hitting direct with a lunge if the distance does not change. If the distance does change and the coach starts moving backwards, the fencer can make an engagement to quarte (4), hitting with a disengage and step lunge, or if the coach moves completely out of distance the fencer can slow down before executing a prearranged attack (two waves).

However, if the blade is not available when making an answering attack, there must be an attack without the blade, which should start with a slow step. If we know the opponent always counter-attacks after stopping, then a direct lunge could be the best option.

Another answering attack is by a false engagement to quarte (4) on the fencer's front foot as it lands (if the coach attacks on preparation, the fencer should be ready to take a counter-quarte (c4) parry as their back foot lands). If there is no counter-action from the coach, the fencer makes a circular beat in quarte (4) as their back foot lands, then disengage before hitting in the sixte (6) line with angulation.

As a further addition to the above exercise, the fencer does an attack on preparation with a lunge, before redoubling at maximum distance. After this, the fencer immediately retreats to a distance from which they attack again on the coach's step-forward, but this time they attack with a step-lunge instead of a lunge. The distance for the beginning of this second attack-on-preparation is larger than the first, as it is done with a step-lunge rather than just a lunge.

Meinhardt

Named after Gerek Meinhardt, the creative US fencer, in this exercise the coach and fencer manoeuvre as in a fight with the fencer ready to defend but at the same time preparing to alternate various first- and second-intention attacks against the coach's prearranged defensive system. When defending the coach parries circular sixte-quarte (6–4). Against the coach's prearranged defence, the fencer has a number of options: they can make a premeditated direct attack, feint counter-disengage, feint counter-disengage-disengage or feint cut-over. These first-intention attacks should then be mixed with second-intention actions such as false attack for counter-parry-riposte or renewal, Romanian, shah-put or submarine. This exercise is a creative workshop. The coach helps with 'polishing' the timing and execution of the fencer's actions. It is important to encourage the fencer to vary the preparations and be creative so as to move as arrhythmically as possible, but at the same time efficiently.

Massialas

Massialas is an exercise named after the prolific US fencer, Alexander Massialas, who likes attacking from a low hand position with angulation to the high and low outside sectors of the target.

When the coach stops the fencer takes the initiative and presses slowly with their hand in the low line with absence of blade. The coach from time to time stops, slows down or attempts a stop hit and the fencer tries to feel the right moment to finish the attack in either the low or high outside line. The delivery of the hit should be relaxed with the point moving first so that the coach sees the action later. To make the exercise harder, in addition to stopping, the coach can also change direction, whereupon the fencer should also change direction, holding distance in defence, ready to take back the initiative again. The fencer must spot the difference between the coach's stop and the coach's change of direction. The coach may also attack from time to time, requiring the fencer to switch to a parry.

Open-eyes attack switching to first-intention or stop hit at full distance while moving back

The fencer follows the coach's steps forward and back and, if the coach attacks, parries circular sixte (6) at the last moment. The correct time to initiate an open-eyes attack is when the coach stops developing their attack. Then the fencer starts slowly with a feint and step forward before dealing with whatever obstacles the coach throws up, such as:

- A first moment beat, on which the fencer does a change beat hit or a simple parry-riposte with opposition.
- A stop hit moving backwards on which the fencer usually finishes the attack direct.
- A counter-attack in quarte (4) opposition on which the fencer reacts with a quarte (4) **croisé** hitting flank.

- One or two parries moving backwards, which the fencer deceives.
- A sudden straightening of the arm against which the fencer does a simple beat attack.

The signal for switching to a stop hit while moving backwards is the coach's step forward with a parry. The fencer disengages and hits at full distance while changing direction and moving backwards followed by a closing of the line before any continuation.

The correct time for switching to a first-intention *prise-de-fer* attack is when the coach breaks distance, the fencer slows down (two waves) and starts from a slightly longer distance with a short step engage and disengage lunge. The coach may ask the fencer to start at a shorter distance and do a one-tempo beat attack (lunge or flèche).

The fencer alternates correct and incorrect attacks and switches to a parry-riposte

This exercise can be done in any situation. The fencer anticipates the beginning of the coach's step forward and can either make a direct attack or an incorrect one. The so-called incorrect attack can be executed by starting it as if it were a direct attack, but just before their front foot lands the fencer takes the blade away by pulling their arm back before hitting direct one tempo after landing. If the coach attacks, the fencer takes a prearranged parry.

From pressing the fencer makes a prearranged correct or incorrect attack when the coach stops. If the coach attacks, the fencer steps back to do a parry-riposte.

Second-intention parry-riposte after compound preparation at various distances

The fencer takes the initiative in the form of fast semi-circular and circular false engagements (invitation) with one step forward. So, the fencer does two movements of the blade during one step forward and offers their chest as available target. The coach from time to time responds and tries to attack or make a stop hit while moving backwards. When the coach attacks, the fencer practises novieme (9) cut-over beats and flicks to shoulder with footwork appropriate to the distance. When the coach does not respond to an invitation, the fencer slows down (two waves) before repeating the same invitation until there is a reaction. If the coach does not react to the first invitation, fencer and coach can prearrange a different subsequent action.

Second-intention one-tempo attacks from engagement of the blade

The fencer follows the coach at lunging distance and the coach arrhythmically changes the engagement of the blades. When the coach stops, the fencer starts an attack by a change of engagement and slides along the coach's blade while waiting for a reaction. If there is no reaction, the fencer executes a fast direct attack. The coach can react with a simple or circular parry on which the fencer does an appropriate disengage. If the coach deceives the fencer's change of engagement and tries to hit, the fencer steps back and takes a circular counter-parry-riposte direct. If, while still moving at lunging distance, the coach initiates an attack along the blade, the fencer takes a circular parry with a step back and ripostes standing still. The coach should remind the fencer to work on accelerating the point as they touch as this will increase their chance of success in a fight.

This exercise develops a feeling for the blade, timing, change of rhythm and the ability to switch from one action to another. A possible alternative is, when the fencer starts an attack, for the coach to break distance, so the fencer has to slow down (two waves) and find the right distance from which to start the same attack again.

Various developments from half-lunge preparation

When the coach stops, the fencer prepares with a beat circular sixte (6) cut-over half-lunge. The coach can react as follows:

- Parry quarte (4) immediately and riposte direct on which the fencer recovers from the half-lunge with the back foot first, takes a circular sixte (6) counter-parry and ripostes direct (the coach may vary the depth of their initial riposte and ask the fencer to make a counter-riposte one-two with a lunge).

- Take any two parries so the fencer chooses to make one or two deceptions and attack from the half-lunge.

- Attack in any sector of the target, whereupon the fencer moves back to a good distance before making the appropriate parry-riposte.

- Hesitate at striking distance, so the fencer attacks with a prearranged action.

- Move back slightly and retake the initiative from the fencer, who keeps distance with good footwork. There are then several options: the coach finishes, the fencer parries; the coach stops, the fencer does a one tempo *prise-de-fer* attack; the coach makes a mistake in preparation by speeding up while taking the point away from the target, the fencer responds with the Romanian.

Open-eyes riposte

The coach simulates an attack, which the fencer parries and holds for a time. Depending on the coach's response, the fencer executes an appropriate riposte, which will vary according to distance, target, and timing. Sometimes the coach's response should require the fencer to take successive parries or even counter-parries and counter-ripostes.

Four lines of defence

The coach presses slowly with absence of blade. The fencer responds as follows:

- First line of defence: the fencer makes feint of counter-attack waiting for the coach to develop attack and ready to step back and parry quarte (4) with disengage riposte.

- Second line of defence (if coach does not react on feint of counter-attack): the fencer makes a false parry and if the coach finishes the attack then the fencer may take a real parry and riposte.
- Third line of defence (if coach does not react to the false parry): the fencer drops his guard (Muhammad Ali) completely, pretending that they are not ready and inviting the coach to finish their attack. If the coach does finish their attack then the fencer takes a parry and riposte.
- Fourth line of defence (if coach does not react to the dropping of the guard): the fencer makes a prearranged beat attack (direct or indirect).

Defence after complex preparation

- Coach presses slowly with absence of the blade; fencer makes two false parries (prime (1), circular prime (1)) followed by a feint of counter-attack.
- Coach attacks after the fencer's feint of counter-attack: fencer steps back before taking a holding parry quarte (4) and ripostes direct or indirect depending on the position of the coach.
- Coach after being parried, moves back to a longer than lunging distance; fencer invites the coach by opening to tierce (3) with a half-step and makes a prearranged parry-riposte if the coach accepts the invitation to attack.
- Coach does not react to the fencer's invitation; fencer starts pressing slowly and chooses the moment to finish with a prearranged attack (often with one feint).

Establishing right of way in near-simultaneous situations

From the distance of 4m or fencing distance, coach and fencer both move forward. The fencer takes a step followed by a half-step. On the half-step the fencer reaches forward for the coach's blade with a round movement, trying to make a beat-cut-over in quarte (4), before withdrawing the blade, and then riposting. In order to maintain right of way, it is important the fencer's blade movement be simultaneous as they take only one step back. The rhythm for this action should be: fast beat-cut-over – slow withdrawal of the blade – fast riposte.

Options to establish right of way:

- Coach continues with the attack in spite of their blade being found; fencer finishes riposting movement after beat-cut-over in quarte (4).
- Coach after their blade has been found, moves back and searches for the fencer's blade; fencer slowly presses with absence of blade and finishes with an attack, which can be prearranged, such as a feint disengage or beat sixte (6) cut over. The fencer can also modify their attack depending on the situation.
- Coach takes his blade away so the fencer fails to find the blade; fencer immediately switches to line as a deterrent while moving back.
- Coach moves for a while and stops at some stage; fencer, when the coach stops, executes an answering attack by circular **false engagement** followed by a real circular beat and hit into a prearranged sector of the target.
- Coach moves forward while searching for the blade; fencer makes a derobement, touching with a step forward.
- Coach instantly executes broken time attack; fencer changes immediately into direct attack.
- Coach opens one line to draw the blade; fencer switches to feint of direct and disengage attack.

The coach continues to mix the above options.

9 | PSYCHOLOGICAL PREPARATION

I share the opinion of many fencing experts, that fencing is fundamentally a psychological game. Some situations can have a negative impact on a fencer's state of mind, but with good psychological preparation it is possible to improve one's mental state. This chapter includes suggestions on how best to deal with those situations. I also provide some examples of psychological preparation practised by top contemporary fencers.

The main objective of psychological preparation for a competition is to replace negative emotions with positive ones and to engage one's full intellectual powers in the game. If this can be achieved, poor and slowly executed decisions, misunderstandings of situations and simple mistakes can be minimized. Coaches should therefore train fencers to engage all their thinking and attention towards the fight and encourage a sense of enjoyment. In this way, fencers can not only reduce errors, but actually enhance their overall performance.

In competition, the impact of a fencer's psychology on their performance is magnified. This is why we see many fencers performing much better or worse compared to their training, and it is down to their psychological preparation. Some fencers are known to raise their game in competition compared to training, while others diminish. A fencer's frame of mind during a competition has a huge impact on performance. Of course, good footwork, technique, tactics and fitness are all necessary, but if a fencer's mind is not focused on the fight in hand they will not be able to fence well. This is particularly apparent in the more important competitions.

A fencer should approach a competition relaxed, focused and confident. Everyone experiences pre-competition nerves to a greater or lesser extent and this anxiety affects how a fencer will perform. However, the ability to cope is critical – the fencers who can manage their anxiety effectively are better placed to fence well.

Cognitive psychology

I believe in the power of cognitive psychology. We can control our thinking to a great extent; how we think affects how we feel, in turn affecting how we perform. Therefore, thinking of yourself as a winner is the first step to being a winner.

Photo opposite by Niki Bruckner.

Coping with pressure is critical – those who can manage their anxiety are better placed to succeed. (Photo: Niki Bruckner)

Mindfulness

In the 1970s autogenic training – a structured meditative-style practice – was popular in sport as a method to bring about mental and physical relaxation. Now mindfulness is the current vogue; if practised regularly it helps an athlete keep their mind on the present. When this happens, there is no room for anything else. Whatever helps an athlete regain the right frame of mind must be used.

THE COACH'S ROLE

Coaches should encourage fencers from the early stages of their involvement in the sport to practise keeping their mind on the present. They should also contribute towards developing the habit of positive thinking and continually remind fencers (and themselves) to check their state of mind and if necessary make corrections.

Optimism is stimulating and positive. Coaches should contribute towards creating a positive environment where the entire process of training and competing fosters maximum optimism and competitiveness.

Having a physiotherapist with the squad usually has a positive effect on players. Some of them like a little help from the physiotherapist before and during a competition. However, one should bear in mind there is a danger of the player overusing the physiotherapist and relying too heavily on their service.

All players, coaches and support staff should strive to create an optimistic mood in the camp, since this stimulates everybody's performance. In summary, coaches should work with their fencers on the following:

- Perceive competitions positively – perceive an opportunity to experience a new level of performance.
- Believe on competition day, the next hit will be theirs and can give an extra 10%.

- Focus on process and performance goals, keeping their mind on the present whilst bearing in mind the outcome.
- Replace negative emotions, such as anger and fear, with positive ones, such as passion and fun.

PSYCHOLOGICAL BARRIERS

The most common barrier is the conviction that your opponent is better than you, with a consequent lack of belief in victory. When this happens, a fencer almost automatically overestimates an adversary so their performance is too cautious. The coach should be aware of such a tendency and help the fencer estimate the adversary more realistically.

Believing in victory is important; however, when a weaker player faces a stronger one, they have to strive to assume the possibility of victory. Experience has shown that lower-ranked fencers can win against higher-ranked ones, given adequate tactics and the right frame of mind. But, if victory is not possible, then the aim should be to experience the maximum level of performance.

Some fencers overestimate the opposition's coaching advice, believing after such an intervention the opponent knows how to win; consequently, they may lose the belief in their own victory. Here the most pragmatic approach is to anticipate how the opponent is going to change and prepare a game plan accordingly.

It is one thing is to be confident when things are going well, but to instil confidence more deeply one has to have experience of being exposed to adversity and responding positively. It can be an opponent's style of play that is frustrating. Sometimes a fencer struggles with a particular opponent; if they can eventually win after a hard fight, then usually they fence much better in the next rounds.

Opportunity

It is possible to reframe almost any situation positively. Every challenge, even fencing while tired or out of form, is an opportunity to perform in a new environment and consequently to become a better fencer.

PSYCHOLOGICAL INFLUENCES

During a competition, or indeed any fight, a fencer's confidence and ability are impacted by their support network, their skill, their opponent, and even the referee. There is therefore an interdependence between a fencer's frame of mind, footwork, technique, tactics, fitness and a myriad of situations before, during and after a fight.

Anxiety-induced tension impairs coordination during a fight; this affects footwork, accuracy, technique, decision making and consequently the entire performance. Therefore, an individually tailored warm-up session and following routines before competing will have a positive effect on a fencer's performance. The familiarity of the routine should help to reduce a fencer's anxiety, while the physical effects of a good warm-up should reduce muscular tension.

During warm-up muscles contract and relax many times, reducing muscular tension and improving coordination and its outcome. An important routine for fencers preparing for competition is the warm-up lesson. An individually designed session can have a hugely positive effect on a fencer's confidence when approaching an opponent. Here the skills of the coach and understanding of their fencer are vital.

For some fencers the way the fight starts can affect their confidence. Starting well usually helps performance later. Likewise, losing the first fight may cause a fencer to perform badly in the next one.

147

Common psychological influences while competing

Before competing	During a match	After a match	Anytime
Confidence in preparation – physical, mental, tactical technical, and equipment	Beginning the fight	The final score	Visualising success
Mental rehearsal	• Being hit • Being hit by an amazing action	Loss of focus after a satisfying match	Nutrition and drinks
Mindfulness & other methods of relaxation	Being on the back line	Stress after a disappointing match	Mood in the camp
Quality of sleep	Scoring a hit	Being distracted by results before the poule is complete. Eg. after winning 5 fights, pressure to win the last one and qualify directly to the last 64.	Relationships with other team members
Warm-up	The actual score	Enjoyment - winning against a strong opponent	Equipment issues
Warm-up lesson	Support: • from the team • from the crowd		General nerves/ excitement
Treatment from the physio	Coaching from the side of the piste		Performance of teammates
Organisation	Time left/approaching the end of the fight		Personal issues
Unexpected changes in schedule	A perceived mistake by the referee		Confidence in fitness
Pressure to achieve a certain result	The last hit		
History against certain opponents	Equipment not working		
	An unexpected break in the fight		
	A vocal opponent		
	Expectation: • being the underdog • being the overdog (expected to win)		
	Environmental factors: • lighting of the piste • noise from the crowd		

There are many factors that can influence a fencer's psychological state during competition. The effect may be positive or negative depending on what it is and how strongly a fencer can focus their attention and thinking on the fight.

A fencer's frame of mind can influence footwork, technique, tactics and fitness. Quiet contemplation can help restore confidence. (Photo: Niki Bruckner)

Move your feet!

The footwork of a tense fencer is often too static. It can, therefore, be helpful in such circumstances for the fencer to force themselves to move their feet more than usual during a fight, thus reducing tension. Coaches will often shout '*move your feet*' during a fight to achieve this.

Sitting low

At the beginning of a competition fencers often make more mistakes and produce more off-target hits, with tension increasing towards the end of the fight. Sitting lower in the on-guard position seems to have a positive effect on a fencer's concentration.

Scoring and receiving hits during a fight affects a fencer's confidence. When receiving a hit, a fencer often tries to hit back immediately by rushing with an often mis-timed action; after receiving a spectacular hit (such as a prime flick to the back) a fencer often experiences a temporary drop in confidence.

Conversely, after scoring a hit, there is a danger of becoming momentarily complacent and over-confident. Winning by a large margin may cause a similar state which is potentially

dangerous for future fights. A successful fencer has to develop the habit of focusing immediately on the next hit.

Knowing one's opponent and what to expect can enable a fencer to make a game plan and can help reduce competitive anxiety.

If a fencer perceives the referee has made a mistake against them, this too might have a detrimental effect on their fencing, particularly if they enter into a debate and become angry with the referee.

149

A successful fencer has the ability to stay focused. (Photo: Niki Bruckner)

A fencer visualizing his best performance before the next match. (Photo: Niki Bruckner)

GAINING CONFIDENCE

When things are not going well, players can be advised to try the following.

Visualize

A fencer should remember their best performances and if possible try to mentally rehearse them to regain a similar feeling. This should give the belief they possess the necessary skills to produce the desired result.

Prepare

Fencers should constantly reflect on their preparation and believe in it. Preparation includes the physical, technical, tactical and mental. If preparation is disturbed by injury or other reasons, one has to rely on strength of character.

> ## Preparation
>
> One of basketball's coaching legends, John Wooden, said, 'Confidence is simply a natural result of correct preparation.' There is a lot of truth in this statement, so both coach and fencer should pay attention to preparation.

Mastery

The fencer and coach should constantly strive to improve their skills, no matter how great their success.

Strengths and style

Recognize and focus on strengths (it is not uncommon for athletes to have difficulty in identifying their strengths). Consider the most effective style of fencing given a particular fencer's game.

Optimism

Optimistic athletes believe what caused failure in the past will not continue to affect them in the future. This is because they have confidence in their ability to learn and improve from past mistakes. It is better to be optimistic than not.

Success of others

In 2010, after Laurence Halsted won bronze in the Tokyo Grand Prix, Richard Kruse, who had had a poor season up to that point, won silver in the next competition in St Petersburg. He said afterwards, Halsted's performance in Tokyo helped him hugely to regain his confidence.

Positive reinforcement

Positive thoughts can strengthen an athlete's confidence. Telling oneself to be patient, to be strong, and to be active, are examples of positive reinforcement. This also includes reinforcement coming from others, such as coaches, fencers, staff and supporters.

Strength of character

Relying on qualities of character – readiness to break the limits of patience, courage, concentration, control, and belief every time – means you can find an extra 10 per cent. The difference between winning and losing is now extremely small in all sports and the winner is the one who finds inspiration on the day; paying attention to details is increasingly important.

> ### Character building
>
> Sport is a great school for character building. In my opinion, sport's influence on character works both ways: we bring our life experience to our sport, but our sport also gives us new experiences to take back into life.

Success

Fencers should think of themselves as winners, as the cream of the crop – and should be proud of it; they can gain confidence from each other by giving support in the form of encouragement and constructive feedback.

Belief

In my opinion, overestimating oneself slightly is a good thing in terms of maximizing performance; however, there is always the danger of becoming arrogant.

Sweat!

Gold medals aren't really made of gold. They're made of sweat, determination, and a hard-to-find alloy called guts.

[Attrib.] Dan Gable (USA), Winner of Gold Medal in Wrestling at the 1972 Olympic Games.

Focus on the moment

Clear your mind of worries – they do not contribute positively to performance. Leave worries to support staff and completely engage in your performance.

Adversity

Gain confidence from adversity: adversity can involve anything which takes an athlete out of their comfort zone. Avoiding difficulties and opting for an easy life does not do your confidence or your ability any good – like a plant grown in a greenhouse that is suddenly exposed to the realities of the natural climate.

Generally, in training and competitions, it is good to be exposed to adversities and deal with them positively – this strengthens confidence. Therefore, introducing various obstacles in training, as well as coping with fencers of different styles, will have a positive effect on confidence.

Coping with adversity

In the 1972 Munich Olympics, Witold Woyda (POL) was not fencing well in the first round of eliminations. He lost 5–0 to the Austrian fencer Losert, and was then 4–1 down to Greg Benko (AUS) in his second fight. However, with the support of his team, he managed to win. From that moment on, he fenced much better, receiving only seven hits against him in the final poule of six and going on to win the gold medal.

THE PATHWAY TO GREAT VICTORIES

- A talented fencer working hard with a talented coach.
- Early experience of fencing against older and more advanced children or adults.
- Many years of being exposed to highly competitive situations with a variety of opponents. This requires travelling to international camps in various countries, as well as taking part in international competitions.
- Constantly improving one's mastery, which applies to fencer and coach.
- Strongly developed self-control and qualities of character, such as courage, determination, competitiveness, initiative and tenacity.
- The right frame of mind, achieved by reminding oneself about previous victories, visualizing best performances, specially designed individual lessons, positive thinking, self-belief, positive emotions and the right tactics.

EXAMPLES OF PSYCHOLOGICAL APPROACHES AT AN INTERNATIONAL LEVEL

Fencing better and older fencers is stimulating for the development of younger fencers, and, at the same time can be very useful for the older fencer. In Italian clubs it is common practice for Olympians to fence the young ones. (Photo: Chris Turner)

At international level, top fencers take a number of different approaches to psychological preparation. Alexander Tofalides (CYP) is well known for his unique psychological preparation, which greatly enhances his performance at major events. Tofalides writes down a detailed plan before each of his matches, which he drafts and then redrafts with his team. In addition to the obvious tactical benefit of analysing opponents, this process of writing out a plan several times helps him to visualize the upcoming match and get him into the right frame of mind.

Final draft of the plan before Tofalides (CYP) match against Garozzo (ITA) in St Petersburg in 2018:

Tactics for Garozzo tomorrow:
In general this is an opportunity to show that with my fencing, my game, I can beat anyone in the world. Make him unsettled from the word go.

Plan A:
Aim to strangle distance and have intense footwork, get him to stop and take over with my running attack.
Attack of Two Waves, and aggressive attacks with prise-de-fer.
Disrupt and disturb his preparation at all times. At the beginning of match look for counterattack but only after intense footwork for at least 8m of the piste.

Plan B:
Play arm-first game from lesson.
Go forward from on-guard, arm first, slow first-step, to take over initiative or to finish.
If too close, run out of distance to start attack.

There is obviously nothing special about the information in this plan. Its benefit lies in the process of creating it. It psychologically prepares and motivates Tofalides for the match at hand.

Other fencers take a totally different approach, and feel focusing on their opponents before a match does not improve their performance. Guilherme Toldo (BRA) once remarked it was psychologically tougher when there was a day's break between the first and second days of the competition. This was because it was hard not to think too much about your opponent throughout the rest day.

Alexander Choupenitch (CZE) often does not try to find out who his opponents are before he arrives at the piste, preferring to focus his preparation around his own fencing.

Of course, fencers' personalities will vary greatly, and so too will their ideal psychological preparation. One of the biggest challenges for any coach is to know how to treat their fencers individually, helping them to discover how *they* can get themselves into the best frame of mind before competition.

10 | PREPARING FOR BEST PERFORMANCE

The best mixture for a successful outcome is an intensive driving force for victory, strong interest in the fencing process and a joy for fighting the opponent.

[Attrib.] Vitali Arkadyev (translated by Z. Wojciechowski)

In sport, we often see fluctuations in performance, with athletes sharper on some days than others. The real challenge for both the coach and the athlete is to achieve the best performance on the day for important competitions, such as the World Championships and Olympic Games. A fencer's form will depend on many factors. Naturally, the talent and expertise of both athlete and coach are key factors, as are the training and competition schedule and the actual training programme.

In this chapter, I endeavour to bring together the various aspects I have found most helpful for producing a fencer's best performance.

Richard Kruse winning Gold at the Shanghai Grand Prix, May 2018. (Photo: Augusto Bizzi)

Photo opposite by Niki Bruckner.

The training and competition programme is particularly important as it is the opportunity for fencers to experience highly competitive situations against a variety of strong opponents representing different styles.

The nature of the **direct phase of preparation** before a major event is critical for fencers – this is what athletes and coaches do several weeks before the event. Fencers who are still developing should follow a direct phase of preparation in the lead-up to a competition, but they must also keep one eye on their longer-term development. Fencers who are more or less fully developed will have both eyes on the competition.

DIRECT PHASE

During this phase it is good to repeat the general trend of the annual training plan:

1. Week 1: Rest and strength and conditioning (S&C) preparation
2. Week 2: More technical training – lessons and footwork + one session of S&C maintenance
3. Weeks 3–5: Tactical and competitive sparring with a possible camp + lessons + weekly session of S&C maintenance
4. Week 6: Tapering just before competing + optional shorter lessons

Training should be frequent, highly intensive and short, with a focus on quality. Participation in international camps with a variety of opponents is the best preparation for weeks 3–5. During these camps, fencers should have two short sessions per day with a decent break between them. A good formula for a weekly micro-cycle would be 2, 2, 1, 2, 2, 1, totalling ten sessions in a week. Both fencer and coach should focus on quality and be prepared to stop a session or even skip one if performance is dropping. Stopping a session when quality drops is particularly important as training

Wanting more

In this period fencers who experience a bad patch should not force themselves to try and overcome it by training more, but rather stop and recuperate. It is important to keep the mind fresh; ideally, fencers should finish every session with the feeling of wanting to do more.

badly in the lead-up to a competition can have detrimental effects. In each session, the fencer should have a 15-minute warm-up lesson (similar to a competition one), followed by the equivalent of three to six fights to fifteen hits.

It is good to mix scored fights with intensive fencing without scoring for about 10 minutes. Matches to five hits or one-hit training are also beneficial. The reason for doing six matches to fifteen is to replicate a competition from the last 64, where a fencer has to win six fights in order to win the competition. At the Olympics often five victories are enough to win a medal, as many players will start the tournament from the top 32. In a training session, the number of fights may be reduced if the quality of opposition is high, as the fights are likely to be more demanding.

During this direct phase of preparation, two international camps of around four or five days, four days apart is ideal. If this can be arranged, fencers should concentrate on recovery and review after the first camp with a final evaluation of performance and goal setting before the second camp, finishing around four to five days before the event.

It can be difficult to arrange two international camps, in which case one is better than nothing, or perhaps one national and one international.

Less is more

In the final week before the competition, fencers should either rest completely or follow their usual routines (light training at home) and have a short session, usually just a lesson, the day before. Complete rest during the week before an important competition is advisable and acceptable but only if there was an intense period of hard work before. If the training was physically and mentally challenging enough, then a period of complete rest before competing becomes almost necessary. Here the formula 'less equals more' applies.

However, a fencer might have too much adrenaline and energy in week six. In this case, then light training is advisable. Experienced fencers should know when to stop or ease off before a competition, while less experienced fencers have a tendency to over-train. Younger fencers can be helped by their coach to monitor the way they prepare for competitions and find the best formula for them. It is crucial to have a winning frame of mind and each fencer has to cope with mental fatigue and recovery times in their own way. Ultimately, a fencer should have complete confidence in their method of preparation for a competition, as this will be reflected by increased confidence on the day.

ADDITIONAL FACTORS

At major events, fencer and coach should prepare for closely fought fights. As more fencers train professionally, the difference in standard between players is diminishing. For example, in the 2016–17 season, there was a different winner for each World Cup and Grand Prix. At the top level, it is often only small fluctuations in performance that determine the winner.

Whilst the outcome of the competition is important, always maintain a focus on process and performance. Fencers improve gradually, and the following areas should be worked on continuously:

• Confidence in yourself and your preparation, and belief in your actions (see Chapter 9).
• Focus on the present, enjoy the here and now (breathing exercises help with this);

Achieving a state of deeper relaxation helps concentration. (Photo: Niki Bruckner)

A fencer clearly feeling she belongs on the piste. (Photo: Niki Bruckner)

be mindful, and take every match one hit at a time.

- Develop a habit of positive thinking and feeling: see the competition as an opportunity to experience a higher level of performance, and not as a threat. You want to be here, you have chosen to be here, this is where you belong, you love your sport and you love competing.
- Believe you will be able to give the extra 10 per cent on the day.
- Work on developing character traits to improve performance: patience, courage, decisiveness, self-control, tenacity, stubbornness, determination, the ability to engage totally, independent thinking, taking the initiative.
- Clear your mind of all worries: if possible, take advantage of your support staff to help you.
- Think of yourself as a winner: this helps with performance. Through cognitive psychology, we can control our thinking to

Always check your weapons, as failure to do so could result in a yellow card. (Photo: Niki Bruckner)

a great extent. How we think affects how we feel, and that in turn affects how we perform.

- Stick to routines, as research has proved this helps with performance.
- Triple-check your weapons and clean your points before and after all competitive matches. Make this a routine.
- Prepare yourself for hard and close fights and gain confidence from them. They are becoming the norm rather than the exception – you have to get used to them.
- Make sure you engage in a fight from the beginning and use your voice, but don't go over the top. Manage your emotions in order to avoid rushing and making unforced errors – this applies particularly to younger fencers in the team.
- Stick to simple things that work! As a fight progresses, a fencer will learn what works and what does not. Towards the end of a fight the pressure grows and fencers should stick to a simple game, using what works rather than trying to perform new actions.
- Play to your strengths. When athletes are asked to identify their strengths, they often struggle to find answers straight away. So this exercise can be helpful, as the more they know about their strengths the easier it will be to use them.
- Have confidence in your second-intention game. Sometimes under the pressure of competition fencers revert to first-intention and reactive fencing, which worsens their performance. Remind yourself to use second-intention actions. Make your opponents react rather than reacting to them (proactive rather than reactive fencing). First-intention actions should be performed from time to time to introduce an element of surprise. Fencers need to be reminded not to react to an opponent's provocation and here it is crucial to differentiate between what is real and what is false.
- We all lose our concentration from time to time. Accept this, and be prepared, if

needed, to take a break in order to regain concentration and focus on tactics. Forcing a break during the match can make an opponent lose concentration and also allow you to regain composure. Only the person who takes the break knows exactly when they are ready to return to the fight.

- Visualize great past performances, as this helps to achieve a winning frame of mind (this can be done during longer breaks in a competition while waiting for the next round).
- Develop correct nutrition and rehydration strategies and habits.
- After scoring, immediately focus on the next hit. Always believe the next hit will be yours. The reason to focus on the next hit immediately after hitting is to prevent any feeling of complacency coming from having scored.
- Approach each fight with plan A and plan B, but also develop the ability to improvise, based on a feeling for the fight and creativeness. Planning should be simple and able to be implemented by the fencer. For instance, plan A: keep pressing slowly and patiently and sooner or later your opponent will make a counter-attack and you should just finish in time with a one-tempo action. Plan B could be to keep provoking your opponent to attack and alternating closing the distance while parrying with defending with distance and answering attacks. A fencer should take any opportunity to discuss their plan with their coach or teammates.
- Move your feet. One of the reasons for moving slowly can be nerves, so force yourself to move your feet – it combats nervousness, you create more opportunities to score, and you will be harder to hit.
- Organize piste coaching during the competition (see Chapter 12) – ideally a coach does this, but a teammate is also useful. A coach can have a positive

It is always wise to check the scores before signing the poule sheet. (Photo: Niki Bruckner)

influence on a fencer's performance by advising the right tactics and helping to create a winning frame of mind. In addition, the coach oversees the referee's decisions and advises on arm judges, video challenges and if the fencer should take a break. In theory coaches are not allowed to communicate with their fencer during the fight, but in practice this is commonplace.
- Find the right lifestyle balance (sport, study or work, and personal life). Finding the right balance between sport and other aspects of life can have a positive effect on an athlete's performance. The right balance will be different for each individual fencer.

11 | TACTICS

In this chapter, my approach to fencing tactics is outlined. I write about how to deal with the four different types of opponents I have identified, as well as many other categorizations and distinctions I find useful when analysing fencers. In particular, I believe these methods of analysis can help fencers and coaches arrive at effective conclusions far more quickly.

Good tactics means the most effective use of one's skills in order to win a fight or achieve the best possible result. Good tactics involve finding and exploiting an opponent's weaknesses, hindering their strengths while utilizing your own. A lower-ranked fencer or team can win against a higher-ranked one by using the right tactics. When considering tactics, it is helpful to think of fencing in terms of action and counter-action.

FOR EVERY ACTION, THERE ARE APPROPRIATE COUNTER-ACTIONS

Against a direct attack
Parry-riposte, **avoidance**, defence with distance, various counter-attacks or point-in-line established before the start of the attack.

Against a parry-riposte
Compound attack, counter-parry-riposte, renewal or defence with distance.

Against a compound attack
Counter-attack, successive parries, defence with distance or avoidance.

Against a counter-attack
Counter-time in the form of a parry, direct attack in time or defence with distance.

Against counter-time
A compound counter-attack or counter-parry-riposte.

Photo opposite by Augusto Bizzi.

Against a counter-parry-riposte

An indirect riposte, second counter-parry-riposte, counter-attack, defence with distance or avoidance.

PREPARATORY AND ACTUAL ACTIONS

When thinking about tactics, I find it helpful to divide actions into two major groups: actual actions, which are those a fencer scores with or attempts to hit with; and preparatory actions, i.e. all other movements with feet and weapon before the start of an actual action. These play an important role in a fencer's tactical game. Examples of preparatory actions:

- Manoeuvring in order to prepare the right distance and timing for an actual action.
- Any action to make an opponent react the way one wants.
- Hindering an opponent's actions.
- Creating false impressions about one's intention. For example, showing a parry before counter-attacking.

Remember!

The ability to read pre-signals (*tells*) and to spot the difference between a false and real action is vital.

It is important to see the difference between a *false* action (preparatory) and a *real* action as early as possible. Reacting to a false action gives an opponent an opportunity to score the hit. If a fencer does not anticipate an opponent's actions, but responds only to what is already happening, it will often be too late.

For instance, seeing the difference between the beginning of a preparatory beat and a real beat, between the beginning of a real attack and a preparation, between the drawing of a coun-

ter-attack and what is simply bad preparation, or between a real counter-attack and a false one.

Equally, making the right decision quickly is crucial: against a false action one can stop the reaction or show a false reaction (calling your opponent's bluff).

FIRST- AND SECOND-INTENTION ACTIONS

Actions can be divided into **first- and second-intention**. These intentions are of huge importance in scoring hits; a first-intention riposte is executed with the intention of hitting immediately, whereas a second-intention riposte is executed with the intention of making an opponent react to a parry in order to perform another pre-planned action.

When considering tactics it is important to understand that fencing actions can be *premeditated* or *partly premeditated*. A **premeditated** action is planned ahead of time and executed from beginning to end no matter what. Simple strokes are harder to change mid-action as they are usually executed at maximum speed. A **partly premeditated** action can initially be premeditated, but change according to the situation. For instance, a fencer plans to parry prime and flick to shoulder after a feint

---

Open eyes

Examples include:

- Engagement to quarte (4); if there is no response or the response is late the fencer finishes direct, otherwise they must disengage or counter-disengage.
- Parry circular sixte (6), but riposte in different sectors of the target at various distances depending on the behaviour of the opponent/coach.

---

of counter-attack, but as they perform this action they see the opponent going to parry the riposte to their shoulder and so the fencer redirects it to the flank or chest. Another partly premeditated action is when the first part of the action is premeditated, but the second part depends on the opponent's response, – I call this **open-eyes**. This approach is a reflexive response to an unforeseen action, from a premeditated start, but with an unknown finish.

Off-hand actions

Off-hand is a fencer's reflex response upon being surprised by an opponent; in other words, an uncontrolled action induced spontaneously as a result of being short of time and usually to avoid being hit. Knowing how an opponent reacts when surprised is highly relevant in the tactical game. For instance, if an opponent always does a wide circular sixte (6) parry when they are surprised, then a fencer can try to set up a surprising feint and counter-disengage attack. Such a feint will be more surprising if presented suddenly from a different line on the opponent's preparation or on the back foot from pressing.

Premeditated continuation

Sometimes a fencer may start a phrase with a partly premeditated action, but change to a premeditated one, depending on the opponent's response. For example, when an opponent stops, the fencer starts a slow open-eyes attack, but if the opponent simply breaks distance, the fencer could slow down, before swapping to a premeditated second-wave attack (two waves).

In a tactical fight, a fencer has to answer two fundamental questions: what to do, and when? Choosing the right action at the right time should result in scoring the hit.

TYPES OF FENCING

- Relying **on a feeling for the figh**t – typical of the intuitive or artistic fencer.
- Using **premeditated actions with first and second intention** – the thinking or tactical fencer.
- Using **open-eyes** – the visual and tactile fencer.
- Using a **combination of the above**.

In my opinion, both fencer and opponent give off subconscious signals, which contribute towards their *feeling* for the fight. Reading an opponent's intentions is of huge importance; sometimes a fencer simply feels what an opponent is going to do and whether it will be real or false. Experience sharpens this feeling for the fight.

From a very early stage, fencers should be encouraged to develop the habit of analysing hits during a fight, drawing conclusions and changing tactics appropriately. For example, if a fencer realizes they are being hit with parry-ripostes, they should conclude that they must either stop attacking or attack differently (by feint-disengage, or second intention for counter-parry). Fencers who do not remember what has happened during a fight will see it as a mixture of accidental actions, whereas the fencer who remembers what is happening, and why, will be in a much better position to anticipate further developments and adjust their tactics appropriately.

If such a habit is established, it will have a positive long-term effect on a fencer's tactical ability. They should be encouraged to apply the same tactical analysis after a match as well as during it. Video analysis is particularly helpful for this.

Comprehension

If a fencer can understand why they won or lost a hit, they will better understand why they won or lost a match.

Re-group, re-focus, re-engage.
(Photo: Niki Bruckner)

THINKING TIME

Thinking time is another important factor when it comes to tactics. Here experience of past fights and intuition is helpful, as is reviewing a specific opponent's behaviour before the fight. During a match a fencer should use the time it takes the referee to call the last hit to think about the next one – the coach should encourage this as there is a tendency for the fencer to get caught up in the referee's decision.

Take a break

A common means of regaining composure when under pressure is by taking a break to tie one's shoelaces or some other excuse; often referees will allow a short break.

FOOTWORK

The value of footwork can never be overstated. In the tactical game, it plays a huge role, as the fencer with the better footwork will have more

Dualism in every moment

Physical – the distance between the two players, the position and movement of their bodies and weapons.
Psychological – the thinking, intent and frame of mind of both players.

time to observe, think and make decisions. If a fencer has good footwork, they are more likely to remain balanced and less likely to be reactive; the fencer with the better footwork is in a better position to make their opponent react to them.

PERCEPTION

Sharp perception and thinking means a fencer correctly judges their own opportunities as well as those of their opponent. The speed in making the right decision has a huge impact on the ability to make a hit. A decision must not only be correct, but must also be taken at the right time.

Decisions are based on a feeling for the fight and tactical thinking; sometimes they have to be made almost instantaneously and at a **critical distance**. For this reason, it is important to develop safety habits – these are highly automated movements with well-developed muscle memory. For example, many top fencers automatically make a renewal after any flicking action.

A feeling for the fight and tactical thinking happen concurrently, yet some players rely more on one than the other.

Senso-motoric and prognostic levels of decision-making in fencing

- **Senso-motoric** is the first level, and concerns making choices in unknown situations as they occur, or when a fencer sees or feels what has to be done.

Sequence of premeditated actions

Some fencers create a sequence of premeditated actions assuming the most probable development of a fight. For example:

- First action: attack by flick to shoulder at the end of the piste.
- Second action: attack to the inside low line.
- Third action: a fast provocation for a parry-riposte.
- Fourth action: attack direct.
- Fifth action: slow preparation and either parry-riposte or attack depending on the opponent's reaction.

- **Prognostic** is the second level, and involves calculating the most probable action from an opponent ahead of time. This is where experience is very important, as is having a premeditated sequence of actions in mind beforehand.

TACTICAL TYPES OF FENCING

As a coach, I find it useful and efficient to divide fencing into four general tactical styles: continuously attacking; manoeuvring attacking; manoeuvring defending; and defending. Of course, a fencer can be adept at two or more of these styles, but in my experience, they tend to favour one over the others. In my opinion, tactically, the hardest of these types to fence against are the continuously attacking and manoeuvring defending.

Continuously attacking

The fencer strives to maintain priority of attack, and scores many of their hits from attacks. This continuous pressing style is particularly preva-lent in modern men's foil. Massialas (USA), Garozzo (ITA), Safin (RUS), and Choupenitch (CZE) favour this style.

Manoeuvring attacking

The fencer is generally aggressive but is willing to give up priority in order to create further opportunities to attack. Meinhardt (USA) uses this style well.

Manoeuvring defending

The fencer is generally defensive but can also attack, usually provoking and feeding off their opponent's mistakes. Kruse (GBR), and Tofalides (CYP) often favour this style.

Defending

The fencer almost exclusively defends, relying on their opponent's errors in preparing and finishing attacks, and occasionally attacking on preparation. Mepstead (GBR) often uses this style to great effect.

Continuously attacking (or pressing)

Here the main tactical aim is to prevent the opponent from developing their attack by using the tactics of confrontation, while

Adaptability

When Richard Kruse (GBR) won his first Shanghai Grand Prix in 2017, he did it with a manoeuvring attacking style, whereas when he won his second Shanghai Grand Prix in 2018 he used his usual manoeuvring defending fencing.

seeking the right time to attempt one's own attack or parry-riposte, in one of the ways described below.

Going for near-simultaneous actions

This prevents the opponent from developing their attack. The most common distance for near-simultaneous actions is 4 metres (at the on-guard lines) or fencing distance when the referee starts the fight. Here there are many possibilities:

- Simultaneous attacks usually result in a draw with both fencers hitting at the same time. Sometimes an opponent may hesitate and there is a chance of winning the hit with a single light or if an opponent pulls their arm back.
- If an opponent attempts to parry during the first phase of their offensive action, then a fast feint disengage or cutover attack, or a fast second-intention attack with a counter-parry-riposte can work. Here, knowledge of an opponent is crucial. If you know which parry they are likely to take, then a feint disengage is appropriate. If you don't, a feint cutover is more effective. A short feint followed immediately by a longer one and disengage is another possibility.
- After a feint attack, take a sweeping parry while stepping forward. This is a higher risk action because if an opponent manages to deceive the parry, there is little time to make further movements. That risk can be minimized by closing distance as quickly as possible and taking the parry in forward direction as much as possible.
- Parrying with a step forward can also be done from retreating. If an opponent speeds up, the fencer can find the blade by stepping in with this sweeping parry. Even if an opponent hides their blade during preparation, this sudden change of distance can help a fencer find it and make a successful parry. A fencer can invite their

Parries with a step forward

In recent years, with the rise of absence of blade pressing, parries with a step forward have become rare and are partially replaced by counter-attacks. However, I believe they still have their place today and their rarity only makes them more surprising and effective.

opponent to speed up by breaking distance.
- After an initial feint attack, a fencer defends with distance and replies immediately. This is difficult and requires a high level of agility. A feint attack has to be convincing, look real and be close enough to really hit, so the opponent commits to finishing their attack early.
- Initiating while lifting the point up with short steps forward, assuming one of the following:
  - the opponent attacks direct into the opening line, upon which the fencer responds by closing in low octave with a lunge and hitting with a bent arm *spike of the cactus*.
  - the opponent hesitates or tries to take a parry and the fencer simply has to finish the attack.
  - the opponent invites the fencer's attack into a particular sector of target looking for a parry-riposte, upon which the fencer performs a feint disengage.

The development of all options in near-simultaneous attack situations becomes more important as fencers become increasingly aggressive in attacking. For these situations, fencers should work on perfecting their game plan.

Permanently threatening the opponent with actions simulating attacks or counter-attacks

Here, distance and the character of false actions matter: the distance has to be such that an opponent is likely to react and believe they have a good chance of hitting, while the defender must still have time to take their defensive actions.

False actions have to look as realistic as possible in order to make an opponent respond. If they do not look credible or they are presented from too far away, an opponent will not respond. If an opponent is not responding, the defender should experiment with the distance and the character of their false actions. Sometimes the defender will see their opponent is not reacting but is still moving forward within the **critical distance**. In this case, an immediate counter-attack has a good chance of success. This is on the condition there is a *latent* reaction to the first false action, as the reaction to a second signal closely following the first is usually slower (see Chapter 1: psychological refractory period). Moreover, if an opponent stops their preparation as a result of the defender's false action, this creates an opportunity for the defender to take back the initiative.

If an opponent refuses to react to the false actions then the defender could look for some way of finding the blade.

Using point-in-line to deter the opponent from attacking

If the line is presented aggressively while maintaining a threatening distance, it is likely the attacker will quickly realize they have to deflect the blade. This might make them stop and hence create an opportunity for the fencer to retake the initiative with answering actions. The line will not always cause an opponent to stop, but if they decide to attack against the line the defender will have a chance to derobe, parry-riposte, counter-attack or stop hit.

Repeatedly breaking the distance while retreating

This makes it more difficult for an opponent to feel the right moment to commit to an attack while giving the defender several options:

Point-in-line

A fencer can use their creativeness to score many different hits from point-in-line; it is a rich and creative addition to one's defence. There is much value in perfecting one's actions from point-in-line, as most fencers do not like facing it. In the future, I hope referees will grow to appreciate point-in-line even more, as it is an effective antidote to the pressing style currently dominating the men's foil game.

- Attack after increasing the distance, as the opponent has to make at least one extra step forward before finishing.
- There is also a chance for the fencer to score from a higher risk action by increasing the distance and then suddenly decreasing it. When decreasing the distance the fencer should quickly open one sector of their target, inviting the opponent to attack in that particular line. If the opponent accepts the invitation then the fencer closes that line with opposition or makes a parry-riposte. This is an energetic but viable way to fence. I believe it is particularly useful against slow pressing because the fencer will have more time and space to implement it.
- If after the fencer breaks distance the opponent pulls their hand away and speeds up, there is a chance to hit with the Romanian.
- An attack after a feint of moving backwards can be effective if the opponent believes the defender will continue moving back. The later an opponent sees an attack beginning, the better chance it has of succeeding.
- If the fencer increases the distance and the opponent speeds up, a fast step forward with a sweeping parry against the opponent's expected attack is another

option a fencer could include in their repertoire, particularly against fencers with a faster attack.

Manoeuvring attacking

Fencers in this group score mainly from attacks with many preparatory actions while changing distance and direction. They find switching to a different attack easier than using counter-time, and generally favour counter-attacks over parry-ripostes.

Force the opponent to defend and reduce their freedom to manoeuvre

This can be achieved by keeping the opponent under constant pressure, being sure to avoid following the opponent as they play with the distance. This tactic has the potential to frustrate an opponent who relies heavily on their freedom of movement, increasing the likelihood they will make mistakes.

Draw the counter-attack and respond by finishing the attack, making a parry-riposte or defending with distance

Usually, an opponent who likes attacking is more likely to counter-attack than parry. Such an opponent is also liable to mistakenly feel they have the right of way while counter-attacking.

To draw a counter-attack, a fencer may use relatively wide openings or multiple actions on the blade – bullying the opponent's blade (blade bully) or a combination of both, depending on the availability of the blade and the fencer's preference. Another way of drawing is to press with absence of blade in any position which is comfortable; sometimes shaking the foil in such a position encourages the opponent to react earlier than they should. In terms of winning right of way, a fencer has to create in the eyes of the referee the illusion of attacking, and in the eyes of their opponent the opportunity to attack or counter-attack.

Drawing counter-attacks

Foilists such as Massialas, Cassara, Chamley-Watson, and many others, base their game on drawing a counter-attack and capitalizing on it.

Once they have drawn the opponent's counter-attack, the fencer should respond in whatever way they are most confident. Ideally, a fencer should be comfortable responding to counter-attacks in a variety of ways, but often the easiest way is just to finish into the available target. The ability to parry a counter-attack comes in useful when the fencer doesn't feel there is a good time to finish, or when they are not confident the referee will see their action as an attack.

Look for an opportunity to attack, alternating between simple and broken time actions

The manoeuvring attacking opponent usually does not have a strong defence. They concentrate on finding opportunities to attack. If they are forced to defend they tend to take advantage of their mobility to defend with distance, and they generally prefer counter-attacking to parries. If expecting a counter-attack from manoeuvring opponent, the fencer should finish with a simple attack. If expecting defence with distance or a parry, then a broken time attack has a good chance of succeeding.

Use of false attacks for reconnaissance and for second-intention

Even though manoeuvring attacking fencers are more vulnerable to attacks, information on their defence still needs to be gathered. A false attack can provide information on how an opponent habitually reacts, which in turn helps the fencer to plan a real attack.

Another purpose of the false attack is to induce an immediate answering attack from the opponent, which can then be parried by the fencer. In a near-simultaneous attack situation, after one or two simultaneous actions, a false attack for counter-parry-riposte can work well provided the fencer is confident in parrying.

Using point-in-line as a deterrent and to prepare various actions

Point-in-line is effective against almost all attacking fencers, as it is the easiest way for the defender to regain priority.

In defence apply a combination of false and real actions

After a false counter-attack, make a real parry-riposte and after a false parry, make a real parry-riposte or real counter-attack.

Manoeuvring defending

In my opinion, these are the most difficult fencers to outwit tactically. This is because they are equally capable of scoring from attack and defence, and pay a great deal of attention to their preparatory actions. They like manoeuvring on the piste in order to discover their opponent's intentions and generally play a highly tactical game. To cope with such a fencer, one has to possess a highly developed technical-tactical level of preparation. A fight against such a fencer should be planned beforehand, taking one's individual style into consideration.

Fence to cause maximum hindrance and decrease the opponent's ability to control the fight

Tactics include breaking the distance, changing the rhythm, using point-in-line, and making false actions. Other options include bullying the blade, giving and taking away the blade, and pressing the opponent.

When involved in a tactical game with a manoeuvring defending fencer, it is good to have a contingency plan for each action

Of course, a fencer should always try to play to their strengths and should be ready with an immediate premeditated second action in case the first action fails when against a manoeuvring defending fencer. The reason for this is that such opponents generally force the fencer to make the first move, and often possess great patience. The same applies after a riposte, making a renewal while closing the distance, or simply blocking out.

Automation

I advocate a high level of automation when it comes to actions immediately following an initial action. Many top fencers have an almost automatic block-out after their parry-riposte, or a renewal following an attempted flick hit. Such a habit works well if the fencer's first action doesn't register, *but also* if the opponent parries the fencer's initial action.

Avoid too much blade work if technically weaker

Manoeuvring defending fencers often have strong blade work; therefore, a fencer who is technically weaker should avoid too much blade work and rely more on timing and footwork. Well prepared broken time actions can be effective.

Play a second-intention game with great attention to the difference between false and real responses

This type of fencer usually likes a tactical game and is experienced at recognizing whether an opponent's actions are second intention or real. When fencing them, it is important not to play their game; if they try to provoke a reaction any counter-action from the fencer should be a bluff or no reaction at all.

Permanently defending

Fencers from this group mainly score from ripostes or counter-attacks and sometimes from attacks on preparation.

Permanently defending

I often refer to this style as **digging in**, much like the trench warfare tactics of the First World War.

Control your distance

Permanently defending opponents prey on a fencer's mistakes, especially those regarding distance. The fencer should try to pay particular attention to this and control the distance at all times.

Be patient and don't rush

Another common error against this patient style of fencing is to rush and prepare too quickly or attack too soon. A fencer must be sure not to lose patience when facing a permanently defending opponent.

Push the opponent to the end of the piste

At the end of the piste, under pressure, an opponent is more likely to react by attacking or counter-attacking out of time.

Push your opponent to the end of the piste. (Photo: Niki Bruckner)

Second-intention parry-riposte

Draw the attack on preparation, or counter-attack.

Second-intention attack and counter-parry-riposte

This attack has to look realistic to induce real riposting actions.

A surprise direct attack can sometimes be effective

This can work by making a compound preparation, thereby encouraging a counter-attack or attack on preparation and then finishing in time with a single tempo action.

When watching fencers it is relatively easy to classify them in the above categories. Specific details can then be added to their general way of fencing and it becomes possible to consider the best way of approaching an opponent tactically. Here performance analysis from previous fights is very useful. Most fencers on the international circuit are well known to each other and the coaches. But new opponents do appear from time to time. They have to be watched carefully and information about them obtained from other fencers or coaches.

Questions to help you understand your opponent

- What is their tactical style of fencing?
- How do they defend against expected and unexpected actions?
- In which sector of target do they like to finish their actions?
- What preparation do they use?
- How do they behave after their attack does not score – searching for the blade, counter-attacking or just using distance?

In the limited time available it may not be possible to answer all these questions, but if an opponent can be put in one of the four categories and some of the questions answered, it will help a fencer's tactical game. It is also very

important to have a plan B in case plan A does not work. If nothing pre-planned is working, a fencer can change completely, but should not forget the option of making smaller adjustments to their existing tactics.

Small adjustments

I have observed many top fencers turning matches around by making small adjustments to the timing and distance of their actions, rather than changing the actions themselves.

OTHER WAYS TO CATEGORIZE FENCERS

There are many other less distinctive ways of identifying types of fencing. Almost all of them are opposite ends of the same spectrum, and most fencers fall somewhere in between. A clear tactical opportunity should arise if an opponent can be identified at either extreme of one of these spectrums.

Active or passive

Look at the degree of activity during a fight. Some fencers move their legs and weapon much more than others. For instance, Meinhardt (USA) is always very busy compared to Baldini (ITA). Generally speaking, against an active fencer, it is better to slow down the tempo of the fight, while against a passive fencer it is better to speed it up.

Efficient or inefficient

This means the amount of effort (energy and time) it takes to execute a movement in relation to the result. Most fencers use too many muscles and too much strength during a fight, resulting in poor coordination and low accuracy. Fencers tend to be less efficient at the beginning of a competition due to nerves, and more efficient towards the later stages as they settle down. Some fencers move a lot before scoring while others move just enough to score. Shorter fencers are usually more mobile and tend to move more than taller fencers, who rely more on reach.

If a fencer notices an opponent is inefficient, it is possible to take advantage of this by holding back and allowing them to waste energy before raising the intensity. A fencer can also render their opponent inefficient by not reacting to their provocations.

Creative or destructive

Another way of looking at fencers is to see whether they actively try to create a situation from which they can score or whether they use an opponent's energy and movements to score the hit.

When dealing with a creative style, second intention is usually more effective than first intention, while against a destructive style simple first-intention actions can often be the best.

High- or low-risk game

Every fencing action involves some degree of risk. Some fencers take more risks in the way they prepare and execute particular actions while others prefer situations where a certain result is almost inevitable. Usually, a fencer who is losing and running out of time takes higher risks in order to win.

Opponents who play a high-risk game can often be more easily invited to take risky actions; a fencer can capitalize on this by using second intention. Against opponents playing a low-risk game, patience is paramount.

Simple or complex actions

Some fencers use lots of complex movements while others keep things simple. In my opinion, simplicity is the most powerful way to fence and fencers who like being complex should be encouraged to simplify their game while increasing their use of distance. I believe a simple game can be executed more successfully under the pressure of competition.

Against simple actions second intention is advisable, whereas complex actions can be more vulnerable to a destructive style of fencing.

Counter-attacks or parries

Some fencers use mainly counter-attacks in defence. They have developed a style capitalizing on gaps in timing which happen during an opponent's preparation; they also move in a way to encourage the attacker to make additional preparatory movements which then gives them the opportunity to counter-attack. These fencers are very much one-sided and usually are unable to obtain a high ranking, but they are always awkward, particularly over five hits. Learning to use parries and ripostes is a long process and the fencer who can master them is far more difficult to fence. Learning attacks is much easier and takes less time than parries. One can observe how certain fencers improve after learning to parry and riposte effectively.

To deal with counter-attacking opponents there are a few options: counter-time, counter-attacking the counter-attacker, extremely simple single-tempo attacks, digging in and forcing the counter-attacker to attack. Against opponents who favour parries, it is advisable to consider cut-over attacks, broken time attacks, compound attacks, or second-intention counter-parry-ripostes.

Technician or fighter

Some like being precise and technical while others are happier with an aggressive and simpler style. Both aspects are important and each type of fencer needs to work on developing the skills of the other. In my experience, this learning process can cause a temporary decrease in performance before an improvement is observed. Both technical and fighting skills are crucial for fencing, especially in competition.

If you think an opponent is lacking technical skills then it can be a good idea to search for technical solutions during the match. Equally, if an opponent lacks fighting spirit, one's own fighting skills should be more useful.

Rich or poor technical repertoire

Certain fencers are one- or two-trick ponies, while others have a much larger repertoire. If you notice your opponent has a limited repertoire, it is best to prevent them from using their favourite strokes. For example, if an opponent only attacks *with* the blade, a fencer should not give their opponent the blade in defence. A fencer may notice their opponent's poor repertoire before a match but also once it is already under way.

Complete or limited tactical repertoire

A complete fencer is one who can do most things well: they are able to attack, parry or counter-attack, use second-intention actions and point-in-line effectively. They score from both open-eyes and premeditated actions. A limited fencer is usually good in just one or two areas; for instance, an opponent might have a good attack and counter-attack but no parries, or a solid defence but a poor attack.

If an opponent has a strong defence and poor attack, the fencer should obviously be patient and encourage their opponent to attack. If an opponent is limited to counter-attacking in defence, one can use counter-time while avoiding fast multi-tempo preparation and attacks. If the opponent is limited to parrying in defence, then cut-overs, broken time attacks, second-intention counter-parry-riposte, and second-intention renewals are all good ideas.

Actions on the blade or absence of blade

Some fencers have more of a feel for the blade than others and they tend to do lots of actions on the blade. Actions on the blade can be more technically complex but tactically they are safer as the fencer who takes the blade will more clearly have right of way. Some fencers, such as Yuki Ota (JPN), have developed amazing accuracy after finding the blade. Other fencers prefer to rely more on absence of the blade and their sense of distance and timing.

These two fundamental fencing skills – finding the blade and avoiding the blade – are characteristic of these two groups. Of course, it would be good to develop fencers who demonstrate both skills equally well, but in practice, it is not that common as fencers vary in their natural abilities. Against opponents who prefer actions on the blade, a fencer should fence with absence of blade, and vice versa.

Premeditated or improvised fencing

Again, these are opposite ends of the same spectrum. Some creative fencers can spot changes in a situation and have the ability to adapt quickly. Other fencers use exclusively premeditated actions: they like to know what they are going to do and they use their preparation to look for a specific opportunity. However, they can find it difficult to cope when a situation changes unexpectedly.

In my opinion, fencers who premeditate their actions can be easier to predict, whereas fencers who mainly improvise are liable to make more mistakes, and it can be easier to get a desired reaction from them.

Cooperative (following) and uncooperative (confronting)

There are fencers who like to take the timing for their actions from their opponent's initiative with lots of answering attacks. They usually follow an opponent's movements and develop their action from them. Conversely, there are fencers who like to cut the distance by parrying with a step forward, counter-attacking or pursuing a confrontational game. Italian fencers are noticeably uncooperative, while Kruse (GBR), Ma (CHN), and many Russian and French fencers could be considered highly cooperative.

Premeditated actions can be more effective against uncooperative opponents because they often do not give the fencer adequate time to make decisions during the fencing phrase.

The cooperative fencer takes more time to prepare their actions, and is therefore usually a lower-risk fencer. The fencer should find a way to get the cooperative opponent to commit to an action or to make a mistake first, before committing to an action themselves.

SPECIFIC TACTICAL SITUATIONS

In a fight certain specific situations can be identified that have their own tactical significance.

Backline

When an opponent cannot move back anymore, the fencer who is pushing is in a better position to finish their attack. However, often the attacking fencer finishes too early and is parried or counter-attacked, or they do not attempt a genuine attack for fear of being parried or counter-attacked and then the initiative changes hand. The attacking fencer should endeavour to be careful and patient, but still courageous. The defending opponent will often expect a first-intention attack, so second-intention attacks (for renewal or counter-parry-riposte) can be a useful option. Otherwise, the attacking fencer should wait for the opponent to search for a parry or start their counter-attack before finishing.

For the fencer who is standing on the backline, one of the most useful actions is to attack with an unexpected action on the blade, or to launch a second-intention attack aiming to make a counter-parry-riposte or renewal, or to execute an attack by counter-time. Offensive actions from the fencer defending on the backline are usually more surprising, and often a better idea than simply defending.

Beginning of the fight

This is tactically important as the fencer who scores first has the advantage and the opponent has to chase, therefore taking more risks. This is particularly important in women's foil, as well as in épée, but also in men's foil against defensive opponents. If a fencer knows an opponent favours defence, then the first hit becomes very tactically relevant; if the opponent loses the first hit they will be forced to *come out of their shell*.

On the other hand, some fencers find hits received at the beginning of the match to be a rich source of information from which they can successfully build their tactics.

Last hit

The match-winning hit creates additional pressure on a fencer, making it difficult to score. A fencer will often receive some hits before being able to finish.

For the fencer who has scored fourteen hits, I advocate a conservative approach. In theory, a fencer's focus for the last hit should not be different from any other hit during the match.

Last hit when the score is equal

This puts even more pressure on both players as they know what works and what does not. In this situation I also advocate a conservative approach: stick to the simple things that have been working, rather than trying something completely new.

Close score with time running out

Often at the end of the third period, a fencer will have less than 10 seconds to score one or two hits to equalize the score and go to the priority minute. Often fencers with a few seconds left perform a flèche or running attack, which can be a useful tactic. Practising 10-second periods of fencing with alternating priorities is useful preparation for such situations.

Last hit with one minute and priority ('sudden death')

When the score is equal at the end of time and the last minute period begins, the fencer with priority knows their opponent has to initiate the attack and pressure mounts as the clock runs down. Again practising time-pressured situations in training is a useful exercise for these situations.

Often an attacking fencer finishes too early and can be parried. (Photo: Niki Bruckner)

2 seconds!

In the last fight of the men's foil team semi-finals between Germany and Japan at the London 2012 Olympics, there were 2 seconds left with Germany leading by one point and Peter Joppich on the backline. With such a short time available, Yuki Ota planned a first-intention attack and a premeditated renewal. Joppich parried but missed the riposte and Ota scored with the renewal. He then scored the winning hit to take Japan to the final.

Fencing a higher-ranked opponent

With the right tactics and the right frame of mind, a lower-ranked fencer can win against a higher-ranked opponent. However, it is crucial to neutralize the stronger fencer's favourite actions and not to play their game. Even if victory cannot be achieved, one should remember fencing a better player helps one to improve and if victory is not possible then striving to achieve the best possible score will still help to develop a fencer's skills. Also, when fencing a higher-ranked opponent a fencer should remind themselves there is *no pressure*, which usually aids performance.

Fencing a lower-ranked opponent

Here the pressure is higher on the fencer as they are expected to win. Higher pressure on a fencer can cause unnecessary tension, but overconfidence can be equally dangerous as it can lead to some degree of complacency. If a fencer feels the pressure of being the favourite for a certain match, they should focus on transforming any fear of losing into a desire to win, as well as convincing themselves to respect the opponent. It is usually a good idea to stick to a simple game.

However, other fencers are often more confident in such situations as they presume to be stronger than their lower-ranked opponent. In order to avoid any complacency, lower-ranked opponents should always be taken seriously, particularly when the fight is for five hits when there is a lower margin for error.

In general, if a certain fight is perceived to be easier, a higher level of motivation is needed for maximum performance.

Fencing when winning

It is possible for a fencer who is winning to feel under pressure because they expect their opponent to step up their game. The winning fencer should stay active, making many false actions to simulate counter-attacks or attacks and hinder the opponent's ability to increase the pressure. The fencer who is winning should stick to things that are working and not change them unless they stop working.

To hinder an opponent's aggression in pursuit of a 'comeback', point-in-line can be an effective deterrent. Every high-calibre fencer should be able to operate with point-in-line, and take full advantage of the rich opportunities it provides, in addition to simple derobements.

A fencer should starve his opponent of the belief victory is even possible. Once a big margin in the score opens up, the next hit is often crucial to the loser's belief. For example, if the score stands at 10–5, the next hit (11–5 or 10–6) could be the difference between the losing fencer thinking they are still in it, or losing belief and consequently the motivation to continue trying to raise their game.

Fencing when losing

A lot depends on how much time is left: when time is truly running out a fencer is forced to go quickly and take higher risks. On the other hand, if there is time, a fencer should be sure not to rush, but to prepare their actions well. It is important to change, rather than keep repeating the same thing if it is not working. Change can mean swapping from attack to defence, or just making small adjustments to the timing and distance, or the line, of previously unsuccessful actions. Equally, one should try to stop the adversary from scoring with the same actions.

Putting pressure on an opponent (without rushing) is a most effective way of reducing a deficit in the score. Being conservative and slowly working towards reducing the difference in hits is a good idea, and particularly important in a team event (apart from the last fight when there are only 3 minutes left).

GENERAL TACTICAL ADVICE

- Top fencers and coaches should be encouraged to keep written information on their opponents. Video material is also very helpful.
- Develop and maintain the habit of analysing why you or your opponent scored the hit, and how you can improve, in training and competition.
- Try to have a tactical plan in both training and competition. It is a good idea to have both plan A and plan B. Having said that, there is value in developing an intuitive level of fencing based on a feeling for the fight, and developing the skill of improvising and responding appropriately to a changing situation.
- In a competition, if you are not succeeding with a particular idea, change it. I would advise trying twice and if things are not working then change. In training it is better to keep working away until the tactic succeeds – practice makes perfect.
- If you succeed with a particular action, there is no reason to change, but leave a little time before repeating it to allow your opponent

> **Remember!**
>
> Never forget the power of small adjustments to the distance and timing, or line of previously unsuccessful actions as a viable alternative to complete changes.

to forget about it, and keep doing this until it stops working. Some fencers and coaches develop a premeditated chain of actions based on anticipating the most probable sequence of actions from an opponent. Just keep doing whatever works.

- Always try to be one move ahead of your opponent by developing the skill of selective perception, allowing you to anticipate what is going to happen before it happens.
- If your opponent has a particularly strong move, try to hinder it as much as possible. If you succeed, you are in a better position, as your opponent will be restricted to weaker actions.
- Generally, fence carefully (not cautiously) but with courage and patience.
- Always continue fighting until the referee calls 'halt' and keep trying even if you are a

Reviewing video footage of previous matches is helpful in tactical planning. (Photo: Niki Bruckner)

Take a break by straightening the foil, changing a glove or tying a shoelace, allowing time to refocus on the match. (Photo: Niki Bruckner)

long way behind. This principle should be followed in training in order to develop it as a habit for competition.

- Be patient and get a feel for your opponent first.
- After each fight in the poule, regardless of the outcome, make a quick constructive assessment of the fencing and then forget the previous match and concentrate solely on your next opponent.
- We lose concentration more easily and quickly than we can build it. It is a difficult but an extremely important skill to recognize the moment when one is no longer mentally in the fight. If you notice you have lost concentration, taking a break is usually the best option. There are numerous options: retying shoelaces, changing your glove or weapon, pacing to the back of the piste, returning slowly to the on-guard lines – depending on what the referee will allow. Apart from disrupting the momentum of

the match, another advantage of taking a break is the fencer who takes the break decides exactly when to return to the fight, while the opponent is forced to wait for them. At any top-level competition, one will see this tactic being employed often with tangible results; after receiving more than two hits in a row most fencers will stop and force some kind of break.

- Try to keep your mind in the present.
- While fencing, apply the fundamental law – an opponent will react more slowly to slower movements and more quickly to faster ones. Also, if you make them react to one signal, their reaction to the one immediately following, will be slower. Even a suppressed reaction can be considered a kind of latent reaction, so an opponent's reaction to the next signal will also be slower.
- Alternate between your actions. For instance, in attack, try alternating between one and two or more tempo actions.

- If you expect an opponent to counter-attack, then a one-tempo attack is a good alternative to counter-time. If you expect your opponent to go back and parry, two or more tempo actions would be appropriate. Also alternate between real attacks and false, correct and incorrect. Very often, fencers tend to always finish an attack; as a result, an opponent knows what to expect instead of being uncertain whether a fencer is going to commit or not. Similarly with parries: if you expect an attack, then alternate, say, between quarte (4) and counter-sixte (c6) or counter-sixte (c6) and defence with distance. Unfortunately, unexpected attacks usually cause all fencers to respond in one particular way, so here alternating between actions is not possible.
- In defence your response should depend on the character of your opponent's movement:
  - If the attack starts with fast foot movements while moving the point away from your target, then a stop hit or counter-attack while blocking the opponent's blade and shortening the distance (Romanian) is appropriate.
  - If the attack starts slowly with a bent arm, then step back while establishing point-in-line. Here there is also the opportunity to steal the hit with a deceptive stop-hit, before closing out the line with the blade.
  - If the attack starts quickly with the blade threatening the target, then parry-riposte.
- Against an opponent who does counter-time, a compound counter-attack may be effective, as well as a second-intention counter-attack followed by counter-parry-riposte.
- If you are winning and there is 1 minute left to the end of the fight, expect your opponent to increase the pressure, so do everything to hinder those tactics, stay active and keep scoring in the way you have been up until that point. I have seen

> ## Risk to win
>
> If nothing succeeds, consider capitalizing on your opponent's mistakes or taking a *risk to win* approach by using unorthodox movements and timing. Examples include: counter-attacks with dramatic displacement of target, submarine, broken time flèche attacks, wild searching for the blade with premeditated flick continuation. Of course, it is better never to be in such a desperate situation, but 'desperate times call for desperate measures'.

many fencers lose matches from winning positions by inviting pressure from the opponent towards the end of time.
- When fencing a weaker opponent, always take them seriously and be fully engaged in the fight.
- When winning by a large margin, try to focus on the next hit even more than usual, as in such situations there is a tendency to relax and let an opponent back into the fight.
- It is important who scores the first hit, particularly in women's foil and fencers with a defending style.
- Always believe the next hit will be yours.
- Create false impressions of your intentions and act in a way your opponent does not expect.
- Keep developing a second-intention game in training and competition. In other words, develop proactive fencing and try to cause genuine reactions from your opponent (provoke a committed attack, counter-attack, parry or renewal) and take advantage of it.
- Some good ways of inducing a real reaction from the opponent are:
  - Presentation of the blade
  - Beat followed by presentation of the blade
  - Beat followed by taking away the blade
  - Sudden presentation followed by sudden taking away

- Threatening point-in-line
- Beat followed by opening of a specific line.

Drawing an opponent's reaction

USA's twelfth hit of the men's foil team final at the World Championships in Leipzig (2017) is a fantastic example of drawing an opponent's reaction: Chamley-Watson (USA) does a beat followed by taking away the blade to induce his opponent to attack without right of way, allowing Chamley-Watson to score with a continuous riposte.

- Take advantage of the ability to differentiate between false and real actions. Against false actions, don't react or give a false reaction (*bluff against bluff*). Against real actions, real counter-actions.
- Move your feet and do not stop too soon. If your footwork is better than your opponent's, engage in many changes of direction and exchanges of initiative, this will increase your chances of choosing the winning moment.
- In defence keep the distance tight or keep breaking it, but in offence keep the distance long and make small slow preparations. Stuttering preparation and breaking the distance are other viable ways of preparing attacks.
- In general, keep changing your rhythm and *breaking* the rhythm of your opponent, as well as hindering their freedom of movement.
- Make sure your weapon only moves when you want it to and you are not forced to search for the blade involuntarily. This can be achieved by keeping control of the distance with your legs. Sometimes when an opponent takes the blade rapidly and moves forward quickly a fencer will panic and search for the blade. To prevent this from happening, stepping forward with

a sweeping movement (for parry-riposte at close quarters) is a good reflex and alternative to the reliable but overused Romanian.

- It is important to remember the tactics a fencer chooses to employ will not only have an effect on the match they are currently fencing, but also on their long-term development. Although counter-attacks can bring much short-term success, it is easy to overuse them and thereby hamper one's tactical and technical repertoire in the long term.
- In general, I advocate the classical principle of keeping the point on target. In defence, the point should always be threatening the opponent's target. In offence, the point can be taken away when preparing at longer distances, or inviting a counter-action from the opponent. However, the fencer should remain diligent about bringing the point back in line as critical distance approaches.
- The more a fencer threatens their opponent's target, the harder it will be to avoid their blade, therefore the fencer who is more adept at avoiding the blade will be better at threatening the opponent's target. I believe fencing with absence of blade is often the *easy option*; however, the fencer who develops the skill of avoiding the opponent's blade, or who reacts positively when their blade is found, will be more tactically complete in the long run. If a fencer is intent on using absence of blade, then I find keeping the point in a low central line creates more time for avoidance, particularly if the opponent's blade is in the high line.
- Often a fencer favours actions on the blade, but their opponent insists on preparing their attacks with absence of blade. In this case, point-in-line will force the opponent to engage the fencer's blade. Deep and threatening presentations of the blade could also have the same effect. Another option likely to induce the attacking opponent to

Fencers often share advice and support — another way to improve tactical development.
(Photo: Niki Bruckner)

Point-in-line

No one can ever stop a fencer from regaining priority by establishing point-in-line. I believe the point-in-line is the natural antidote to absence of blade pressing; fencers, coaches, and referees should have more faith in it.

react by searching for the fencer's blade, is to suddenly present them with the blade before suddenly taking it away. If the opponent does indeed search, then the fencer will have the opportunity to regain right of way and hit in the opening sector.

- If your opponent is stronger in defence than they are in offence, obviously try to encourage them to attack you. If they do not oblige, then your attacks should be mostly second-intention to draw ripostes and capitalize on them by defending with

parries, distance or by counter-attacking. One more reliable way to force a defensive opponent to attack you is by pushing them to the backline.

- If your opponent is a strong counter-attacker, encourage them to attack you. But, if you have to attack, make it one tempo or, after increasing the distance, start slowly. Alternatively, a *prise-de-fer* attack can be effective as, during that action, your opponent's blade is removed from the target. Another option is to provoke the counter-attack and parry, finish the attack or defend with distance.
- In my experience as both a fencer and a coach, I have often found playing an opponent's game against them can be a highly successful tactic. This could mean, for example, counter-attacking the counter-attacker, or attacking the attacker. The wider a fencer's repertoire, the more useful this tactic can be. Fight fire with fire!

181

12 | COACHING DURING COMPETITION

I have been involved in coaching at an international level for over forty years; coaching fencers during competitions has provided me with a constant source of learning and inspiration, and has always been a fascinating and enjoyable experience. In this chapter, I offer my insights on how a coach can be the most helpful to their competing fencers.

OVERVIEW

Coaching covers both specific and non-specific actions and situations. Most people consider coaching to be mainly tactical in nature; however, anything to help a fencer achieve the right frame of mind and improve their performance should be encouraged. The coach–fencer relationship is critical: the coach has to know what a fencer likes or dislikes, and when to intervene or when not to. These soft skills underpin the fundamental premise of coaching, whether in training or competition, which is the ability to deliver pre-agreed process, performance and outcome goals, as agreed between the coach and fencer. To become a good coach takes many years of experience; it is a long journey and one's coaching will continuously improve over time – a good coach is also a tactician and psychologist.

Coaches should remind fencers that any situation or competition is an opportunity and not a threat. Throughout a fencer's preparation it is vitally important to establish a habit of positive thinking and confidence. This also includes body language – especially not showing an opponent any symptoms of stress or fatigue.

Tactical advice. (Photo: Karen Saunders)

Photo opposite by Niki Bruckner.

I advocate a democratic relationship between a fencer and a coach. The relationship should be a partnership in which both agree on a course of action, rather than 'Do what you are told.' A coach is there to support and build confidence, both psychological and tactical – and yet a fencer should not be dependent on a coach's input. Fencers should be encouraged to think independently and solve problems for themselves; for some experienced fencers little intervention is required, whereas the less experienced or younger fencer may not even have understood a coach's advice (but still be too shy to tell them), leading to a poor performance. Since competition communication (coaching) happens under pressure, as a general rule, less is more. Remember what works and keep it simple. Good interventions occur when a fencer is able to understand the advice from the coach and change, leading to improved performance.

The coach should encourage anything to enhance a fencer's performance, such as: be in the moment and focus on performance and process goals rather than outcome; believe in your ability to give the extra 10 per cent in competition; let go of negative emotions such as anger and replace them with positive emotions such as joy and passion; develop patience and calmness; focus on the fight and don't be distracted by things such as a referee's bad decision or an opponent's attempt to wind up a fencer; and stick to simple things that work.

Yet, there are occasions when a coach's interventions do not have an impact on the fight. Potential reasons for this include: a fencer is unable to change (they have a limited repertoire or are off-form); an opponent is still very good; a fencer has stopped believing in victory; the coach's advice is

Body language can have a positive impact on a referee's decision. (Photo: Niki Bruckner)

not right for the situation; a fencer cannot understand the coach's advice because it is too complicated, or because they are too emotional at the time and need to be calmed down before they can be advised further; or a coach becomes too emotional and their judgment is distorted.

Listed below are some quite general, yet valuable coaching observations:

- Fencers should be encouraged to fence with second intention wherever possible. This means forcing an opponent to react in a particular way and then taking advantage of the situation, rather than reacting to the actions of the opponent.
- A versatile fencer is better than a one-trick pony. A fencer who is versatile can do many things well, and is more likely to follow coaching. The key thing is they are unpredictable, therefore an opponent is never sure what will happen next.
- Coaching during competition can occur:
  Before a fight: fencers usually know who their opponent is going to be at least one day before; review video analysis and/or written information about the opponent, or watch them fencing someone else during the same competition.
  During a fight: although this is generally prohibited it still happens. A coach should be prepared to do it, if it feels right.
  During the 1-minute break.
  After the fight: review and conclude what was positive and what needs to be improved.
- Generally, if an opponent has a particular strength (and most good fencers have), the coach should advise their fencer to try and prevent the opponent from using it.
- In my personal experience, if a fencer is able to fence in the same way as their opponent, it often works well. For example, if an opponent favours attack-remises, then hitting him with attack-remise could be a successful option.

Coaching during a competition occurs under pressure – remember what works and keep it simple. (Photo: Niki Bruckner)

- It is better for a fencer not to look at their coach during a bout, as this reduces dependency on outside help and increases independent thought. However, in cases when help is really needed, it is useful to pre-agree simple hand signals so a fencer can quickly see what the coach is suggesting.
- Distance and moving the legs are important areas of the coach's focus. Coaches should remind fencers to keep a particular distance and move their feet. Often changes in distance can greatly affect performance.
- Coaches should look for an opponent's patterns of behaviour during a fight. For example, some fencers tend to counter-attack after a short or unsuccessful attack; others tend to parry.
- Last but not least, one of the basic roles of the coach during a fight is to watch the referee's decisions and advise the fencer when to call or not to call for a video replay, when to ask for arm judges and to warn them when they are approaching the backline.

ENCOURAGEMENT AND COACHING DURING COMPETITION

Coaching during the bout

Referees are generally tolerant towards some verbal or visual signals coming from the coaching corner, even though it is technically against the rules. However, there are occasions, such as at the Olympic Games, when a referee may be very strict and not allow any signals from the coach. This happened when I was coaching Richard Kruse at the Beijing 2008 Olympics. Having said that, piste coaching is considered an important part of developing fencers, particularly in the USA where it is normal practice during domestic events.

Most of the following advice is of a general nature. Specific advice will depend on information about a particular opponent, and some examples of this are given below.

Encourage the fencer to stay in the moment.
(Photo: Niki Bruckner)

Advice can be divided into four categories: psychological, tactical, physical, and technical.

Psychological advice

'One hit at a time' or 'One touch'

This reminds a fencer to focus on the present, helping with performance.

'Next one'

To avoid the risk of complacency after scoring, this refocuses attention and full engagement in the bout.

'With (the) voice'

Most coaches encourage fencers to use their voice while fencing, particularly immediately after a successful action. This increases engagement in the bout and improves performance.

'Be ready'

This reminds fencers to prepare and be ready to fence.

'Too casual, sharper' (process goal)

This draws the fencer's attention to the level of intensity during the fight and often helps with their performance.

'Initiative'

This reminds fencers to be more active if the coach considers their game too passive.

'Positive'

This is a general reminder to be more positive in every aspect of fencing, including being more decisive.

'Believe in your action'

This stimulates a fencer's confidence.

'All your powers'

This is motivational encouragement drawing a fencer's attention to their strengths, as fencers should always rely on these.

'Keep calm'

A good reminder if a fencer displays symptoms of nervousness.

'Patience'

Many fencers have a tendency to rush and consequently choose the wrong moment to act. This advice is especially useful for fencers with good footwork.

Tactical advice

'Slow beginning'

This is an important reminder which usually leads to increased effectiveness of attacks. Fencers have a tendency to start their offensive actions too quickly, which gives opponents a better chance to score.

'From their mistakes'

Fencers can provoke opponents to initiate actions and choose the right moment for a counter-action. This advice is helpful against fencers who make mistakes in preparing their actions, and against opponents who are effective in defence.

'Use opponent's initiative'

Similar to the advice above, this applies to any action executed when an opponent has the initiative, including:

- Attack on opponent's preparation – usually the most effective timing.
- When the opponent stops.
- First- and last-moment parries and counter-attacks. Here a fencer uses their opponent's energy to score.

'Backline'

This warns the retreating fencer when they are close to the backline. At every stage of a tournament, fencers score hits by pushing opponents over the backline. The coach should shout to the retreating fencer about 1 metre before the line to allow enough

'Use the voice!' This increases engagement and improves performance. (Photo: Augusto Bizzi)

time to stop or change direction. Often coaches give a warning too late. Some adjustment in the timing of warnings has to be made during a fight against particularly fast attackers, when *breaking distance* is going to take longer.

'Take a break' (if hit by an opponent too quickly too often)

Taking a break may help a fencer collect their thoughts and refocus on the 'what to do and when'; it can cause an opponent to lose concentration and allows the fencer taking the break to know exactly when they are returning to the fight whereas the adversary does not.

'Change'

Change tactics. It is counter-productive when a fencer is repeatedly unsuccessful with the same move and just tries to do the same thing harder and faster. I would advise not to change immediately but after at least two attempts, because the action could be right but not succeeding for different reasons.

'Small preparation' or 'Keep it small'

There is a general tendency to make rather large preparations and fencers need to be reminded to make small movements. This also applies to footwork.

'Good preparation'

This reminds fencers to focus on preparing actions well – anticipating the correct distance and timing, and making all movements small and in the right rhythm.

'Keep your distance'

Every fencer has an optimal effective distance. Sometimes fencers need to be reminded. This is also true when an opponent tries to upset the feel for the distance by constantly changing it.

'Shorter distance in defence, longer in offence'

Coaches need to remind fencers to keep the distance tighter in defence and longer when preparing attacks. Fencers are often not aware they are too far away when defending.

'Break the rhythm'

Every fencer likes a particular rhythm of movements and the coach should encourage a fencer to *break* an opponent's rhythm, taking them out of their comfort zone.

'Pressure opponent'

Standard advice meaning moving carefully forward while sometimes breaking the distance or even stopping while waiting for an opponent to react with a parry, counter-attack, attack on preparation or simply just a preparation and then performing an appropriate counter-action.

'Mix second-intention with first'

Mix first- and second-intention actions from time to time as an effective tactic. First-intention actions are always a dangerous alternative as they are done relatively seldom and are less expected.

'Draw an opponent', 'Make them react', or 'Set it up'

Tactical instructions meaning the same thing. The coach must stop a fencer being reactive to the opponent and take the offensive – to make the opponent react and take advantage of it.

'Break the distance'

This advice can work well if a fencer receives too many hits on preparation. Breaking the distance is useful as it can upset an opponent's feel for distance and hence timing. It can be highly effective although very tiring.

'More hindering'

There can never be too much hindering, but this must not distract a fencer from choosing the right moment for their actions. Using a straight arm is an effective way of hindering an opponent's preparation, as are actions to simulate attacks, counter-attacks and false parries, in addition to breaking the distance and rhythm.

'One-tempo attacks'

Some fencers use multi-tempo actions too much and they are susceptible to counter-attacks, so the coach should encourage more one-tempo foot actions. Fencers with less explosive legs or with a shorter reach may find this difficult to implement.

'Avoid being hit with counter-attacks'

This is tactical advice against an opponent who is mainly counter-attacking. Here a fencer has to consider various options:
- Don't attack at all – in this situation the counter-attack cannot exist.
- Only make one-tempo attacks or *prise-de-fer* with one foot action, so one lunge or flèche.
- If using more than one tempo, start slowly after stepping back.
- Make a second-intention parry-riposte.
- Draw the counter-attack and defend with distance.

- Draw the counter-attack and finish in time – here it is important to keep the right distance (not too close).

'Deceptive timing'

This reminds the fencer to disguise their actions – cover pre-signals by acting unexpectedly so the opponent sees them at the last minute, or by showing the opponent a different action to the one planned. For instance:

- Before attacking with a lunge, move backwards.
- Before counter-attacking, make a false parry.
- Before parrying, make a feint counter-attack or another false parry.

'Choose the right moment'

As above, advise the fencer to be more selective in choosing the moment to hit. Fencers should believe it is possible to find the right timing to hit against every opponent.

'Stick to simple things that work' or 'Keep it simple'

Sometimes fencers try new things, particularly towards the end of a fight when it is too risky. It is better to stick to the simple things that work.

'Vary your actions'

This works well if a fencer is too repetitive.

'Your game'

This reminds a fencer to play to their strengths and should improve performance.

'Parry-riposte'

This is for the fencer who overuses counter-attacks, allowing the opponent to know what to expect. If the opponent is afraid of being parried, the chances of scoring increases.

Physical advice

'Move your feet' or 'Hard footwork'

Sometimes fencers are too nervous and their legs become slow and unresponsive. In these circumstances, if fencers do move their legs, they have more opportunity to find the right timing for their actions and are consequently less likely to make counter-attacks out of time. Also, hard work on the legs causes tiredness, which in turn relaxes the muscles, hence improving coordination and consequently timing. This is an example of how physical advice can help improve coordination and concentration through relaxation.

'Change the rhythm'

Fencers have a tendency to fall into the trap of using the same rhythm and therefore become predictable. Coaches should work with fencers to help them change their rhythm – making them more difficult to fence.

'More acceleration at the end'

Accelerating a movement at the end increases the chances of success. This has to be practised in lessons too, but in competitions fencers sometimes move their point just before landing on target at the same speed or even slower. Therefore a reminder to accelerate can have a positive effect on point accuracy.

'Keep your balance'

Sometimes fencers lose their balance and the position from which they can launch an immediate attack. This can be due to faulty footwork, slow reactions or losing too much ground while retreating. Such a reminder can be more effective in training bouts, as fencers require time to improve their balance.

Technical advice

'Keep point-in-line with target'

This is particularly important while closing the distance. It is usually good advice if a fencer is receiving too many counter-attacks.

'Small movements' or 'Keep it small'

Fencers always have a tendency to make big movements.

'Use your fingers'

This reminds fencers not to hold the weapon too tightly; instead, to use optimal strength and consequently improve the quality of hitting.

'Parry first-moment quarte (4) riposte direct'

An instant parry-riposte can be very effective if the opponent's blade can be found at such a distance when there isn't any time to make a counter-parry.

'Attack on preparation by beat-disengage'

This is specific advice against fencers who have a strong tendency to parry quarte (4).

'Sudden feint and counter-disengage attack'

This is specific advice against an opponent who reacts by parrying counter-sixte (c6) when surprised.

'Finish in the outside high sector'

This is against fencers who have strong quarte/seconde or octave (4/2–8) parries and do not cope well with defending hits in the outside high sector.

Coaching during the 1-minute break

The choice of advice is dependent on what has happened thus far and what can be anticipated in the next period.

This is when communication is most pressured and the coach must be both a tactician and psychologist. The coach should deliver no more than two key messages, keeping it simple, with positive body language in a calm, clear manner. Tone of voice is critical and will be dependent on the fencer's needs – motivation, confidence, or re-focusing on the match. Ultimately the coach must know if the fencer will be able to follow the advice given.

To less experienced coaches I would recommend keeping a written record of each hit as a good way of memorizing the fight and drawing logical and objective conclusions in readiness for a debrief with the fencer. For example, during the first period the opponent scores with an attack, attack-renewal, attack; our fencer with a riposte, stop hit and an attack. Conclusion: more offence – choose the moment to attack and hinder the initiation of attacks by the opponent.

However, during important competitions experienced coaches will probably be more effective without writing things down as often the fight moves quickly, as this is time consuming and distracts from the actual play during which the coach needs to be alert for video calls and anticipating an opponent's further actions.

Below are some examples of messages from the coach during the 1-minute break.

Physical advice

- Increase manoeuvring and slightly increase (or decrease) the distance.
- Since your footwork is superior, try to unsettle your opponent by making short attacks and frequently take the initiative back, using this mobility to choose the moment for your actions – mainly attacks on preparation or answering attacks.

- Focus on hindering while using good footwork and choose the right moment to make an answering attack beginning slowly.

Advice for particular opponent characteristics and styles

- Your opponent is reluctant to finish an action and tends to make a counter-attack after stopping, so keep your distance until there is a pause and make sure that you start your answering attack slowly and finish in the opening line.
- Since your opponent always moves forward and either takes a quarte parry (4) or finishes direct, perform a first-intention feint disengage.
- When surprised, your opponent always reacts with a circular sixte (6) parry; this is an opportunity for a sudden feint counter-disengage.
- All attacks stem from your opponent's initiative, so vary attacks on preparation with answering attacks while manoeuvring.
- After your opponent's short or unsuccessful attack, they tend to counter-attack so make sure your answering attack is in one tempo and you finish it.
- Your opponent is shorter than you, so offer the blade and outreach them with a stop hit at your maximum distance against their riposte.
- Your opponent is tall; attack only at the end of the piste (avoid attacking tall fencers who have good footwork in the middle).
- Your opponent tends to always riposte to shoulder and defends the shoulder well, so try a second-intention counter-riposte to flank.

Tactical advice

- React only against real actions; read your opponent's intentions.
- Maximum hindering as your opponent initiates an attack, but at the same time

During the 1-minute break, the coach should give reassurance with a maximum of two clear messages, which the fencer is able to perform.
(Photo: Niki Bruckner)

Any competition is an opportunity and not a threat – always encourage positive thinking and confidence.
(Photo: Niki Bruckner)

actively look for an opportunity to initiate your attack knowing your opponent reacts with a circular sixte (6).

- Do not give your opponent opportunities to hit you with a counter-attack, so focus only on aggressive defence and invite your opponent to attack you.
- Your chosen tactics are good, but find more variation in defence, so your opponent does not know what you are going to do next. Vary your parries and their timing, mixed with stop hits or counter-attacks and defence with distance.
- Apply the tactics of confronting your opponent and wherever possible score hits by going for near-simultaneous actions.
- In defence keep a closer distance so you can find your opponent's blade even if it is being drawn back.
- Mix real attacks with false ones so your opponent is uncertain when you are going to finish, and after a false attack look immediately for an opportunity to find the blade and hit.
- Do not let your opponent dramatically increase the distance to set up an attack; when they try, follow with an invitation and when they respond, close the distance with a parry-riposte at close quarters.
- Anticipate when your opponent intends to counter-attack, so attack by taking the blade with one lunge and, when they move back and parry, continue with a feint cut-over while making a two-tempo foot action.
- When you prepare attacks try finishing earlier as you have a tendency to make another step. But when you are in defence then you have a tendency to stop too soon; use the whole piste with good footwork to hold your opponent for longer.
- Keep mixing defence with distance and counter-attacks, but be selective and counter-attack only if your opponent starts fast with wide blade actions as a result of effective defence with distance or after your attack finishes short.

- Keep a high intensity of preparation while pursuing an aggressive defensive style. If you anticipate the beginning of your opponent's committed action, parry-riposte but, if you anticipate the beginning of a preparation, attack at this moment.
- You can hit with a second-intention counter-riposte.
- After the referee starts the fight, move forward then give your opponent the initiative and hold them at a short distance while looking for the timing of an answering attack and when you take the initiative back try to finish your attack, so forwards, backwards and forwards.
- You will have a better chance to score by manoeuvring while mixing premeditated attacks with second-intention attacks for counter-ripostes.
- Try to score hits in your opponent's half of the piste, keeping them away from your half as much as possible.

Pressure your opponent

- Keep pressing your opponent while breaking the distance and make simple one-tempo attacks on preparation if they respond to your breaks; otherwise, make the same attack at the end of the piste when you get to the critical distance.
- Keep slowly and patiently pressing your opponent with an absence of blade and eventually they will counter-attack; anticipate the moment and just finish your action. Be patient, as your opponent will often counter-attack after many of your steps forward usually at the end of the piste.
- Slowly put your opponent under pressure and only attack on preparation when they try to push back fast. Be selective if you anticipate a slow beginning with absence of blade, then put point-in-line to deter the development of their attack.
- Provoke your opponent into parrying and go for a counter-riposte or counter-

attack depending on the character of their riposte: if direct, counter-riposte; if delayed or two-tempo, then counter-attack.

Tactical advice for fencing from a winning position

There is no need to change a winning formula. However, one has to anticipate an unsuccessful opponent will be trying to change their game; therefore a fencer has to be prepared to adjust, if the winning formula stops working, in order to maintain intensity and domination. If an opponent adapts successfully to a winning tactic, it is better not to make immediate changes, but rather make small adjustments in terms of distance, timing, or technique.

It is important to remember, an opponent who is losing is under more pressure to score, and there is therefore a greater possibility of feeding off an opponent's probable mistakes. If possible, one has to increase intensity even more while building a lead. Of course, a fencer should always be looking to score and not simply *maintain* their lead. Options include the following:

- Stick to the same final action, but use different preparations.
- Change tactics for one or two hits, in order to distract the opponent before returning to the previously successful action.
- Maintain intensity but never fully commit, forcing the opponent to make a mistake since they are under more pressure to score.
- Explore actions from point-in-line.
- Maintain maximum intensity to ensure neither you nor your opponent gets too comfortable.
- Remember to prepare actions adequately; do not become complacent.
- Focus on the present hit, try not to be distracted by the outcome.

Tactical advice for fencing from a losing position

If a fencer is losing, something has to change in order to create a better chance of winning. The change might be a small adjustment in any or all of the following: distance, timing, rhythm, intensity. Equally, it could be a major shift in tactics, such as changing predominantly from defence to offence. With every change, there has to be an increase in intensity and domination. It is common for fencers to become impatient and rushed when facing a losing position. Providing there is ample time remaining, one has to adopt a patient and low-risk strategy.

- Stick to simple things that work.
- Press aggressively, forcing the opponent to 'come out of their shell'.
- Use more second-intention actions, as they bear a lower risk of unforced error for the fencer, and rely on forcing errors from the opponent.
- If time is short, using 110 per cent intensity, take advantage of the fact pressure is also on the fencer with the lead, who suddenly has something to lose.
- When there are only a few seconds left, in addition to aggressive offensive counter-time, a very fast flèche attack can come in handy.

Finally, a coach should avoid developing a fencer who is dependent on them during competition. In theory, developing a fencer who is tactically self-sufficient and does not need external advice should be the ultimate goal of every coach. Therefore, coaches should use every opportunity to encourage and guide fencers to solve tactical problems by themselves; during competition be prudent with advice (less means more), with the focus on deciding when the video replay or arm judges are needed and when to warn against crossing the backline.

13 | THIS IS TEAM FENCING!

I was the GB national team coach from 2007–2013, including the 2012 London Olympic Games. Here, I outline my views on how to build a team culture and produce strong team performances, as well as exploring some specific team-fencing tactics.

TEAM VISION

When a new team is being formed, all potential team members should share a vision of what they are trying to achieve. Such an exercise is an important part of building team spirit and cohesion. Training camps are often the best place to do this, as there is more time to sit down and have a meeting; otherwise, it can be at the end of a regular training session.

The vision should include answers to the following question: what qualities should our team possess, and how do we want to be seen by the rest of the world?

Here are some answers I have heard from the GB squad in the past:

- The best competition preparation – a unified team, before, during and after the event.
- A great team unit, with strength in depth, not just a collection of individuals.
- A tenacious team, fighting for every hit and scrapping well at close-quarters; a team that dominates on the piste and will not be bullied by opponents, keeping fencing even if halt is called.
- A team that earns respect.
- Conditioning: to be known as the fittest team in the world.
- The favourites: to be the tough draw for everyone else.
- Professional: to be the best-organized team, getting to the venue on time and following set routines; to have working equipment at all times; to show the younger generation of fencers how to train and compete professionally – leading by example.
- A mix of styles: to have no single style like other teams, but a mix of different styles, being therefore more unpredictable and difficult to fence.

Photo opposite by Chris Turner.

195

- A versatile team, able to adapt to any situation in the fight and playing to individual strengths in fights.
- The most efficient team: to have other teams know that any mistakes they make will be punished at all times.
- A patriotic team: doing our job for our country and being proud to do so.
- Unshakable under pressure: a team that thrives in pressurized situations, for example when the score is tied at 44–44.
- Everyone takes equal responsibility for every match, rather than relying on certain fencers in the team.
- A team constantly reviewing their performance after every match in order to improve.
- A team dreaming of winning.
- A team that sticks to things that work under pressure and sticks to a winning formula.
- A proactive team that doesn't react but provokes opponents to react.
- A team that can steadily come back from a deficit in small increments.
- A team in which everyone performs to their best ability.
- A team with patience and control under pressure (coaches too!).
- A team that smells blood and takes

advantage of any weak fencer on the opposing team.
- A team with a strong finisher and a belief in every member (no matter what the score is in a fight).
- A team continually striving to improve.
- A team of great performers who raise their game under the pressure of the crowd and media.
- A team that sees every situation as an opportunity to excel.
- A team capable of taking breaks if necessary (particularly if the momentum is with the opponents).

This is not a complete vision but a good start. A similar exercise can be done by coaches or jointly to create a team vision.

Team performance issues

In a team event, the maximum time limit of 3 minutes per fight is a key factor. Some players perform better in a team environment than they do in individual competitions and sometimes fencers are selected for a team ahead of higher ranked teammates. One potential explanation for a difference in individual and team performance is a fencer is more motivated in a team, or they perform better when the fight is shorter. Of course, there are many common areas, which affect performance in both individual and team events.

Fencers should forget they are individuals and should think of themselves as a part of the team. Team members should have full confidence in each other and accept each person as they are, rather than judging each other,

It is important for the non-fencing team members to be focused on the match in progress.
(Photo: Chris Turner)

One good routine

A warm-up match for 20 hits (two against two) starting 30 minutes before the real match.

as this often produces negative feelings. My experience shows, when this happens, the team performs better.

It is hugely important to foster the habit of positive thinking – to regard the match as a chance to improve and to enjoy the occasion. Every competitive match is an opportunity to improve team performance, team cohesion and to prepare for European, World and Olympic events.

In a team match competition conservative fencing is generally better: taking lower risks is advisable – this means going after small gains rather than big ones. It is important to have a good start rather than being under pressure to chase. Developing patience and eliminating rushing is an important goal in team fencing and generally contributes positively towards performance, as actions are more likely to be better prepared.

The whole team should be totally engaged in every fencer's fight, supporting whoever is fencing at the time. Sometimes in a match, the team loses a bit of focus resulting in one poor fight, which can badly affect the result, as there may not be enough time to repair the damage.

Develop routines as a means of coping with anxiety and enhancing performance. The team should establish certain routines for preparation and behaviour during a match. Review performance after each match and focus on what went right and what needs to be improved. This is an important routine and should be done quickly even if there is not much time.

Triple-check equipment. This is a generic problem, but getting a yellow card and sometimes a red because of faulty equipment is clearly unprofessional and should never happen.

Everyone is a leader. It is important every member of the team takes equal responsibility for the result. If members rely on one particular person to score most of the points there is a danger other fencers will shirk responsibility and underperform. Having said that, there is often a case for someone to take a particular role, e.g. the finisher or holder.

Roles

Roles can be a good way of encouraging fencers to take on responsibility and increase engagement.

The strategy of taking regular breaks applies also to team events, particularly when a fencer receives several hits in a row. The coach, and also teammates, should be ready to tell a fencer they should force a break and refocus.

The whole team should think of themselves as winners (cognitive psychology). This has been discussed in Chapter 9 (psychological preparation), and applies to teams as well. The team should have the goal of having all three members perform at their best in the same match; this way they have the best chance of achieving an ice-breaking result.

Belief

A lower ranked team can beat a higher one if they *all* perform well, have the right frame of mind and follow good tactics.

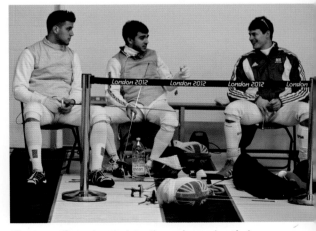

The team discussing their tactics and agreeing their positions. (Photo: Chris Turner)

TEAM TACTICS

Before the match starts there is a draw to determine which position the team members will occupy: top (numbers 1, 2, 3) or bottom (4, 5, 6). Generally, I think it is better to be at the bottom as number 5 (usually the strongest) fences the second match where they can repair any damage incurred by the opposition number 3 (usually the strongest), who fences the first match. Another consideration for being at the bottom is that number 4 always has one fight on and one fight off through the middle five fights of the match. Some fencers are more suited to this role, particularly if they need more time to warm up, or are very fit. The last fight is crucial and most teams put their strongest player in this position.

The anchor

American coaches call the finishing fencer the anchor.

A good *holder* can have a huge influence on the result of a match without scoring many hits. Some fencers are difficult to hit but do not produce many hits. One strategy could be to give the best player the number that does not finish last (1, 2 or 4, 6), hoping to gain a lead, and then put the fencer who is a good holder afterwards, hoping the opposing team, being behind, will take more risks and so give the holder more chance of scoring.

One should also take the opposing team's likely order into consideration and then determine the most effective order for themselves

Holding fencers

When a team has a lead, holding fencers become remarkably more effective.

Passivity

Sometimes going for passivity may be the right tactic, particularly when leading – after 1 minute without any hit the referee can stop the fight and the score is taken over by the next pair.

based on results from previous fights with those fencer(s). Although all teams keep the order of their fencers secret, it is possible to make assumptions based on previous matches. Of course, it is good for fencers to get used to fencing in a certain position, particularly the finisher, but I also had success experimenting with the order in search of better performances.

It is important to have a lead at the beginning so the other team has to chase and take higher risks. In the case of having to chase, small gains over multiple matches are better than taking too many risks in one particular match.

Team tactics against specific teams, supported by video reviews, should be discussed several days before the event, usually at a preparatory training camp or at the end of a training session. Some team training sessions can be designed in preparation to fence a particular team, in which case the coach sets specific training conditions. For instance, any hit on preparation is worth two points against a team known to over-prepare; any counter-attack out of time is worth two hits for the opposing team. Or, if a particular team scores with lots of counter-attacks, *our team* members would have to do five press-ups for every successful counter-attack they receive. There are many possibilities.

Often it is advisable to make a tactical substitution when you believe one fencer on your team will be particularly effective against a certain member of the opposition. Knowledge of past performance is vital.

Substituting fencers for poor performance is a rather delicate issue. The question for the coach is when to do it. Does the coach pull

Substitution

In the Olympic Games, in order for all four players to receive a medal, it is necessary for all of them to fence; however, once a change has been made, it is impossible to reverse, even in the case of injury. Consequently, in order for all players to have a medal, a team in the medal zone must make an irreversible substitution, which could result in losing the match.

the fencer off after just one bad fight, or do they give the fencer a chance to recover and improve? Here the coach's knowledge of the fencer from previous competitions comes in handy. If the coach makes a change after the first bad fight, this might adversely affect the player's confidence. Waiting until after the second fight is usually better, as this gives the fencer a chance to improve as well as providing more information about the player in question, so the coach is more likely to make the correct decision.

Pre-competition team meeting

A team meeting should take place the day before an event to ensure information has time to be assimilated. The agenda for this meeting could be:

Reminder of basic performance issues

It is useful for the coach to remind fencers of performance-enhancing strategies, as repetition is a basic teaching method. Basic performance issues could include: everyone being a leader and taking responsibility; the whole team being focused on the matter at hand; or every member keeping their mind in the present.

Discuss specific tactics

The coach should remind fencers of specific tactics against the first team they will fence,

which will be known by the afternoon of the day before. Video material can be useful here too. Fencers should focus on one match at a time. Tactics against all team opponents should be discussed in earlier team meetings, but the day before a competition the focus should be on the next match. I believe it is distracting for fencers to imagine and plan for the entire tableau at the beginning of the competition. After winning the first match and making a quick review of it, there is usually enough time to remind fencers about the tactics against their next opponents.

Logistics

What time is breakfast? When to leave for the venue? How to get there? Where will the team put their bags? And the physio table? How long before the match to arrive at the venue (usually, fencers like two hours)? And, if applicable, what time will warm-up lessons be? What time to do a warm-up match?

It is important to answer these questions decisively, and well in advance. Teams should have a strong routine, so they are doing more or less the same thing before each team competition.

Selfie time! The winning team and coach.
(Photo: Chris Turner)

	1	2	3	4	5	6	7	Signature
1	▓	V5	V5	V5	V5	D1	V5	
2	D1	▓	V5	D2	D2	D1	D1	
3	D0	D3	▓	V5	D3	D1	D2	
4	D1	V5	D1	▓	D3	D4	D4	
5	D2	V5	V5	V5	▓	D3	D4	
6	V1	V5	V5	V5	V5	▓	V5	
7	D1	V5	V5	V5	V5	D1	▓	

order

IM Alex V5
UDDERICK Felix D2
OTUSER Marek V5
ASKOW Luca D2
RAUK Maria D3
NITO Matteo V5

14 | PERFORMANCE ANALYSIS

Performance analysis is vital to improve and enhance outcomes. Analysis can be qualitatively based on observations or quantitatively based on factual or statistical data. This chapter looks at both approaches, and includes a section contributed by Jamie Kenber (GBR) outlining his own methods of analysis. Most of this chapter refers to performance analysis of competitive matches.

In analysing performance it is helpful to register all hits as they happen. Such analysis can be carried out live, with instant conclusions, or after watching the video replay.

The following abbreviations are used:

A	Attack
Ap	Attack on preparation
Ar	Attack-renewal
Af	Flèche attack
Ab-t	Broken time attack
Aan	Answering attack
R	Riposte
Rr	Riposte-renewal
cR	Counter-riposte
cRr	Counter-riposte-renewal

Photo opposite by Niki Bruckner.

C	Counter-attack without blocking the line, which could be a stop hit
Cr	Counter-attack Romanian
Cl	Hit scored from point-in-line
Coot	Counter-attack out of time
BL	Hit scored by pushing over the backline, classified as an attack
Ye	Yellow card (make a note why)
Red	Red card hit (make a note why)

Other notes may include injury time and technical problems, and potentially the intention behind any hit scored.

In every analysis, there has to be some room for error. One of the most common errors occurs when differentiating between an attack on preparation (Ap) and a counter-attack (C) out of time when the opponent misses. Naturally, it is more difficult to judge while analysing a live fight.

While analysing, I draw a horizontal line with the names of the fencers above and below the line. This line represents the length of time the fight takes and gives information about the dynamics of the fight. Hits for are always registered as they happen above or under the line depending on who scored them. A vertical line with the score is drawn to indicate the 1-minute break. Thus the score in each period can be seen.

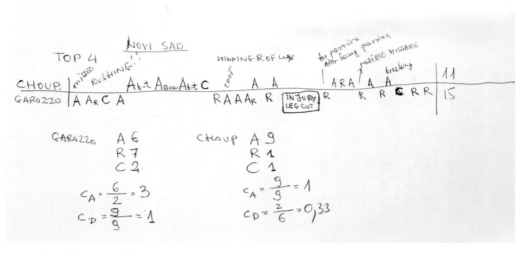

Match analysis notes. This shows the very simple way of analysing the dynamics of the fight in note form. The symbols are used to describe the type of hits scored by both fencers. For example, here you can see Choupenitch (Choup) scored nine attacks, one riposte and one counter-attack. The efficiency of attacking and defensive manoeuvres can be worked out by comparing their scores; the effectiveness of Choupenitch's attacks was 1, and the effectiveness of his defence was 0.33. (Photo: Niki Bruckner)

It is helpful to write any additional relevant observations underneath – for example, how many hits are scored at the end of the piste, whether a fencer is left-handed, likes to break the distance most of the time, takes mainly a quarte (4) parry, after an attack always searches for the blade in prime, mostly prepares in the low line, is a 'blade bully', likes close-quarters fighting, or tends to hit under the arm.

If coaching is required during the 1-minute break, it is helpful to quickly look at the hits and draw conclusions for any advice which can be given. For example, if a fencer receives numerous hits from attacks but also scores mainly with attacks, the advice should be to try and prevent the opponent attacking by going for near-simultaneous actions and, if forced to retreat, hinder the timing of attacks by using point-in-line, breaking the distance and making false actions to simulate counter-attacks or attacks.

When the fight has finished, it is possible to work out the efficiency of attacks or defence for both fencers and write out more observations.

EFFECTIVENESS OF ATTACKS AND DEFENCE

The following formula is very helpful:

Effectiveness of attacks eA = A for / (R ag + C ag)

Effectiveness of defence eD = (R for + C for) / A ag

(A = attack, D = defence, e = effectiveness)

A   Attacks scored by particular fencer
R   Ripostes scored by particular fencer
C   Counter-attacks scored by particular fencer
A ag   Attacks received by particular fencer
R ag   Ripostes received by particular fencer
C ag   Counter-attacks received by particular fencer

The higher the coefficient of effectiveness, the higher the effectiveness of attack or defence.

For the purposes of these equations, if fencer A is attacking, then fencer B can only score with defensive actions of ripostes or counter-attacks. When their coefficient of effectiveness of attacks is higher than one, that fencer should favour an attacking game. If effectiveness of attacks equals 1 it means attacks are neutralized by defensive action. Apart from how strong a particular player is in certain areas, further observations can be made, and all of this information can be used in planning tactics before fencing a particular fencer or team. These observations may include:

- The score in each period.
- When most hits are scored or received; for example, some players have a tendency to receive hits at the beginning of a period, or at the end, or both.
- Whether there is any pattern of scoring or receiving (for instance, three hits in a row).
- The overall percentage of attacks, ripostes and counter-attacks.
- If a fencer mainly attacks or counter-attacks, whether the opponent mainly defended with a mixture of ripostes and counter-attacks, or just one of the two.
- Whether a fencer counter-attacks out of time too often (address in training).

- Whether there is a tendency to receive a yellow card, for example, covering with the head (this would need to be addressed in training).
- Whether a fencer has an effective flèche attack.
- Whether there is a pattern between a particular fencer's results and the distribution of hits produced; for instance perhaps the best results were achieved when most hits came from defence (60 per cent) and that more parries were used than counter-attacks.
- Whether a fencer usually starts a bout with counter-attacks and only attacks and ripostes after getting a feeling for their opponent.

Some actual examples from past competitions are shown below.

GBR Hits		Against FRANCE	Against RUSSIA	TOTAL
A	68% (30)	51% (23)	66% (29)	62% (82)
R	27% (2)	20% (9)	27% (12)	25% (33)
C	5% (2)	29% (13)	7% (3)	14% (18)
GBR scores	44	45	44	133

Hit analysis from the Olympic test event, November 2011. Hits scored.

Choupenitch (CZE) against Janda (POL)

Choupenitch (CZE) against Janda (POL) scored with 10A, 3R and 2C. Janda scored with 4A, 2R and 2C. So the effectiveness of Choupenitch's attacks (eA) was $10/4 = 2.5$. The effectiveness of his defence (eD) was $eD = 5/4 = 1.25$. On the other hand, Janda's effectiveness of attack (eA) was $4/5 = 0.8$; and defence (eD) was $4/10 = 0.4$.

We can conclude that Choupenitch was effective both in attack and in defence, but his attacks were more effective. Janda had a poor defence; his attacks were better, but he was losing in both areas.

GBR Hits		Against FRANCE	Against RUSSIA	TOTAL
A	46% (20)	48% (12)	47% (16)	47% (48)
R	25% (11)	32% (8)	35% (12)	30% (31)
C	28% (12)	20% (5)	18% (6)	22% (23)
GBR scores	43	25	34	102

Hit analysis from the Olympic test event, November 2011. Hits received.

GBR against	CHINA	FRANCE	RUSSIA
cA	1.3	1.8	1.6
cD	0.7	1.8	0.9

Hit analysis from the Olympic test event, November 2011. Effectiveness of attack and defence of GBR against China, France and Russia.

Against GBR	cA	cD
China	1.4	0.8
France	0.5	0.6
Russia	1.1	0.6

Hit analysis from the Olympic test event, November 2011. Effectiveness of attack and defence of China, France and Russia against GBR.

OLYMPIC TEST EVENT, NOVEMBER 2011

Observations

- GBR made more attacks.
- GBR scored few counter-attacks against China and Russia because they prepared their attacks well.
- Against China and Russia, the majority of GBR hits were attacks (nearly 70 per cent).
- Against France, counter-attacks worked well.
- Chinese attacks were quite effective (1.4). More pressure should have been put on them by keeping them in their half, going for near-simultaneous actions, looking for more opportunities to attack and increasing the range of hindering actions in defence, including the line.
- GBR's defence against China and Russia needed to be more effective.
- Russia did more parries than counter-attacks.

In summary, 235 hits were analysed, 55 per cent were scored by attacks, 27 per cent by ripostes and 17 per cent by counter-attacks, showing a trend for more ripostes over counter-attacks in men's foil at senior level.

DIRECT ELIMINATION FIGHTS FROM INDIVIDUAL EUROPEAN SENIOR CHAMPIONSHIPS, ZAGREB 2013

Observations

- Davis scored with eight attacks, four counter-attacks and three ripostes against seven attacks from Majewski, two ripostes and one counter-attack. So Davis's attacks were very effective, $8/3 = 2.7$, and his defence was equal to Majewski's attacks, $7/7 = 1$.
- Davis started well, with Majewski catching up during the later stages of the first 3-minute period, before Davis finished strongly in the second period.
- Davis's fight was more balanced as he scored seven hits from defence and eight hits from offence, while Majewski mainly scored from attacks, trying to draw Davis's counter-attack out of time (Coot), which succeeded four times.
- Recommendations for the future: Davis should attack Majewski more and hinder the timing of Majewski's attacks; he should also be more selective with counter-attacks and use more parries and ripostes.
- The fight was of average duration, finishing during the second period. Both players scored twenty-four hits in just over 5 minutes.

Davis (GBR)		RCCA	C	coot	coot	5	cR A Aa	A coot coot A C A	A R A	15
Majewski (Pol)			cR	A	R A	A5		A A A	C A	9

Example of performance analysis during a top 32 match: James Davis (GBR) vs Janusz Majewski (POL) 2013.

Observations

- Kruse's fencing was highly intensive with a manoeuvring defensive style, only producing four attacks, the majority of his hits coming from defence (six ripostes and five counter-attacks).
- Cassara did not score with a single counter-attack and managed four ripostes and three attacks.
- The effectiveness of Kruse's defence was very high: 11/3 = 3.7.
- Cassara's defence equalled Kruse's attack: 4/4 = 1.

- Kruse was sharp in the beginning and also had a strong finish.
- Twenty-three hits were produced in just under 5 minutes as the fight finished in the second period.
- Recommendations for the future: maintain the initiative while putting pressure and breaking distance, provoke the opponent into initiating an attack and then riposte or counter-attack. Second-intention attacks to make counter-parry-ripostes are possible.

Kruse		C	cR Ab-t	C A C R	7	R A A	C C R	cR cR	15
Cassara		Aan	R	Ap	3		CR A cR	R	7

Example of performance analysis during a top 16 match: Richard Kruse (GBR) vs Andrea Cassara (ITA) 2013.

One important factor in this fight which is not reflected in the notes is the fact that both fencers scored mainly from actions with the blade, and Kruse was working particularly hard in defence to provoke Cassara's actions with the blade. The conclusion made from statistics should always be complemented by more general, qualitative observations. As mentioned earlier, it is advisable to write down such observations underneath the statistical analysis.

There are other ways of analysing performance, such as the Jamie Kenber Method. This involves registering every hit with three or more digits from 0 to 10, each digit having a particular meaning. This can generate considerable information about a hit, but needs to be learnt and is time-consuming. This method is laid out in more detail below; the remainder of this chapter is a contribution by Jamie Kenber.

PERFORMANCE ANALYSIS

My experience of fencing performance analysis was with the GB foil team during the period 2008–2012. Before and following this period, most of our performance analysis would involve watching footage of ourselves and opponents, forming strategies and identifying weaknesses. There was a huge amount of experience in our video sessions and it was great to hear from our teammates and coaches.

During a long spell of injury, I started to wonder how a data-driven approach could be applied to fencing. Statistical approaches are popular in many fields: football and cricket betting, where companies such as Opta Stats are dedicated to data capture; US sports drafts, as popularized in the film *Moneyball*; and in online poker where most professionals will use software such as Hold'em Manager or PokerTracker. It is likely some nations are applying data and statistics to their fencing performance analysis. We took on a project of that nature, converting video footage into data for analysis.

We need to capture the most valuable information possible in our data. The challenge here is to preserve information without being too labour-intensive. I'll explain the approach I took, but if your goals are different you may need to adapt this. There are a near infinite number of fencing phrases: at least four common parries, a huge number of footwork combinations, body positions, lines of attack, misses, off-targets, cards. Recording all of this information isn't practical. To collect the right data, we need to know what we're trying to answer.

I believe specific movements are best addressed using video analysis – experts in a room looking at footage, and discussing how to approach the situation. If a particular opponent has a very strong low-line attack, counter-attack, stop-hit, I would consider these specific movements. The aim of our data capture was to pick up upon more general themes:

- Identify your own weaknesses to be addressed in training/tactics – 'you're weak in close quarters', 'you're hitting off-target too often', 'you're picking up too many yellows', 'you attack too often/not often enough', 'you're weaker against left-handers'.
- To give practical advice about your opponent – 'he's strong up close, avoid it', 'he's susceptible to a remise', 'he's strong on preparation, keep it disciplined', 'initiate the hits, because he's weak in response'.

Given that this was our aim, we omitted 'specifics' from our data capture. We did not collect data describing which line of attack or which parry. Statistically, I believe this is the right thing to do. In order to achieve insight at that level of detail, the data capture would be very time consuming, and the sample sizes you're likely to collect would be too small.

With these goals in mind, and limited time on offer, this is the data we chose to record:

1. **Who are the two fencers?**
   Pretty obvious, but along with the names, I recommend recording whether they are left-/right-handed, tall/medium/short and their region/nationality. Recording nationality may seem controversial, however, some regions do have distinct traits. For example, I believe the hand-speed of Asian region trained fencers is noticeably faster and this is a different skill set to oppose.

2. Who initiated the hit? From what distance did the hit take place?

This is essential; it's the easiest thing to adjust when going into a match. It can be hard to implement advice from a coach describing which parry to take or which line. By contrast, it's easier to influence whether you wait for the opponent or not, and whether to get in close or not. *Note*: we recorded the distance from which the hit landed, not the distance when the action began.

3. What was the phrase?

As mentioned, we will not be recording lines of attack or lines of parry, but otherwise, we will preserve as much information as possible. We're aiming to answer questions of this nature:

- Should you be looking to draw a counter-attack or be cautious of one?
- Should you attack on preparation or is your opponent effective against this?

For foil fencing, I found these actions the most common and relevant, during the 2008–2012 period:

- Simultaneous
- Attack vs counter-attack
- Attack vs attempted parry (or vs no action)
- Attempted attack on prep, successful or not
- Attempted stop hit, successful or not
- Riposte vs counter-attack (or remise)
- Riposte vs attempted counter-parry

Bout ID	Bout Type	Green fencer name	Green fencer hand	Green fencer height	Zone	Green Fencer name	Green fencer hand	Green fencer height	Zone
1	Team leg	Halstead	Right	M	Eu	Lei	Left	T	Asia & Oceania
2	3 hits	Kruse	Right	T	Eu	Le Pechoux	Left	S	Eu
3	15 hits	Jefferies	Left	M	Eu	Cassara	Left	T	Eu

Dataset 1: Matches. A row should be entered into this table, for each bout that we record.

Bout ID	Phrase ID	Code	Agressor distance	Action	Outcome
1	1	115	1	1	5
1	2	222	2	2	2
1	3	121	1	2	1
2	9	251	2	5	1
2	10	231	2	3	1
2	11	162	1	6	2
2	12	163	1	6	3
2	13	231	2	3	1
2	14	281	2	8	1

Dataset 2: Hits. A row should be entered into this table, for each time the referee calls halt (including those that do not result in a hit awarded). The last three columns in this example aren't necessary – they can be calculated afterwards – but will be helpful for analysis. You will need to be familiar with the coding system that follows, or devise your own.

DIGIT 1 – Agressor/Distance		DIGIT 2 – Action		DIGIT 3 – Outcome	
1	LHS initiates, finishes at regular distance	1	Simultaneous	1	LHS scores
2	RHS initiates, finishes at regular distance	2	Attack vs counter-attack	2	RHS scores
3	LHS initiates, finishes at close quarters	3	Attack vs attempted parry (or vs no action)	3	LHS off-target
4	RHS initiates, finishes at close quarters	4	Attempted attack on prep	4	RHS off-target
		5	Attempted stop hit	5	Simultaneous (any two lights)
		6	Riposte vs counter-attack (or remise)	6	LHS yellow card
		7	Riposte ve counter-parry	7	RHS red card
		8	Counter-riposte vs counter-attack (or remise	8	LHS yellow card
		9	Riposte vs attempted counter-parry	9	LHS red card
		0	Line	0	No lights

Although this coding system looks complicated, it quickly becomes possible to enter these codes at the same speed as watching footage.

- Counter-riposte vs counter-attack (or remise)
- Counter-riposte vs attempted counter-parry

4. **Who had priority at the final action? What was the outcome? From what distance?**
This is essential to record. An example is shown in the tables following.

How did we record this data?

We actually have two separate datasets: data describing the bout (the fencers and their info), and data describing each hit. It is good practice to store these separately, joining them together using an identifier column. This column is 'Bout ID' in the examples that follow.

Analysing the data

It's best at this point to get somebody on board with an understanding of data and/or stats. The capture you'll have done so far lends itself to a lot of analysis. You might want someone with data and stats experience on the project, since it is easy to draw a conclusion from a mere coincidence.

Converting the data into insight can be done using Microsoft Excel, since our data volumes will be modest. However, it will take someone

The team discussing their performance with their coach. (Photo: Niki Bruckner)

with no experience quite a while to convert raw data into stats on each fencer. If analysing the data yourself, be careful not to draw any strong conclusions from less than fifty observations.

Our project recorded about 20,000 fencing phrases. We managed to obtain a healthy sample size as some of the team coded up their own bouts. The sheer size of the database is not important; what matters is the number of phrases for whichever fencer we are analysing.

The project allowed us to see a very wide variety of information, including:

- which fencers had higher percentages in attack vs defence or vice-versa, coupled with their ratios attacking:defending;
- which fencers' accuracy was weak; which fencers were weak at close quarters;
- who suffered losing streaks; a fencer's defending percentages, parrying vs counter-attacking;
- split any of the above vs left-handers/ right-handers.

The data volumes were not sufficient to identify opponents' weaknesses: we only had the sample sizes to cover ourselves. With the FIE footage available today, and with enough time invested, samples for any of the top fencers in the world are attainable.

Observations about our own fencing were intended to guide a training plan, and a few did just that. However, we didn't address an age-old dilemma: should we focus on capitalizing from our strengths, or protecting against our weaknesses?

15 | CONCLUSION

Just like any other sport, foil fencing continues to develop and change. There are many factors influencing modern foil: changes in equipment; creation, interpretation and enforcement of rules; physical fitness and stamina. I also believe that men's foil is importing many elements from sabre. Those who are succeeding have adopted an offensive game, and phrases seem to have become shorter – below are a few observations on how I believe the sport is changing.

Men's foil fencing is heading towards the continuous development of a second-intention game based on drawing a counter-attack, parry or attack on preparation and capitalizing on it. The tactics of confrontation with premeditated or partly premeditated actions have to be continuously developed, because more and more fencers are performing a pressing style with absence of blade, which is hard to defend against. I believe Stefano Cerioni's influence on the Russian team was to make them considerably more confrontational in their style of fencing.

Footwork has increasing importance, as there is greater use of distance to pressure an opponent, to defend with, and to keep changing both distance and rhythm to create more opportunity for scoring the hits; competing with the opponent to win right of way by starting a fraction of a second earlier. A good example of this was the semi-final at the 2017 Long Beach Grand Prix between Safin (RUS) and Avola (ITA).

The length of time of a fight and the average time for scoring one hit is becoming increasingly short, and fights often finish in the first period. It occurs to me men's foil is following sabre in this respect; the battle for priority immediately after the referee says *'Allez!'* is crucial, and many fencers often defend with distance. Before the timing change in 2005, men's foil was much faster. It slowed down after 2005, as fencers adjusted to the new requirements for hitting. Recently, I would say fencers have begun to speed up again.

As the hits in men's foil get faster, it is becoming much harder for judges to referee. Close calls are very common, and referees are often divided in the big matches. The usage and review of video refereeing is a constant source of conversation and confrontation on the circuit.

Photo opposite by Chris Turner.

Fights are getting faster

Garozzo (ITA) vs Davis (GBR) in the 2015 European Championships only took 1 minute 28 seconds. That's an average of 4 seconds per hit.

The 1968 Olympic Games were at high altitude in Mexico City, where only the fittest athletes were able to produce good performances. This led to an emphasis on physical preparation for athletes across the world. For the past fifty years, I have heard how fencing is 'now much more physical than before.' Athleticism was and is still essential. However, I believe the classic principles of foil should always come first.

Today, attacks are a dominant feature at the highest level of men's foil fencing. The new generation of top World fencers (Garozzo (ITA), Massialas (USA), Safin (RUS)) play a highly offensive game, scoring mostly from attacks. A majority of the previous generation of top fencers (Joppich (GER), Baldini (ITA), Le Pechoux (FRA), Kruse (GBR), Ma

(CHN), Cheremisinov (RUS)) played a longer game, and were more willing to give their opponents priority.

There is more in-depth strength today in international fencing. More nations train professionally, and it is almost impossible to predict a winner in any competition. I feel close fights happen on a scale not seen before. Garozzo (ITA) was the only fencer to win two competitions in the 2016/17 FIE season, and we regularly see top-16 fencers losing in the first round of international competitions.

The distribution of hits has always interested me, so from time to time I take random samples of hits from senior world competitions, and try to identify any trends. Technically speaking, a parry-riposte is a more difficult movement than a counter-attack or a simple attack. This is because it consists of two movements: a parry and then a riposte. Additionally, many fencers specialize in drawing a parry and counter-attacking against the opponent's riposte; this makes riposting even more difficult. This can cause young fencers to rely mainly on attacks or counter-attacks. Parry-ripostes tend to emerge in the later stages of their development.

	A % Attacks inlcuding their renewal	R % Parry-ripostes including their renewal	C % Counter-attacks with their renewal	Total number of hits
World Champ 1983 Final	62	16	22	?
World Champ 1985 Final	52	21	27	?
Worl Cup San Jose 2015	53	24	23	435 all stages
World Cup Tokyo 2016	48	31	21	272 all stages
Tokyo 2016	37	38	25	73 finals and semi

Analysis of hits 1983–2016.

In my analysis, I divide the hits into three categories:

A – attacks including their renewal
R – parry-ripostes including their renewal
C – counter-attacks with their renewal

From the results in the table above we can draw some interesting conclusions. Firstly, the probability of scoring from defence is similar to offence; however, when a larger sample is reviewed (San Jose) the trend indicates a move towards a more attacking game. Secondly, in the 1980s, when flicking was very popular, attackers could prepare in such a way that it was virtually impossible for their opponent to parry. I believe this was the reason there were many more successful counter-attacks than there were ripostes. However, after the 2004 Olympics when timing changed, the proportion of ripostes in relation to counter-attacks gradually increased. This finding contradicts the common perception that there are still more counter-attacks than parry-ripostes. Of course, it is easier to counter-attack, especially against the absence of blade pressing of today; however, these facts show parry-ripostes are indeed still effective. Parry-ripostes are still

playing a significant role in foil, therefore fencers should continue to work on them and emulate the legendary Yuki Ota (JPN): 'When Ota finds the blade he always hits!'

In the semi-finals and final of the 2016 World Cup in Tokyo the distribution of hits was very interesting: A – 37 per cent, R – 38 per cent and C – 25 per cent. The top four were Chamley-Watson (USA), Le Pechoux (FRA), Paroli (ITA) and Avola (ITA). It surprised me there were more ripostes than attacks. This could be explained by the tactical orientation of these particular players, or perhaps they were also too tired to push an effective attack and relied instead on finding the blade.

Coaches and fencers will always be at the mercy of the rules and their evolving interpretations, and it is therefore vital that coaches and fencers stay up to date with modern trends in fencing and refereeing. On the other hand, it is often easy to get distracted by the latest fashion. As Kruse (GBR) once remarked, one's system of fencing 'has to work with everyone.' Equally, I believe fencers should never neglect those eternal principles which will serve them well, whatever the current trend in fencing may be.

GLOSSARY

In this book, apart from generic terms, I use some terms created by my fencers during our journey to the top.

Airborne riposte

A way of riposting while jumping. It moves the valid target from its usual place and increases access to the opponent's upper target for the riposte. Can be surprising and spectacular. Andrea Baldini (ITA) was famous for this stroke.

Avoidance

A way of defending by moving one's target out of the way of the opponent's point. Maximilien Chastanet (FRA) often avoids being hit by moving his target.

Avola steps

Steps executed in an unorthodox way, named after Georgio Avola (ITA), who sends confusing messages to his opponents by sometimes initiating steps forward with the back foot, or steps backward with the front foot. In particular, stepping forward by moving the back foot first is a classic way of discreetly gaining distance and disguising the length of one's attack.

Bear hug

Sometimes called *scoop*, this is a way of hitting an opponent at close quarters where the foil hand tracks around the trunk of the opponent as if giving them a bear hug.

Beating the blade

A rapid action of blade against blade, usually medium part against weak (it can be any part, but if it is weak against strong, and both fencers hit, the referee may interpret the action as a parry-riposte for the opponent). If a fencer plans to hit directly after their beat, their beat should be strong. If they plan to hit indirect then their beat will need to be lighter. Also, the shorter the duration of the beat, the faster the beating blade will move. Tactically, a beat can be a parry, attack or counter-time. Technically, it can be a simple beat, return beat, change-beat, circular beat, semi-circular beat, diagonal beat, or a beat from any other position.

Bow and arrow

Usually a fencer should be encouraged to keep arm and body movements separate. However, sometimes it is helpful to think of the trunk and legs as a bow and the sword arm as an arrow. This can be achieved by lowering the legs while rotating the trunk and moving the head and sword arm back; when the moment comes to strike, the movement of the weapon can be accelerated considerably taking cumulative power from the legs, trunk and sword arm – like an arrow being shot from a bow.

Bully the blade/blade bully

The way of making various, usually strong actions against the adversary's blade in order to force them to respond. This response could be an attempt to beat back against the fencer's blade, or any other reaction of which the fencer can take advantage.

Central line

A hypothetical line created when the fencer lines up not only their point, but also their whole body, with the middle of the opponent's target. The middle of the opponent's target is not necessarily the middle of their chest, but the centre of the target as it appears to the fencer. Usually this will be in the middle of the breast of the fencing arm, but of course it changes as the opponent moves their body. Awareness of how to create and maintain this central line with the opponent's target helps a great deal with accuracy. It also aids the fencer in defence, as it gives them a useful bearing should they wish to avoid the opponent's attack. If a fencer's point is on target, but the rest of their body is orientated elsewhere, they have a higher chance of missing.

Champley

A specific way of hitting at close range, introduced by the USA fencer Miles Chamley-Watson (USA). This hit involves wrapping the sword arm over the non-fencing shoulder and around the neck so the hit arrives from an unexpected angle.

Choice reaction

An exercise when fencer has a limited number of specific choices (usually two or three). For example, there is a choice between attack on preparation and parry-riposte; or there is a choice between stop hit at maximum distance and last moment parry-riposte; or after feint of counter-attack there is a choice between going back or beat attack or direct attack depending on the signals from (the coach/opponent).

Counter-time

This is any hit in response to an opponent's counter-attack, often *second-intention* in nature. It can be in the form of any action with or without the blade, even defence with distance. I believe when the attacker is deliberately drawing an opponent's counter-attack in order to finish their own attack without the blade, this attack should also be considered as a type of counter-time. Garozzo (ITA) is known for scoring in this fashion.

Critical distance

Distance at which the opponent is very likely to react as it seems that the fencer is close enough to hit them with a single action.

Croisé

Hitting by transportation of the blade in the same plane from high to low line or vice versa.

Digging in

An aggressive-defensive way of fencing. The fencer stays active while provoking their opponent to initiate some genuine action. This strategy is inspired by the trench warfare of the First World War.

Double engagement

This is when the fencer's blade makes two contacts with opponent's blade, one on each side; the first one is usually short, and the second longer. Actions like this usually prevent the opponent from deceiving any attempt by the fencer to engage their blade. Double engagements can be effective against opponents who are adept at deceiving the blade. In addition, they are a splendid way of improving one's technique and usage of fingers.

Engagement of the blade (taking the blade)

This is when the fencer's blade makes and maintains contact with the opponent's blade. It should be done in such a way that the fencer can control the opponent's blade. Attacking with a blade is very useful, as it prevents counter-attacks and can override an opponent's parry. Taking the blade can also have a tactical purpose, drawing a reaction from the opponent. Technically, an engagement of the blade can be simple, semi-circular, circular, diagonal, or from any position.

False engagement (false search)

A movement that looks like a real engagement, but the engaging fencer's blade actually goes round the opponent's blade. The false engagement appears to invite the opponent to thrust and can be a very effective preparation before a real beat or engagement. The round trajectory of the point distinguishes this action from a cut-over.

False parries

False parries are essentially parries with no riposte. Instead of riposting, the fencer either holds the opponent's blade, or suddenly releases it. These actions are usually designed to invite the opponent to follow up with some response upon which the fencer can capitalize.

Fencing distance

This is a distance between the fencers from which the referee allows them to start. The only exception to this is at the beginning of the match, or following a successful hit, when the fencers start at the on-guard lines. In theory, fencing distance is determined by both fencers extending their sword-arms, and then adjusting their position so that their points are just touching each other.

Garbushka

A famous action performed frequently by the Soviet World Champion in 1966, German Svieshnikov. Svieshnikov was aggressively inviting the opponent's blade and parrying with seconde or prime, before riposting on the back. In Russian, the word 'garbushka' means the crust of a loaf of bread; however, in this context it takes its meaning from 'gorb' ('garb' in Polish), meaning 'hump', referring to the opponent's back, where the hit lands.

Half-lunge

A partly developed lunge from which a fencer can recover by either moving backwards initiated with the back foot or developing any continuation of the attack: lunge, step-lunge, patinando, flèche.

Half-step flèche

An attack started by moving the front foot forward, before pushing off into a full flèche. By initiating with a half-step forward, the fencer not only gains distance, but also disguises their flèche as the opponent initially recognizes only the beginning of a step forward.

Hop-lunge

An attack in which a fencer does a very long step forward, and then immediately after landing on their front foot, hops even further forward (without crossing the legs). A hop-lunge will cover roughly the same distance as a step-lunge but in less time. In sabre this is called a 'flunge'. Some top fencers use this method of attack. For example, Alexander Massialas (USA) and Gerek Meinhardt (USA).

Ironing board

The original name of a type of counter-attack when, immediately after the hit, the fencer blocks the attacker's hit arriving either by making a windscreen-wiper type movement or leaving the point on and moving the guard to stop the blade getting through. Also known as a Romanian.

Jault

Hitting from behind at close distance by moving the sword arm behind the back and hitting the target from the side of the opposite arm mainly into the low line. Named after the French fencer Jerome Jault who made this move popular.

Knitting

A lesson exercise. On the coach's engagement of their blade, the fencer executes a change of engagement while slowly sliding along the blade towards the coach's target. The coach then takes either a simple or a circular parry, which the fencer deceives before hitting. If the coach increases the distance while taking another simple or circular parry, the fencer should make another deception and hit with a lunge. If the coach deceives the fencer's attempt to retake their blade, the fencer should make successive circular parries with a step back and riposte while standing still.

Learning bouts

These are bouts where fencers have a particular task to fulfil in order to learn and perfect technical and tactical skills. For example, this could be a fight where counter-attacks do not count.

Looking step

After an opponent's initial attack falls short, answering with one-tempo foot actions (like a single lunge or a flèche) is the best way for a fencer to avoid receiving a counter-attack. Alternatively, if a fencer *does* wish to answer with a step, it should be slow, and small, while looking for the opponent's reaction. Italian coaches refer to this type of step as a 'looking step'.

Magic of direct thrust

A lesson exercise where both coach and fencer manoeuvre and the fencer's task is to disguise a direct thrust so the coach sees it too late to parry. The coach should genuinely try to parry.

Mashing grapes

In the old days, all Soviet fencers could be easily recognized, even from a long distance, by the way they kept their legs moving up and down on the spot as if they were 'mashing grapes'. The purpose of this action was to relax the muscles in the upper body, in order to have the most efficient and best coordinated movement. It also helped athletes to change direction quickly and disguise the beginnings of their actions.

Massialas

A lesson exercise named after Alexander Massialas (USA) and the way in which he prepares his attacks. The fencer presses the coach with their hand in a low wide position on their own inside line, before finishing in the coach's outside line, either low or high.

Meinhardt

A lesson exercise named after Gerek Meinhardt (USA) due to his unique combination of high intensity and creativeness. The fencer takes the initiative and alternates first- and second-intention attacks with the coach checking the fencer's readiness to switch to defence. The coach and fencer agree beforehand on the coach's defensive system so the fencer can prepare both first- and second-intention attacks. For *second-intention* attacks, the fencer mixes counter-parries, counter-attacks and defence with distance. The fencer is asked to prepare with high intensity while constantly changing rhythm and direction. When a fencer becomes exhausted, they can terminate the exercise by making a second-intention attack, with a premeditated flèche renewal, running past the coach.

Mincemeat

A lesson exercise where a fencer, without moving their feet, hits repeatedly. The coach varies between close-quarters and riposting distance, continuously taking various parries as well as rotating their target. The coach can also introduce their non sword-arm as an additional obstacle. The fencer's objective is to keep hitting perpendicular to the target, with optimum strength and in time, into the opening sectors of the target.

Muhammad Ali

Fencing from a low hand position when the opponent does not have access to the blade, named after the famous boxer who often fought with his hands low.

Near-simultaneous actions

These actions occur when both fencers are attacking immediately after the referee says 'Allez!' Both fencers confront each other with either premeditated or partly premeditated action.

Off-hand actions

These are all actions executed automatically without conscious control, usually when there is a severe deficit of time.

Open-eyes/eyes open

Starting with a certain movement and waiting for the opponent's response. The fencer decides on an appropriate counter-action as the opponent responds to their initial action. The fencer does not know beforehand what their opponent will do. Although 'open-eyes' refers to the sense of sight, it can also apply to the sense of touch. For example, a fencer can take the blade and wait to feel their opponent's reaction.

Partly premeditated actions

These are actions with a single known beginning, with either a choice reaction or open-eyes ending. This can also refer to a completely premeditated action a fencer is forced to change due to something unexpected happening.

Patinando

Attack with step and lunge executed in such a way that when the back foot touches the floor on the step forward, the front foot immediately executes the lunge. Once their back foot moves the fencer is fully committed to the attack. This attack has a very distinctive rhythm and significant acceleration.

Pavlina

A type of riposte from high prime. The fencer moves their hand over their head and the foil around their back, keeping the blade vertical, so the arm is cocked back in a bicep-curl, and the foil ends up hitting down the outside of the fencer's elbow into the opponent's low line. This is hard to execute but is a truly surprising move. It was first introduced by the coach Artur Wojtyczka and his student Pavel Warzycha, hence the name 'Pavlina'.

Pensa alla punta

An Italian term meaning 'think of the point', which focuses a fencer's mind on feeling where the point of the foil is in relation to the target.

Point-in-line

Defensive-offensive position where the sword arm is straight and the point is threatening the opponent's target area. If point-in-line is established before the commencement of the opponent's attack, it has priority over that attack. Most referees agree that point-in-line should be presented before the final step lunge or step flèche of the attacker, in order to have priority.

Premeditated actions

All actions fully planned in advance.

Psychological refractory period

This term refers to the period of time during which the response to a second stimulus is significantly slowed because a first stimulus is still being processed.

Referee friendly parries

These are all the circular movements against an opponent's blade. They are much easier for the referee to identify as parries.

Romanian

A type of counter-attack when, immediately after the hit, the fencer blocks the attacker's blade. This can be done by making a windscreen-wiper type movement or by leaving the point on the opponent's target and moving the guard. Named after the Romanian foil team that scored many hits with such counter-attacks, in particular Ion Drimba, who won the individual Olympic gold medal in 1968 mainly using this movement.

Scorpion

A common way of hitting at close quarters when the fencer's hand travels above the head with part rotation of the trunk, in imitation of the way a scorpion strikes.

Second-intention

Drawing an opponent's reaction before executing one's final action. This final action could be an attack, parry, counter-parry, counter-attack or counter-time.

Shah-put

Defence with distance normally followed by a direct reply. It was named after a 6-year-old Persian prince who could not focus on his lesson while the GB squad members were practising defence with distance.

Spaghetti arm

The ideal fencer's arm. Above all a fencer's arm should be loose, like a strand of cooked spaghetti. Because it is relaxed, it can move independently from the legs, and involve only those muscles that are needed for the movement (mainly fingers and extenders of the elbow).

Spike of the cactus

A way of hitting from a low wide-sixte position with the hand below the fencer's hips. The fencer's hand is in supination and the blade is directed upwards to the low line, usually at close or lunging distance. This stroke is too low to be defended by a typical quarte parry. It can also often collect the opponent's blade in opposition on its way through to the target.

Stuttering preparation

A very advanced way of pressing the opponent where fencer changes the rhythm of his actions in order to unsettle the opponent. It includes many very short moments where the fencer stops completely, hoping to induce a reaction from the opponent.

Submarine

Another name for the ducking stop hit.

Sweeping parry

A parry that covers most of the space in front of the fencer's target. It is often taken with a step forward, and is very difficult to deceive. Technically speaking, sweeping parries tend to be high or low prime (1), low prime-sixte (1–6), circular sixte-high prime (6–1), quarte-octave (4–8) or seconde (2), circular sixte-septime (6–7), high septime (7) (effective against an opposite-hander), wide sweeping seconde (2) when the sword arm moves up first, low quinte (5), and high neuvieme (9). Probably the most common is low prime-sixte (1–6) and high prime (1). In recent years low quinte (5) has become popular.

Tactical steps

Steps with a feint involving moving in one direction before actually going in another.

Tochka

A Russian term referring to the change of distance that happens when, or just before, a fencer tries to hit. The opponent will often change this distance very late and the fencer must be ready to cope with this change and adjust their hitting action. When a fencer is about to hit, their opponent can stand still, move back or move forward. In these cases the fencer can hit by medium tochka (lunge), long tochka (step-lunge), or short tochka (hitting with just the arm). The specific hitting action is relative to each fencer; tochka is a dynamic term, referring specifically to the challenge of anticipating and adjusting to late changes in distance just before hitting the opponent. It is important to anticipate not only what action an opponent will choose when threatened, but also how they will try to change the distance in critical moments.

Two waves

Refers to the situation when, while developing an attack (first wave), a fencer feels the opponent is too far to reach. The fencer slows down, creating the impression that they no longer have the intention to attack. But, after getting to attacking distance, they speed up for a second time and launch an attack (second wave). There can be more than two waves, of course.

Vezzali steps

Constantly doing half-steps forward and backwards without actually moving along the piste. The order is: front foot forwards, then back foot backwards followed by front foot backwards and back foot forwards. Any slight movement forwards or backwards will depend on the difference in length between the actions of the feet. Such steps can keep the opponent confused and the fencer who does them is ready to attack or retreat quickly. They can also help to disguise slight changes of distance. Named after the greatest female fencer ever, Valentina Vezzali (ITA). This type of movement is also very popular in footwork drills.

Vo$_2$ max

A measure of the maximum volume of oxygen that an athlete can use. It is measured in millilitres per kilogramme of body weight per minute (ml/kg/min).

BIBLIOGRAPHY

Arkadiev, V. *Tactics in Fencing.* pubmix.com, Moscow, 1969.

Czajkowski, Z. *Tactics in Fencing.* Warsaw, 1982.

Czajkowski, Z. *Tactics and Psychology in Fencing.* Katowice, 1984.

Czajkowski, Z. *Fencing Foil.* SKA SwordPlay Books, Warsaw, 1987.

Czajkowski, Z. *Fencers Training I and II,* Katowice 1988.

Czajkowski, Z. *Understanding Fencing,* SKA SwordPlay Books, 2005.

Płocharski, F. *Level of aerobic fitness among foilists of Sietom AZS-AWFiS Gdansk.* Gdansk, 2014.

Ponomarev, A. *Fencing from the Novice to the Master.* Moscow, 1987.

Soza ski, H. and Witczak, T. *Speed Training.* Warsaw, 1981.

Taylor, J. *Train Your Mind for Athletic Success.* Rowman & Littlefield, 2017.

Tissler, D. *et al. Fencing.* Moscow, 1978.

Turecki, B. *Duel of Fencers.* Kiev, 1985.

Ulatowski, T. *Theory and Methodology of Sport.* Warsaw, 1981.

Wojciechowski, Z. *Theory, Methods and Exercises in Fencing.* London, 1991.

INDEX